THE MAD BISHOPS

The Hunt for Earl Anglin James and His Assassin Brethren

JAMES DAY

Published by:
Trine Day LLC
PO Box 577
Walterville, OR 97489
1-800-556-2012
www.TrineDay.com
TrineDay@icloud.com

Library of Congress Control Number: 2023943215

Day, James.
−1st ed.
p. cm.

Epub (ISBN-13) 978-1-63424-449-7
Trade Paperback (ISBN-13) 978-1-63424-448-0
1. Earl Anglin James 1901-1977. 2. Kennedy, John F. 1917-1963, Assassination.
3. *Episcopi vagantes*. I. Day, James. II. Title

FIRST EDITION
10 9 8 7 6 5 4 3 2 1

Printed in the USA
Distribution to the Trade by:
Independent Publishers Group (IPG)
814 North Franklin Street
Chicago, Illinois 60610
312.337.0747
www.ipgbook.com

PUBLISHER'S FOREWORD

Good Lord, what madness rules in brainsick men,
When for so slight and frivolous a cause
Such factious emulations shall arise!
— William Shakespeare, Henry VI, Act 4, Scene 1

As time goes by, and the murder of our 35th President recedes into the mists of memory, will *we* still care? Will there still be a desire/need to see/hear/feel the truth? Is it an obsession or is there a purpose? The last "validated" living North American born before the Lincoln assassination was Rachel Hannah Bateman (née Bailey; 16 January 1865-18 March 1976; 111 years 62 days).[1] So by that measure the last Kennedy assassination "survivor" will be around until 2075 maybe 2076. Just in time for our country's tercentennial, I know I won't be there, but I do hope our country will still stand in liberty – free and brave...

A path forward is understanding the perfidy despicably done to our country, our body politic, our souls. The 1963 Kennedy assassination has many authors – and a long gestation. Once the path was set, many forces camped along the path and many got on board – for various reasons. There were those who had no idea they were involved until the operation was completed. And then there is US, a shell-shocked nation – ripe for the picking.

James Day's *The Mad Bishops: The Hunt for Earl Anglin James and His Assassin Brethren* is a deep-nether dive into one of the avenues used by this ongoing treachery of mulitiple knives and ancient vengeance. Secret actions and societies may come and go, but there is a "power" residing in our tales, history, myths, and futures.... As President John Fitzgerald Kennedy spoke on June 11, 1962, at Yale's commencement:

> [John C] Calhoun in 1804 and [William H.] Taft in 1878 graduated into a world very different from ours today. They and their contemporaries spent entire careers stretching over 40 years in grappling with a few dramatic issues on which the Nation was sharply

 https://gerontology.fandom.com/wiki/Rachel_Bateman

and emotionally divided, issues that occupied the attention of a generation at a time: the national bank, the disposal of the public lands, nullification or union, freedom or slavery, gold or silver. Today these old sweeping issues very largely have disappeared. The central domestic issues of our time are more subtle and less simple. They relate not to basic clashes of philosophy or ideology but to ways and means of reaching common goals – to research for sophisticated solutions to complex and obstinate issues. The world of Calhoun, the world of Taft had its own hard problems and notable challenges. But its problems are not our problems. Their age is not our age. As every past generation has had to disenthrall itself from an inheritance of truisms and stereotypes, so in our own time we must move on from the reassuring repetition of stale phrases to a new, difficult, but essential confrontation with reality.

For the great enemy of truth is very often not the lie – deliberate, contrived and dishonest – but the myth – persistent, persuasive, and unrealistic. Too often we hold fast to the cliches of our forebears. We subject all facts to a prefabricated set of interpretations. We enjoy the comfort of opinion without the discomfort of thought.[2]

Kennedy understood what our country needed. He was trying to move us forward. It didn't happen…. Why? Are there those that do not care for our secular democracy? That do not hope for "a more perfect union"?

Was there a clique of "fake" bishops in New Orleans in 1963? What's with all the racisists and racism … even fascism? Who are all these "people?" Are they true-believers or simply scamming charlatans or …? Do spooks take advantage of this underworld?

James Day takes you beyond the myth and takes a broad look at at the questions, with a spotlight on Earl Anglin James and his mainly ignoble associates. James consecrated and some say de-frocked the infamous JFK assassination scoundrel, David Ferrie. TrineDay is honored to present: *The Mad Bishops: The Hunt for Earl Anglin James and His Assassin Brethren!*

Onward to the Utmost of Futures!
Peace,
RA "Kris" Millegan
Publisher
TrineDay
September 2, 2023

2 https://www.jfklibrary.org/about-us/about-the-jfk-library/kennedy-library-fast-facts/rededication-film-quote. Empahsis mine.

For My Daughters

The day that they killed him, someone said to me, "Son
The age of the Antichrist has just only begun"
                                              - Bob Dylan, "Murder Most Foul"

ACKNOWLEDGMENTS

I am deeply grateful to Kris Millegan for his encouragement and support. Thanks also to the following authors for their correspondences: Robert Hutchison, Peter Levenda, Gary Hill, Doug Valentine, Jim DiEugenio, John Kowalski, Anthony Summers, Fred Litwin, James Lateer, Gillian McCann, Hugh Wilford, Phillip Willan, Dan E. Moldea, R.M. Douglas, Jerome Aan del Wiel, HL Arledge, Tom Nevin, and the late Daniel Hopsicker. To those at many institutions: Alejandra Estrada Martínez, Marymount Cuernavaca; Nathan Jordan; National Archives at Atlanta; Tom McAnear, Eric Van Slander and David Castillo, National Archives at College Park; Special Collections at Graduate Theological Union; USC Office of the Registrar; USF Libraries Tampa Special Collection; Linda Smith, Eisenhower Presidential Museum and Library; Mary-Lou Gelissen, Windsor Public Library; Toronto Reference Library; Sarah Coates, University of Florida, George A. Smathers Libraries; Kaitlyn Price, Dallas Historical Society; Christina Jensen, Southern Methodist University Special Collections; Cathy Smith, Haley Memorial Library & History Center; Library & Archives Canada; Daniel Cook, Atascadero Democratic Club; Jason McCaig, Jerusalem Shriners; Robert Austin, Denver City Council; Texas State Library & Archives Commission; Courtney Welu, University of Texas at Austin; Cynthia A. Shenette, Robert Hutchings Goddard Library, Clark University; Jacob Baker, Saint Louis Public Library; City of Vienna Public Library; Professor John Kersey (Prince-Abbot Edmond III of San Luigi); Diana Kohnke, San Francisco State University, Sutro Library; California Genealogical Society; Monica Sperabene, Biblioteca Nazionale Centrale di Roma; Laura Ricci, Sovereign Military Order of Saint John of Jerusalem, of Rhodes, of Malta; Dallas Public Library; His Eminent Highness Jose Cosmelli, Prince, Knights of Malta, Federation of the Autonomous Priories; Sophia Southard, Kansas City Research Center; Special Collections, Texas Tech University; U.S. Embassy, Bern, Switzerland; LBJ Presidential Library archivists; and Robert Ellsberg, son of the late Daniel Ellsberg.

This book was researched and written in Orange County, California, a nexus point for many incidents in this narrative. I am deeply indebted to the staff at the Garden Grove Main Library in the Orange County Public Library system for all the ILLs and general good humor. Also thanks to the Richard Nixon Library and Presidential Museum in Yorba Linda, the United States Marine Corps Aviation, the Museum of the Republic of Vietnam in Westminster, the Vietnamese American Oral History Project of the University of California, Irvine, and the general resources available in Little Saigon (particularly Lily's Bakery on Bolsa Ave. and the Vietnamese iced coffee at Lee's Sandwiches).

As always, to my wife Christina, and the joys of our life, Isla Rose and Elsie Grace.

CONTENTS

DRAMATIS PERSONAE

Earl Anglin James alias Mar Laurentius (1901-1977): Old Roman Catholic Church bishop, spiritualist, forger, claimant to 2,100 honorary degrees whom David Ferrie phoned on a number of occasions in 1962.

David W. Ferrie alias Francis Maria D.W. Ferrie (1918-1967): suigeneric Jesuit-educated figure; at once an airline pilot, hypnotist, occultist, Mafia paralegal, paramilitary strategist, contrabandist, cancer researcher, both failed seminarian (Roman Catholicism) and phony bishop (Old Catholicism), sexual offender, mentor to Lee Oswald in Civil Air Patrol, member of Stanley's Orthodox Society of Jesus. Claimed purpose of 350-mile road trip from Louisiana to Texas the night of JFK's assassination was for weekend of goose hunting and ice skating with two males, ages 18 and 20.

Walter Myron Propheta alias Wolodymyr I (1912-1972): former Ukrainian Orthodox priest and founder of Crusade Against Communism campaign; launched American Orthodox Catholic Church in 1965.

Carl Jerome Stanley alias St. Christopher Maria (1902-1967): consecrated bishop by Earl Anglin James; ecumenical observer at Second Vatican Council; consecrated David W. Ferrie as bishop in the Primitive Catholic Apostolic Orthodox Church of Antioch of the Syro-Byzantine Tradition; purportedly told by Ferrie and Bishop Jack Martin while bar hopping in Louisville, KY in November 1961 of plan to assassinate JFK. Pastor of the Orthodox Society of Jesus.

Charles Brearley alias Tau Ignatius Carolus (1894-1978): auto mechanic/archbishop of Old Holy Catholic Church who introduced New Age practices into church; advocate of British Israelism. Chaplain of phony Sovereign Order of Cyprus.

Frederick C. King alias Prince of Vilna and All of Byelorussia (1917-1985): bridge between radical right and phony bishops. Member of Orthodox Society of Jesus; member of John Birch Society and host of radio program, Bishop King Crusade. Consecrated by same bishop who consecrated Propheta and Stanley (Homer F.F. Roebke).

Charles Dennis Boltwood (1889-1985): English bishop in Free Protestant Episocopal Church; champion of Spiritualism, Theosophy and occultism.

Hugh George de Willmott Newman (1905-1979) alias Mar Georgius of Glastonbury: First Catholicos of the Catholicate of the West. Elected Earl Anlin James exarch of the Canadas; consecrated Charles Dennis Boltwood; corresponded with occultist Aleister Crowley.

William Bernard Crow (1895-1976) alias Mar Basilius Abdullah III: Consecrated Hugh George de Willmott Newman; corresponded with Aleister Crowley who made Crow Sovereign Patriarch of the Ecclesia Gnostica Catholica; ordained priest in Liberal Catholic Church in 1935.

James Ingall Wedgwood (1883-1951): Founding bishop of Liberal Catholic Church, an Old Catholic microchurch infused with Theosophical, Rosicrucian, and Masonic ideas; consecrated C.W. Leadbeater in 1916.

Charles Webster [C.W.] Leadbeater (1854-1934): Disciple of Theosophy foundress Madame Blavatsky; bridge between Theosophy and Old Catholic movement. Sirhan Sirhan requested book by Leadbeater in prison.

Raymond O'Brien alias Earl of Thomond (1905-1977): Mentally unstable sex offender and associate of Earl Anglin James; launched United Christian Nationalist Party in Ireland heavily based on Gerald L.K. Smith's Christian Nationalist Crusade.

Gerald L.K. Smith (1898-1976): Anti-semitic white supremacist preacher who promoted notorious Protocols of the Elders of Zion which warned of a pending global Jewish conspiracy.

Wesley Swift (1913-1970): Southern California-based reverend and leading proponent of Christian Identity; influenced worldview of Joseph A. Milteer and Edgar Eugene Bradley.

Joseph A. Milteer (1902-1974): White supremacist and Klansman with apparent foreknowledge of the JFK assassination.

O.B. Graham (d. 1974): Pentecostal revival preacher who owned Abundant Life Temple in Oak Cliff neighborhood of Dallas.

Guy Banister (1901-1964): Former FBI agent who later ran New Orleans private investigative firm as front for racist, anti-integration activities.

Delphine Roberts: Both employee and mistress of Guy Banister; excommunicated from Catholic Church for opposing integration policies of the archbishop of New Orleans. Proponent of British Israelism.

Jackson Ricau (1918-2001): Former investigator for Banister and publisher of racist newsletter Citizens' Report. Excommunicated with Delphine Roberts and Leander Perez.

Leander Perez (1891-1969): Louisiana judge, pro-segregationist, financial backer of JFK assassination, per informant Willie Somersett.

Jack Martin alias Edward Stewart Suggs: Investigator for Banister, heavily involved in independent Catholic movement and friend of Earl Anglin James (per Martin acolyte Thomas Beckham).

Kerry Thornley (1938-1998): Fellow Marine with Lee Oswald, wrote *The Idle Warriors* based on Oswald; Identified by Thomas Beckham as member of Banister's cell. Founder of Discordianism.

Pericles Voultsos-Vourtzis: Grand Master of phony chivalric order. U.S. lay representative of Old Holy Catholic Church.

Ngo Dinh Thuc (1897-1984): Brother of deposed South Vietnam president Ngo Dinh Diem and high profile Roman Catholic bishop; later makes series of dubious consecrations and announces himself sedevacantist; excommunicated by Rome but apparently reconciles before death.

Leopold Ledl: Austrian swindler who ingratiated himself within high-ranking Vatican prelates as part of "Vatican Connection" fraudulent securities scheme of the early 1970s.

H.L. Hunt (1889-1974): Powerful Texas oilman with little affection for the Kennedy clan. Obtained first edition copy of Abraham Zapruder's 8mm film of JFK assassination.

Edwin Walker (1909-1993): Texan, Army general, John Birch Society member, and passionate conservative who whipped up swaths of the radical right on speaking tours.

D.H. Byrd (1900-1986): Powerful Texan who owned building from which Lee Oswald allegedly shot President Kennedy on November 22, 1963.

Robert Morris (1914-1996): President of University of Dallas, one-time attorney for General Walker.

Nelson Rockefeller (1908-1979): Coordinator of Inter-American Affairs who championed initatives such as the Good Neighbor Policy, an outfit that fronted for personal and lucrative ventures in Mexico for wealthy Texans, many from Dallas.

William J. Byran (1926-1977): California hypnotist, author of *Religious Aspects of Hypnosis*; per author Peter Evans, suggested to have hypnotized Sirhan Sirhan prior to shooting RFK on June 5, 1968.

Xavier von Koss (b. 1910): Reverend and hypnotist who treated James Earl Ray in Southern California prior to assassination of MLK.

Jerry Owen alias Oliver Brindley Owen; alias The Walking Bible (1913-1993): Reverend who was seen in presence of Sirhan Sirhan just prior to RFK's shooting.

INTRODUCTION

We are not here to curse the darkness, but to light a candle that can
guide us through the darkness to a safe and sure future. For the world is
changing. The old era is ending. The old ways will not do.
                                            –John F. Kennedy, July 15, 1960

In the days leading up to President John F. Kennedy's planned stop at the world's largest wholesale trade center, the Dallas Trade Mart, for a luncheon address on Friday, November 22, 1963, the Secret Service was not worrying about assassins lurking along the route to the Trade Mart or the 34 known threats on the president's life out of Texas alone. Instead, their concern was the sirloin steak that was on the menu for the luncheon. Trade Mart chefs intended to cook the best steak available for the president, but the Secret Service rejected the idea: the chefs were to prepare all 2,000 steaks for those in attendance, and an agent would randomly select one of those steaks for the president's plate. "A would-be assassin couldn't be sure of poisoning the President's meal unless he put poison in every steak served at the luncheon," an organizer said.[1] A dispensation was given from the Catholic bishop of the Dallas-Fort Worth diocese allowing Catholics in attendance like the President and First Lady to eat the steaks if they wished (in the pre-Vatican Council II era – in session that very day in Rome – Catholics were required to abstain from eating meat every Friday throughout the year).[2]

Of course, there never was a luncheon. The motorcade was already behind schedule leaving Love Field and snaking its way past 250,000 people for its 40-minute parade through downtown Dallas, the financial heart of Texas's oil industry, which the Nixon/Lodge ticket won by 60,000 votes over Kennedy/Johnson in 1960. At the urging of his vice president, Lyndon Johnson, President Kennedy agreed to a southern swing in late 1963, in hopes of uniting Texas Democrats ahead of the 1964 general election. The political cavalcade passed through San Antonio and Houston the day

---

1   "No Special Steak for Kennedys," *Brownsville Herald*, 21 November 1963.
2   "Meat Okay for Catholics," *El Paso Herald-Post*, 21 November 1963.

before; on the morning of November 22, the president breakfasted with the Forth Worth Chamber of Commerce. First Lady Jacqueline Kennedy, who rarely made such trips, was on hand, but arrived to the breakfast late, wearing a pink dress with matching pill box hat. On arriving in Dallas after the short flight from Fort Worth, hospitality representatives presented Mrs. Kennedy with a bouquet of red roses – she had received Texas yellow roses in each city before Dallas.

At the Trade Mart, the steaks were ready, the 2,000 guests were seated, the event was supposed to begin at 12:30 PM. But at 12:30, the motorcade was heading into a trap set in Dealey Plaza, a high noon ambush in Texas.

Two days later, while 45-year-old David W. Ferrie and two male companions, ages 18 and 20 respectively, were spending a peripatetic weekend ice skating in Houston – a much needed vacation, Ferrie said, after working on the defense team of Carlos Marcello's deportation trial – on the day Jack Ruby silenced accused Kennedy assassin Lee Oswald forever in the basement of Dallas police headquarters on live television – the Dallas Cowboys were playing on the road. They were in Ferrie's hometown of Cleveland, where they encountered the Browns at windswept Cleveland Municipal Stadium off Lake Erie. When the NFL made the tone deaf decision to hold games the weekend of the president's assassination, it was as if the anguish and anger of a shocked nation all thundered down on the Cowboys. "When we went out to warm up, there were strong boos," Cowboys VP Gil Brandt remembered in 2011. "And when we were introduced, they made a point of not saying 'Dallas.' They just called us the Cowboys. There was a smaller crowd than normal, but they were booing."[3] The decision not to say "Dallas" came from Browns owner Art Modell, who somehow thought it was a sign of respect.

55,000 cold and subdued fans were in attendance in a cavernous stadium that seated over 80,000. There were no player introductions, no usual fanfare from marching bands, the flag flew at half staff. A moment of silence for the slain president stretched to beyond two minutes – little resemblance to the usual thrilling tension of a Browns football game. The Browns defeated the Cowboys, 27-17.

* * *

Thirty years later. Nine miles from Municipal Stadium an eleven-year-old boy was getting a haircut. Big band music was playing on Cleveland's 850 AM. "Put that book away," Nick the barber barked. "And look up."

---

3   "Cowboys fielded boos, anger after JFK's assassination in Dallas," nfl.com, 23 November 2011.

Scholastic's *They Shot the President* by George Sullivan had just arrived at St. Michael's School, just behind Nick's barber shop. I was that boy, and couldn't put that book down. I revisited that paperback preparing this book. Tiny brown hairs were buried in the binding around the chapter on President Lincoln's assassination, "Murder in Box 7." I flipped over to the rather lengthy chapter "Who Killed JFK?" It is worth quoting the chapter's concluding paragraphs in full:

> "[S]uspicions that Oswald was not the lone assassin have been fueled by other books and by Hollywood films. When the movie *JFK* was released in 1991, it triggered a new wave of controversy. The film declares that a vast web of political, government, and corporate interests were behind the killing. But many critics say the film is as fictional as *The Wizard of Oz*.
>
> A poll conducted in 1992 by *Time* magazine and the Cable News Network reported that three quarters of Americans believe there was a conspiracy behind the assassination. The leading suspects are the CIA, the Mafia, the Cuban government, anti-Castro Cuban exiles, American military leaders, and the Dallas police.
>
> Perhaps the truth about President Kennedy's assassination will never be known. Perhaps there was more than one gunman. Perhaps the president was the victim of an enormous conspiracy. But there are mere theories, and a theory is only an assumption or guess based on limited information or knowledge. Until believable evidence is presented to support any of the theories, it is fair to assume that Lee Harvey Oswald, acting alone, shot President John Kennedy."[4]

It wasn't until film school in 2005-2006 when I finally devoured the Stone epic. A few of us pored over that film. This was during the time when Stone was just down the hill from school, at the former site of Howard Hughes Aircraft shooting *World Trade Center* on a full-scale recreation of Ground Zero.

More time went by – a whole fifteen years until I could no longer outrun the nagging question: who *did* kill JFK? There was a cognitive dissonance in grasping not only the actual facts of what happened on November 22, 1963, but our own country's position on the murder of our president: if Congress deemed a conspiracy likely took place, as it concluded in 1979, why was the mainstream media still pushing Oswald as a troubled, lone

---

4   George Sullivan, *They Shot the President: Ten True Stories* (New York: Scholastic, 1993), 149-150.

nut assassin? Overwhelmed by one too many conspiracy cliches about the grassy knoll? Occupied by problems in our own time?

But what if the inherent corruption in our own time is perpetuated because of the killing of three major American figures of the 1960s: John F. Kennedy, Robert F. Kennedy, and Martin Luther King, Jr.?

I found it too tantalizing a coincidence that David Ferrie, whom Joe Pesci so memorably played in *JFK* and dubbed by New Orleans DA Jim Garrison as "one of history's most important individuals," attended my own high school, the Jesuit-run Cleveland St. Ignatius – Ferrie of the class of 1935, me of the class of 2000. We both went on to nearby John Carroll University, also a Jesuit school, both wrote for *The Carroll News*, and even roomed in the same dormitory (Bernet Hall). Ferrie was also a noted member of the college debate team; he continued public speaking throughout his life.

What particularly intrigued me, touched on briefly in *JFK*, was Ferrie's religious conviction. Like me, Ferrie was Roman Catholic. We were raised in similar neighborhoods. He was from the city's west side, under the roof of devout Irish Catholic parents, a family of Cleveland firefighters and policemen. The eldest of James Howard Ferrie and Burdett Coutts Goldrick's two sons. Leaving John Carroll in his last year to attend Cleveland's diocesan seminary, St. Mary's, he was released for "emotional instability" after suffering a nervous breakdown. With his father's help he tried again at the now-closed St. Charles Seminary in southwestern Ohio, run by the Missionaries of the Precious Blood. For one reason or another, Ferrie's temperament was simply not suited for the Roman Catholic priesthood. Nor was he suited as a lay teacher: in 1946, Ferrie was removed from his aeronautics teaching position at Cleveland's all-boys Benedictine High School for escorting students to a brothel, among other sundry things.

It was a bit mind boggling: How did someone with such a strong family and faith background wind up in New Orleans conducting paramilitary training exercises for anti-Castro Cuban exiles, providing legal advice and flying planes for New Orleans Mafia boss Carlos Marcello, purportedly teach cadet Lee Oswald how to shoot a rifle, and publicly speculate how to ambush the president of the United States?

Most perplexing, however, is how such a sexual predator was allowed such latitude by those around him to carry out his acts. His habitual molestation of young adult males remained a damaging pattern of behavior throughout his life, with little legal consequence, even if it resulted in his firing as a commercial pilot. It is not out of the realm of possibility Lee Oswald was such a victim. While that accusation remains unverified, there are too many verified cases of young men who were literally mesmerized by Ferrie, who were seduced by the allure of the occult, and were thus taken advantage of by the older man. Ferrie was also a drug abuser, provided alcohol to underage partygoers, and frequently screened pornographic films to his young companions as a kind of blackmail to keep their silence.

Not exactly a candidate for alumnus of the year.

"All I ever wanted to be was a priest," Pesci's Ferrie laments in *JFK*. Through Ferrie, an entirely new world was about to open up. One both somewhat familiar and yet altogether unknown, if not downright bizarre. But perfect for those who never quite fit in with the status quo. This was the world of independent Catholicism. Such renegade "clerics" are known in Christian history as *episcopi vagantes*, "wandering bishops," unaffiliated with the official Roman Catholic Church. The movement's existence was largely justified by its rejection of the primacy of the Roman pontiff, particularly the Chair of Peter's claim to papal infallibility. Splitting off from Rome's authority, the Old Catholic Church developed and formed its own subsects. It mutated with Protestantism and Eastern Orthodoxy, sometimes freely blending characteristics of New Age and New Thought practices, as we will see. With no adherence to the pope, they became highly creative with their own vision for their church, even if their cathedral often was nothing but a parlor room.

For those who ventured into the Old Catholic Church, becoming a bishop was an obsession. Ferrie was no exception. And many the New Orleans cabal that District Attorney Jim Garrison suspected plotted to assassinate President Kennedy were, in fact, bishops in these rogue churches.

When we go through this looking glass, we find a world of curved mirrors, refracting reality in a distorted, mystifying way – a dualistic viewpoint of how the world works. There's the organized religion of the Roman Catholic Church and other mainline denominations, and then there's the Old Catholic Church and its various nomenclatures. There are recognized colleges and universities, and there are fake colleges and phony diplomas and worthless degrees. There's the Sovereign Military Order of Malta, and there are imposter orders, like the Sovereign Greek Order of St. Dennis of Zante. And even, on one hand, there's government – and invisible government. Most disturbing, however, is when the fantasy world blurs with the real world, and respected, legitimate institutions and organizations become infiltrated by the pretenders and usurpers creating cognitive chaos, so much so one has found themselves trapped in the zone of relativism, wondering what is truth.

This aspect of Garrison's investigation into what he called "odd sects" was entirely left out of Oliver Stone's film. It delineated too far from the director's intention to expose the military-industrial complex in the assassination of the president. Beyond the Garrison probe, this religious element has been little researched aside from Peter Levenda's *Sinister Forces* trilogy. Even as a cradle Catholic, who spent nineteen years in Catholic education, plus another twelve years as an employee for Catholic organizations, I knew nothing about the independent Catholic movement and the phenomena of the wandering bishops. With David Ferrie as my guide, this was a journey into the grotesque and esoteric, ritualistic and sacramental, composed of individuals nearly all with criminal backgrounds. Little wonder why it consumed Jim Garrison.

David Ferrie made a number of phone calls to an unlisted Toronto phone number in 1962. The number belonged to a two-bit shyster who later denied knowing or ever hearing the name Ferrie. Through never before revealed connections and a thorough exploration into this man's two *modi operandi* – issuing phony academic honors and degrees, and his membership in an eccentric religious milieu – a portrait emerges of a puppetmaster of chaos, a sponsor of political assassinations and coup d'etats. His name was Earl Anglin James. In the pages ahead, he will become known as the mad bishop, harbinger of the occult and esoteric, which brought so great a spiritual torrent upon the United States of America on November 22, 1963 that nothing thereafter was ever the same again.

CHAPTER ONE

IN THE BEGINNING

The officials of Zoan have become fools,
the leaders of Memphis are deceived;
the cornerstones of her peoples
have led Egypt astray.

– Isaiah 19:13

E arl Anglin Lawrence James was born in Memphis, Tennessee into the Anglican faith on April 23, 1901 (some sources say 1904). His father was Elmer Anglin James (1878-1959) and Marguerite Elena James (nee Taber). Elmer was born in Missouri to Frank James and Molly Burns. Later, Earl claimed he was the grandson of infamous outlaw Frank James, brother of Jesse James. Although like so much of what James proclaimed, it was a complete fabrication.[1] His mother was French Canadian, daughter of William Taber and Gertrude Lawrence. Earl had two siblings. His brother, Frederick Lawrence James, died in infancy. His sister, Alma Gertrude James Reynolds, died in 1932 at age 27.

Due to his profession, father Elmer frequently moved. He was a horse groom and jockey, although his son championed him as "the famous sportsman, worthy of Merit and Honor," and dedicated his supposed missionary organization, EAJ Peace Missions, "to Perpetuate and Commemorate the Memory of Our Elmer Anglin James. Who gained Fame of Queen's Plate of England and Duke of York Stakes, being Associated with Baron de Rothschild of France … etc."[2]

---

1   James definitely made it a point in his CV to mention his famous "ancestors": On speaking of a cross he wears: "[A] Little 200 year-old 2 ½ in. Christ on the Cross in Old Ebony and Silver" that my Uncle Jesse James carried about his neck – he was a good Man, for no doubt you recall him making straight on the wall a sign-motto that read: "God Bless Our Home" – at the time when he was shot dead. Not only this Fact, but it has been proven many times that "Uncle Jesse James robbed the Rich to Pay the Poor! This was the method employed by Good Robin Hood of Merry England. And, did you Know that one of the Governors of a State in United States of America, named Governor Cristtenden, pardoned and freed him? That was so, as it was proven many times over he and Grandfather Frank James were BROTHERS definitely not to blame and guiltless of Body-Crime to anyone, and that distorted and fictitious stories existed. That's Right!"
2   Barbara Moon, "Prince of the Degree Merchants," *Maclean's*, 6 April 1963.

By the time young Earl was ten, the family home was 199 St. Patrick in Toronto, Ontario, Canada, a city which would serve as Earl's home base for the rest of his life. He attended Ryerson School in Toronto from 1907-1915. In 1921, the family lived at 62 Wroxeter, the future address of Earl's unaccredited diploma mill outfit, National College (sometimes referred to as National University) of Canada. Also, 62 Wroxeter will be the address for the unlisted home number David Ferrie will phone in 1962.

However, in the 1940 *National Reference Book on Canadian Men and Women*, James claimed his early life "was spent in France, Germany, and England with his illustrious father."

James was not an athletic young man; he was obese and of average height. He struggled academically. Yet, he displayed a penchant for the arts: a love for music, tutoring piano lessons, a talent for drawing and design, playwriting and acting, and a certain eloquence which would serve useful in the art of forgery and earning his living manufacturing elaborate, if worthless, degrees.

In his "curriculum vitae," likely written – or dreamed up – at the behest of a certain Bishop Walter Propheta, who we will see was connected with J. Edgar Hoover of the FBI, James characterized his teen years as a renowned piano instructor, whose pupils numbered in the "hundreds."

Throughout the 1920s, when he should have been wrapping up his education years, James continually was flunking first-year exams at the University of Toronto. For three straight years he could not pass the tests. Then, a shameless reinvention: at 28, James awarded himself a fellowship in music degree. At thirty, enforced by a relentless marketing blitz, advertisements with James's picture began popping up in local newspapers. He was now Earl Anglin James, president of the National College of Music, Arts and Language. While he managed to obtain a charter for the National College from the Ontario Provincial Government, it was not permitted to confer degrees of any kind. The Canadian embassy in Rome tersely summarized the college this way: "[It] ha[s] no legal status, and its diplomas or degrees are without value." Still, James claimed the institution had sixty branches and staff of over a hundred. And he was already on the way to giving himself phony degrees: such as a degree in music from Loyola University of New Orleans in 1925.

In 1932, James married. The marriage was not to last, and in this relationship with one Mary Kozak we get a rare look into the private, dysfunctional life of Earl Anglin James. It is a glimpse that will help shape our understanding of his public actions in the ensuing decades.

Mary Kozak was a student of National College, secretary to the president, and finally its registrar. "Although she is only 20 years of age, Miss Kozak has accomplished more than most people would have done by the time they were 40," Ontario's Sault Ste. Marie newspaper reported in its "Woman's Page." Kozak was born in Vienna, Austria to Nicholas Kozak and Ilena Drabit. The family relocated to Canada in 1925, to Goudreau, a small gold mining village in northeastern Ontario. Goudreau was one of many ghost towns in the Algoma region which popped up and quickly vanished by World War II. Here Nicholas Kozak proved a successful prospector in gold mining – nearby Kozak Lake was named after the Viennese prospector. This was before Canada came off the gold standard, enabling young Mary and her mother to enjoy a privileged lifestyle for a time, characterized by frequent trips to Europe, namely Paris. The trip lasted four years.

OUR E A J EMBLEM!

EARL   ANGLIN   JAMES
Laurentius 1

CURRICULUM VITAE

Medical-Missionary   Archbishop-Primate

"Amicitiam Confirmo"

PAST————PRESENT————FUTURE

(OBSERVE: All information in this CV is definitely AUTHENTIC, LEGALLY SOUND & SUBSTANTIATED in DETAIL & PROOF. TRUTH is here, under AFFIDAVIT — CANADA, U.S.A.)

The "Who's Who" of Europe

It begins: At 16 yrs. of age, until 20, my class of piano pupils, weekly numbered 50 to 75; I taught piano and theory to many hundreds of them. My specialty was Chopin, Liszt and Beethoven. Great Masters taught me: Paderewski, Virtuoso MARK HAMBOURG, his Father Prof. Michael. I gained knowledge by studying under Guerrero, Conradi, Boyce, Farmer. My pupils not only played piano but also composed, and I delighted in having them compose a hymn in 7 minutes. Numerous recitals were given at the University of Toronto and Conservatory, in aid of Orphans, Homeless, Aged, Disabled and Maimed 1914 to 1918 War Veterans, in Music Halls, everywhere. One of my 8 year old pupils electrified and astonished University Professors and Graduates by giving a 2 hr. recital of Chopin at Wymilwood, U of T. My own personal recital of the 24 Preludes of Chopin was a Victory and Gloriously Acclaimed Triumph. Medals, Honors, Merits found their way to us — my Pupils and their Teacher. But, eventually, and I do not know why, though it seems, I oddly would become a Medical Doctor and Missionary, fashioned into the Status of a Medical-Missionary.

Page one of James's sprawling CV, likely produced on order from Walter Propheta, for all intents and purposes an FBI informant for J. Edgar Hoover.

Nicholas and Ilena settled for a time in Kozah Township outside Sault Ste. Marie on the Canadian side of St. Mary's River, an area populated by many such emigrated Austro-Ukrainians, across from the smaller Sault Ste. Marie, Michigan. The *Sault Star* glowed at her visit from the metropolis of Toronto to her parents in the summer of 1931, "where she received her A.C.C.M. degree in modern languages, and now has a position in the college." The languages of her degree included her native Austrian, along with Polish, Roumanian, and Russian, all of which she fluently spoke. Another article on Mary Kozak indicated she took creative writing classes as well, which will later prove beneficial in her vindictive novel, *Scars*, that demonizes her former husband, Earl Anglin James.

On the surface, Mary Kozak seems to be a fine fit for Earl: a flair for languages, music, both Spanish guitar and piano, and painting. They each list Anglican as their religion on their marriage certificate, dated June 29, 1932. They married in Sault Ste. Marie; the *Sault Star* indicated a July 16 wedding ceremony. Earl was 29 and Mary was 22. Their address was 512 Danforth in Toronto, the official mailing address of the National College of Canada. A Mr. and Mrs. Albert R. Wood are the two witnesses named on the marriage certificate, names which will resurface when the disastrous marriage explodes into chaos.

MISS MARY KOZAK

Mary suffered a scare earlier in the year when she was attacked by three collies whilst riding a horse-drawn sleigh near her family home. The dogs slashed "her legs and thighs with their teeth." Kozak downplayed the incident in the newspaper account, but was certain to mention her job: "What worries me most is that I should be back at the National College of Music, at Toronto, where I am employed as registrar. You know, in these days, no one likes to lose time and jobs are very scarce. I wired my office the cause of my delay, but I must return to Toronto as soon as I am able to move." Missing work was such a priority for Mary Kozak that the owner of the attacking collies offered to both cover her medical expenses and personally cover the amount of pay lost from the injury. Two of the three dogs were put down because of the assault.

But what is odd is that Kozak was married only a few months after the accident – an incident that received a wealth of coverage for the sleepy town – and there is no mention of any engagement in the *Sault Star*, as was customary in small-town newspapers, or a puff piece about the summer wedding, another staple of local reporting, especially given the high profile of father Nick and the frequent appearances of the photogenic Mary in the *Sault Star*.

Rather, the wedding between Earl Anglin James and Mary Kozak had the makings of an hastily arranged, if not forced, marriage.

A son was born on March 1, 1933, named after his father. Research has uncovered little about this individual. His mother said her son studied art and psychology at the University of Southern California in the 1950s, and residential records put an Earl Anglin Jamees in Hawthorne, California, in southwestern Los Angeles County throughout his adult life. However, on request from this author, the USC Registrar's Office could not verify an Earl Anglin James attended the university.

Things for Mr. and Mrs. Earl James took a bizarre turn in 1934. On December 24, Earl arrived home with a small Christmas tree to find Albert R. Wood, the best man from his wedding, visiting and chatting with Earl's wife. This innocuous scene incensed Earl Anglin James, who so took the presence of Wood as a great affront that he stormed out of the apartment. Wood, by all accounts an upright citizen, manager of a Sault Ste. Marie gas station and active in local parliamentary politics, followed Earl outside. Wood explained he wanted help with a speech he was preparing. James ignored him. (Indeed, within the year Wood would become president of Sault Ste. Marie Board of Trade – today's Chamber of Commerce – and unsuccessfully campaign as a Liberal Party candidate in the federal elections). But Earl Anglin James wanted nothing to do with the man – or his wife Mary. He did not return home that night. Though he eventually did return, the young couple and little boy lived together another five weeks, until Mary took their son and disappeared. Earl later claimed he did not see his infant son for five years.

Earl was convinced Albert R. Wood was the cause of the loss of consortium between he and his wife. In March 1940, Earl filed a heart balm tort in a Toronto court – accusing Wood and Mary of having an affair – and sought $100,000 in damages. Wood was named as the defendant. In the claim, Earl James identified himself as a teacher of public speaking. "My wife invited him to come up for an evening and from then on my troubles began," he testified. In his own testimony, defendant Wood provided some more context, indicating the marriage was in trouble throughout 1934: "James had written Mrs. Wood and myself to come and see if we could 'straighten matters out.' Mrs. Wood and I visited James at his Bay Street apartment for about an hour and a half, when James discussed all his domestic troubles, and blamed Mrs. James for all sorts of things. He named one or two men. On another occasion that year we discussed his troubles again. Mrs. Wood and I advised them to quit fighting and go back and live together peaceably."

A month later the case was dismissed. Justice G.F. McFarland found no evidence Albert R. Wood attempted to alienate the affections of Mary Kozak James.

"Good women are hard to find," James warned a Y.M.C.A. group at the University of Toronto in 1935. "You can marry all your happiness and regret it for years to come if you are not more careful." On the other hand, Wood died in 1968, outliving his deceased wife Annie, and leaving a paternal legacy of five children, six grandchildren, and a number of great-grandchildren.

In the same year as the death of Wood, the man who accused Wood of breaking up his marriage so many years earlier, Earl Anglin James, since divorced and estranged from his only son, found himself the subject of inquiry from the New Orleans District Attorney in relation to the shocking assassination of the thirty-fifth president of the United States.

2

A Bishop's Crook

In all labor there is profit;
But the talk of the lips tendeth only to penury.
– Proverbs 14:23

While he continued issuing fellowships and degrees via his National College, Earl Anglin James was also pursuing an ecclesiastical career. In reality, it was his first foray into religious cultism, his initiation into esotericism, and his association with magicians and spiritual charlatans. This was the Metaphysical Spiritualist Church in Windsor, Ontario, sometimes referred to as the Metaphysical Alliance Church or Canadian Metaphysical Alliance, headquartered in Winnipeg. Advertisements billed him as a lecturer, speaking on "The Christmas Spirit" and "Psychological Aspects of Home, Marriage and Family Life." By now, James referred to himself as Rev. Earl A. James, D.D., LL.D, as in Doctor of Divinity and Doctor of Law. He claimed he was made a bishop by the Metaphysicians of Winnipeg. The church was the interior of Windsor's Palace Theatre Building. In most ads, James is named as Minister, and Pastor is one Rev. Harry Gaunt. But the collaboration between James and Gaunt did not extend more than a few years. While Gaunt continued preaching at the Palace Theatre Building, James disappeared from Windsor by 1941. This short-lived partnership nevertheless left an impression on James in a subject that will emerge again as a major theme of our study: the practice of hypnotherapy.

It also is the first indication of James's association with the New Thought movement. Dubbed by William James as "the religion of healthy mindedness," the movement was popularized by the spiritual works of two 19th-century American women, Mary Eddy Baker and Emma Curtis Hopkins. Less interested in organized religion and a systematic theology, it advocated goodwill with others, mental and bodily healings, and personal prosperity. The latter gave rise to the prosperity gospel teachings of such evangelists as Norman Vincent Peale and Joel Osteen.

At the 1940 commencement ceremonies for Staley College of the Spoken Word, an award was given *in absentia* to Earl James, "Archbishop of the Province of Ontario."[1] The Brookline, Massachusetts school of public speaking closed its doors in 1960, but not before one of its professors, Benjamin Stolow, helped prepare presidential candidate John Fitzgerald Kennedy for his first televised debate with Republican nominee Dick Nixon.[2]

But James' degrees-by-mail racket finally caught up with him, if only for the time being: the Ontario Department of Education effectively told James to go legitimate or face up to $25,000 in fines. He popped up in the obscure mining town of Sudbury, renting hotel rooms and hitting on diner waitresses. He now referred to himself as "Doctor" instead of "Reverend." Shortly after checking into the Fontenac Hotel in Sudbury, a number of underage girls were found in James's room. He was kicked out, but not before sputtering obscene language at the hotel manager.

He even surfaced in Akron, Ohio as an unlicensed marriage and family therapist, charging twenty-five dollars a visit.[3] In this role, he claimed to be director of something called the National Academy of Education. And not only was James frequently moving around at this time, shuttling between the U.S. and Canada, but so was his estranged wife. What became of Mary after the heart balm charge?

During World War II, Mary Kozak worked as a representative for a U.S. soft drinks firm. The position sent her around the United States with her small dog, Jinxie, as her companion. In 1952, a border crossing document for Earl Anglin James, Jr. tells us the younger James entered Canada with his mother, cited on the manifest as "Mrs. Mary Johnson." The young man's permanent address in the record is the apartment of his grandparents, Nick and Lena Kozak, 490 Queen St. in Sault Ste. Marie, where the former prospector was now proprietor of a cafe below the apartment. Earl Anglin James, Jr.'s address in the United States, according to the same manifest, was 826 Fern Ave. in Dallas, which he shared with his mother. The 19-year-old's occupation was a stock manager.

The elderly Kozaks were ailing by now, and ownership of the Queen St. apartment in Ontario passed to Mary. Lena died in 1954; her obituary cited she was the mother of "Mrs. Mary Johnson of Los Angeles, California."[4] Nick Kozak died six months later.

---

1   *Boston Globe*, 15 May 1940.
2   *Boston Globe*, Benjamin Stolow Obituary, 15 June 2004.
3   See Moon, "Prince of the Degree Merchants."
4   *Sault Star*, 2 April 1954.

In 1959, under the pen name Diane James, Mary Kozak published her semi-autobiographical, if hopelessly melodramatic novel, *Scars*. Kozak wrote the novel over the course of two years at the 490 Queen St. apartment. The fictional protagonists, the Kovall family, bear many similarities to the real-life Kozaks, including their emigration from the old country to Ontario mining towns. The novel's plot even incorporates "an unfortunate marriage which ended in divorce."[5] The novel's antagonist, the evil Professor Henry Ignace, is an unequivocal surrogate for Earl Anglin James. He is a vile and base fat monster, a rapist and murderer.

> She enrolled in a small private school to study the English language further in an evening class. She met Professor Ignace, a fat-bellied man with brown hair and a bald spot. He had piercing black eyes. Professor Ignace taught a small group in English and was forever favoring Marusia with extra help in her work. His soft voice, almost like a woman's, irritated Marusia and she wished he didn't pay her special attention, for it was embarrassing to her in front of the other students.[6]

Marusia, Mary Kozak's stand-in, goes home for vacation. It is not a happy home, dominated by an overbearing father. There is a knock at the door.

> "Hello," said a mild, womanlike voice, "is this where the Kovall family lives?"
>
> Marusia recognized Professor Ignace's voice and she froze where she sat.
>
> "Your daughter studied in my school in Toronto and we became good friends. Since she said she was going to visit her parents and since it's vacation time I thought I'd come out here and visit with you folks for a few days."
>
> Mr. Kovall motioned Professor Ignace in and said, "I want to hear about my daughters' activities. You might as well tell me what it is she's been doing."
>
> "Oh, she was in my school and we spent many evenings very privately together over a period of six months."
>
> "In that case you ought to marry this man, daughter."
>
> Mrs. Kovall stood by the round table and her color was almost purple. She held a bread board in her hand and Marusia grabbed the bread board from her mother and with a great swing slammed it over the professor's head. He whirled, and cursed her, "You stuck-up, foreign little ass, I'll make you suffer for this!"

---

5   *Sault Star*, 03 March 1959.
6   Diane James, *Scars* (New York: Pageant Press, 1959), 135.

Swept up by the professor's false implications over relations with Marusia, Mr. Kovall storms his daughter down to City Hall, where Ignace and a preacher await. A hasty marriage takes place, against Marusia's will. Ignace immediately shoves Marusia into his car, tying her to the seat by rope. "He slid behind the wheel and started driving. His fat belly wobbled at every bump on the road. His greasy face poured sweat down over his dirty collar. Marusia's mind worked feverishly on how to kill Ignace."

Ignace effectively rapes Marusia on their "honeymoon" camping trip. It is a hellish sequence. A pregnancy results, and a son is soon born. Ignace has nothing to do with the boy. At the end, convicted of murdering Marusia's gentlemanly soulmate, Peter, he is sentenced to hang. Earlier, Ignace does five years of hard labor for raping an underage girl. He is completely one dimensional, the hate from the main character – and its author – spewing forth with all its vitriol.

Under her pen name, Mary Kozak showed no lack of ambition when she sent a signed copy of *Scars* to gossip columnist Hedda Hopper. The inscribed note included a postscript hoping the novel might be adapted as a Hollywood motion picture. It never was.

The book jacket for *Scars* confirms some details: "[Diane James] has traveled extensively in the United States and lived in Dallas, Texas, and Los Angeles, California, for a period of some twelve years. A mother of a grown son, she was able to take time from her occupation in the real estate business to pursue her literary interest. Mrs. James is planning to return from Sault Ste. Marie, Ontario, Canada, to the United States, of which country she is a permanent resident. She will live in Los Angeles, where her son is now studying psychology and dramatic arts."

* * *

The ex-husband of Mary Kozak/Diane James was keeping busy in his own way – so much so the Royal Canadian Mountain Police alerted FBI director J. Edgar Hoover about James. According to his United States draft card, dated February 16, 1942, James was in Chicago. His residency was the now demolished Brevoort Hotel, an architecturally classic, early 20th century downtown hotel famous for its ornate, marble lobby and crystal bar. On another occasion, he stayed at the Morrison Hotel in Chicago. James provided "McKinley-Roosevelt University" as his place of employment on the draft card, its address on Chicago's North Side, 4610 Sheridan Rd., a mile north of Wrigley Field. An early 1940s map of Chicago places the address in a residential area, the home of a Mr. and Mrs. Taylor, today a cluster of low income apartment housing. James signed the draft card "Dr. Earl A. James."

The exact date is unclear, but based on that draft card signature James "earned" his medical degree from First National University of Naturopathy and Allied Sciences, another diploma mill, out of Newark, New Jersey.[7] The fraternity amid those within the diploma mill/correspondence school business becomes clearer with this particular association, as if those in the business were part of their own underground network. First National University of Naturopathy and Allied Sciences was a project of one Frederick W. Collins, known as the "Consulting Drugless Physician of America." The university's website today proclaims Collins "the first Naturopath, Osteopath, Chiropractor, in fact, the first and only drugless physician to receive the nomination for President of the United States."[8] In a 1944 sworn affidavit, the secretary of the New Jersey State Board of Medical Examiners stated: "[T]he First National University of Naturopathy has [n]ever been recognized by the New Jersey State Board of Medical Examiners, nor have any physicians, surgeons, osteopaths nor chiropractors, been licensed from said institution."[9] But that did not deter Collins, a frequent lecturer at conventions for groups like the Society of Human

---

7   *Toronto Star*, 10 February 1968.

8   First National University of Naturopathy website (https://www.fnun.edu/collins/history. html).

9   Supreme Court of the State of New York, Appellate Division – Second Department (1944), 106.

Engineers. Kevah Deo Griffis, a Hollywood occultist from the 1920s, also spoke on astrology at the same gatherings.[10]

Naturopathy has long been derided as pseudoscience, what a contemporary ex-naturopathist termed "essentially witchcraft."[11] For James, there is a similarity between his association with naturopathy and his past foray into the trance preaching of the Metaphysical Spiritualist Church. In the decades to come, when hypnosis emerges in our analysis of the JFK, MLK, and RFK assassinations, we find a connecting thread back to both naturopathy and trance - and, in turn, the world of the occult.

* * *

When asked on his draft card to name a person "who will always know your address," Earl James provided the name "Brig. Gen. Gustavus Blech." It is an odd answer to a question effectively asking for next of kin – the usual place for names of spouses, siblings, and other family members. James, however, names an aged medical doctor, surgeon, and veteran of numerous American military campaigns, including the Spanish-American War and World War I. Blech was from Riga, the capital city of Latvia off the Baltic Sea, another White Russian whom James apparently considered within his limited circle of intimates, after his ex-Austro-Ukrainian in-laws, the Kozaks. While Blech was a colonel in the United States Army, his rank in the Illinois National Guard was in fact Brigadier General. Blech died in Chicago in 1949 and is buried at Arlington National Cemetery.

According to the RCMP file on James, he had sought out Blech in order to be treated for asthma, and remained under his care for three years. James's CV sheds further light on this interesting relationship – if there really was one – as well as providing an insight into James's habit of using people's names as endorsements, *without their knowledge*:

> I prefer to know the Soul of a Person long before I meet his Physical Body; One of my Best Friends, General Gustavus Blech of the United States Army of First World War ONE, I did not see "in flesh ever," for ten long years, though I wrote to him almost every week – I knew His Soul 1st. – and then I met the FLESH – The GENERAL! How much better it is this way! Far better than meeting the Person 1st.[12]

10   *Los Angeles Evening Citizen News*, 11 Sept. 1929.
11   Megan Thielking, "'Essentially Witchcraft': A former naturopath takes on her colleagues," *Stat*, 20 Oct. 2016.
12   EAJ Curriculum Vitae, 33.

It is not clear what kind of job – again, if there really *was* one – James held at McKinley-Roosevelt University. As with the other institutions in James's life, this one was no different. McKinley-Roosevelt was nothing more than a correspondence school operating out of the home of W.R. Taylor and wife Jessie. It came under fire in 1947 by the Federal Trade Commission for misrepresenting the sale of correspondence courses, among other infractions.[13] William R. Peacock, secretary of the school, issued a statement of compliance with the FTC to cease "representing itself as an institution of higher learning authorized to confer degrees."[14] Peacock mentioned the school had on staff "seven or eight professors." It's possible James was one of these professors, but Peacock offers no further detail on the qualifications or courses taught by these "professors."

In a blistering, terse indictment against James and his livelihood, the Better Business Bureau of Hartford, Connecticut exposed his fraudulent practices.[15] Based on the plethora of degrees James accumulated by 1943 – 112, the "world's record for college degrees" he boasted, which would explode to 2,000 twenty-five years later – he was well into the business of not only dishing out diplomas for $50 as the Hartford BBB claimed, but also amassing degrees and titles for himself, suggesting a *quid pro quo* relationship between James and his "students."

While by all accounts a compulsive liar, James enjoyed name-dropping and displaying photographs of the both familiar and nameless. "That's me with Mae West," he volunteered to *Toronto Star* reporter Earl McRae in 1968. He claimed to have performed the wedding ceremony of Al Capone's son and his bride (in reality, Albert Francis Capone and Diana Ruth Casey were married at St. Patrick's Catholic Church in Miami Beach). Then, just a beat later, he uttered with great seriousness, "I own all of these buildings from here to Broadview," gesturing grandly.

The Hartford BBB was well aware of James' antics, and shows a thorough grasp of his time at McKinley-Roosevelt University: "[S]ome of his alleged 112 degrees were granted by a so-called 'university' in Chicago, operated by a man and his wife in a couple of rooms, and that others were obtained on an exchange basis between 'Dr.' James's National College, Toronto, and some trade schools and other minor organizations in the United States."[16]

Now, prohibited from operations by the Board of Education in Ottawa, an undaunted James saw an opportunity to go on the road across

13   *The Gazette and Daily*, 08 July 1947.
14   *Chicago Tribune*, 09 July 1947.
15   *Hartford Courant*, 11 July 1943.
16   Ibid.

the border. It was wartime, and like a true door-to-door salesman, Earl James visited U.S. Army camps peddling his briefcase of homemade diplomas and other accessories. Three months before the BBB of Hartford published its warning against his practices, the U.S. War Department became privy to James's wandering around military compounds. Most of the Better Business Bureau claims against James are lifted directly from a May 8, 1943 communique and dispersed out of Fort Sumter to all bases five days later:[17]

> Information has been received that a man by the name of "Dr." Earl Anglin James is traveling over this country selling fake "College Degrees."
>
> This so called "Dr." Earl Anglin James claims to be a distinguished Canadian educator, President of the National College of Canada, and rector of an Episcopalian Church in Canada. He has been known to gain some publicity by claiming close blood kin to the former notorious bandits Frank and Jesse James.
>
> "Dr." Earl Anglin James was checked by the Toronto Bureau and found to be a big "faker."
>
> "Dr." James was last seen in Fort Wayne, Indiana, driving a Dodge sedan with Canadian license plates. He informed newspaper reporters that he was making a tour of U. S. Army camps.
>
> Any information regarding this "Dr." Earl Anglin James should be reported to the nearest FBI Office.

In spite of the Army's alert on James, he continued to find willing "students." One such pupil was Capt. Sam McCluney, a native of Waxahachie, Texas south of Dallas, and an educator at Houston's Jefferson Davis High before the war. Over the course of World War II, McCluney rose to the rank of lieutenant-colonel, leading an ordnance battalion in the Italian theater. But in the summer of 1943, at the same time as the Army's communique on James, McCluney received a Ph.D from the National College, complementing the earlier – and legitimate – undergraduate and postgraduate degrees McCluney had obtained from Texas A&M. McCluney met James in 1941 while he was stationed in Detroit. At the time the two met, McCluney was the only member of the government's Office of Production Control, set up "to control distribution of critical materials so that all manufacturers received their share."[18] These critical materiels ranged from engines to tanks. By war's end, McCluney oversaw a forty-member department.

---

17   U.S. War Dept. Communique, May 8 1943.
18   *The Waxahachie Light*, 13 February 1946.

James somehow found McCluney's work of interest and recommend-ed he turn it into a doctoral thesis. But McCluney was pressed for time, so James accepted the official report McCluney wrote for his government supervisors in 1943 in lieu of a thesis paper. From there, courses were waived, and McCluney was awarded a doctor of philosophy. "The Cana-dians thought his work was so good that along with it came an honorary LL.D degree from the Canadian Therapeutic Society," McCluney's home-town newspaper glowed.[19] It is questionable if such an institution as the Canadia Therapeutic Society even existed: this author uncovered only one other mention of it, also from 1943, when a Windsor, Ontario resi-dent, Ralph Caliguire, received a Ph.D. We can safely assume that it was another product of the imagination of Earl Anglin James.

* * *

As the war drew to a close in 1945, Earl James was in Edmonton, Al-berta, renting a room at the Selkirk Hotel, where he entertained Air Force officers and sought a relationship with a juvenile delinquent. Now James entered a new phase, one that would satiate his desire for fame and inflate his self-esteem while placing him in a new orbit of equally strange individ-uals. The small-time Anglican who dabbled in spiritualism and naturopa-thy was to become, at last, an ordained bishop. A prince of the church. But of what church? And who was his flock?

---

19   Ibid.

American Orthodox Catholic Church

✠

ARCHBISHOP WALTER M. PROPHETA
Primate

CATHEDRAL CHURCH OF THE HOLY RESURRECTION
675 East 183rd Street
New York, N.Y. 10458
Phone (212) FOrdham 7-1961

September 12, 1967

Hon. James Garrison
4600 Owens Dr.
New Orleans, Louisiana

Dear Mr. Garrison:

Our friend Jack Martin has submited to us your Address and it is an honor and privilege to write this letter to you.

We want to take this opportunity to congratulate you for the fine job that you are doing in trying to unmask the Communist conspiracy that killed our President Kennedy.

It takes an outstanding man with real courage to do what you are doing and we are praying for more men of your calibre.

As Founder and President of "Crusade Against Communism" for the past 38 years, I know from personal experience what you must be going through - denunciations, calumnies, vicious slander, threats etc., but be cheer and keep up the good work. Please rely on our full cooperation and please accept our deep admiration and sincere gratitude.

Gratefully yours,

✝ Archbishop W. M. Propheta

Archbishop Walter M. Propheta

P.S. If at all possible, please send Jack Martin to us on the 30th of this month.

CHAPTER THREE

CHURCH BIZARRE

They wandered in the wilderness in a desert region;
They did not find a way to an inhabited city.

– Psalm 107:4

As discussed at the outset, the Old Catholic Church generally refers to the practices, rituals, liturgies, and rules developed by schismatic sects that largely formed as a rebuke against papal infallibility. This dogma of the Catholic Church was defined at the First Vatican Council in 1870. The relationship with the Orthodox Patriarchate of Antioch is particularly important for our purposes, a line of apostolic succession that will ultimately take us to a secret society opposed to the Kennedy vision for America.

By rejecting the doctrine, those who identified with the schismatics were duly excommunicated by the Church, including breakaway bishops validly ordained. These men of the episcopacy exercised their claim of apostolic succession – an unbroken line of bishops they claim stretches to the time of the first apostles chosen by Christ – resulting in an enormous catalog of names not unlike genealogies detailed in the Bible: "Enoch fathered Irad, and Irad fathered Mehujael; Mehujael fathered Methushael...," etc. (Gen. 4:18). Apostolic succession is so important that in the Roman church three bishops lay hands over an ordinate – triple assurance of the validity of the consecration.

However, the official history of the Old Roman Catholic Church prefers to date its origins to the 18th century, when the diocese of Utrecht broke from the Vatican following accusations from the region's Jesuits that the Jansenist heresy was alive and well. The archbishop of Utrecht was suspended, and Rome, having dissolved the diocese, recognized Utrecht as mission territory. Of course, the Old Catholic Church of the Netherlands, the mother church of the Old Catholic Union of Utrecht, viewed themselves as the true Catholic Church, neither schismatic nor heretical. Once independent of Rome, ecumenical unity became a major

objective for the Old Catholic Church. Two acts of union with the Orthodox Patriarchate of Antioch and another with the Orthodox Patriarchate
of Alexandria were enacted in 1911 and 1912, respectively.

This theme of ecumenism is mirrored in New Thought's pillar of goodwill and unity to others. It also dominates Earl Anglin James' writings.

The Old Catholic Church's history points to an untitled papal bull promulgated by Pope Pius X in 1911 "which reveals and recognized beyond
all possibility of question, the absolute validity of the Orders of the Old
Roman Catholic Church. The group recognizes the Papal Roman Catholic Church as the first true Church of Jesus Christ, and the Pope of Rome
as the center of Catholic Unity."[1] The author has not been able to confirm
the existence of this papal document of Pius X, but *A Practical Commentary on the Code of Canon Law* (1939) states:

> A validly consecrated bishop can validly confer all orders from the
> minor orders to the episcopate inclusively, though he be a heretic,
> schismatic, or deposed and degraded from the episcopal digni
> ty, for he nevertheless retains the episcopal character in virtue of
> which he can validly ordain, provided he observes the essentials of
> the form of ordination and has the intention to do what the Church
> does in performing the sacred ordination rites. For this reason the
> ordinations performed by the schismatic (Orthodox) bishops of
> the Greek Church, by the Jansenist bishops in Holland, and by the
> Old Catholics in Germany and Switzerland are considered valid.[2]

The 1931 Bonn Agreement, which established communion between
the Church of England and the Old Catholic Church of Utrecht, further
adds to the possibility of valid ordinations.

This validity carries enormous portent for those vying to become ordained and hopefully raised to the episcopacy in the Old Catholic Church.
As we will see, for men otherwise ill-suited for such a vocation, like David
Ferrie, becoming a bishop was a fixation. From a theological standpoint, a
valid ordination confers such men into the royal priesthood: One can say
Mass, with the power to turn bread and wine into the Body and Blood, Soul
and Divinity of Christ in the Eucharist. One has the power to baptize, to
marry, to give last rites to the dying. One has the power to forgive sins. And,
most importantly in this case, if one becomes a bishop, one has the power to
create new priests – and new bishops. From a secular standpoint, confident

---

1   "The Old Roman Catholic Church in Europe and North America." From the files of Robert
Arthur Burns.
2   Stanislaus Woyod, *A Practical Commentary on the Code of Canon* Law, par. 881.

their rise to the priesthood is wholly and canonically valid, these men can wear their Roman collars or bishop miters publicly and proudly. They can travel abroad without the general public – or, more importantly, customs agents – thinking twice. They can raise money for their tax-free churches or missions without much explanation. Since there is no oversight from Rome, such men are thus free of extensive hierarchical oversight. And, if you are so inclined, you can simply form your own version of the Old Catholic Church. You are your own bishop, your own pope.

Not a bad setup when you spend your life associating with the underworld.

In his 1947 work, *Episcopi Vagantes and the Anglican Church*, mentioned by Earl Anglin James in his CV, Henry R.T. Bandreth paints the following example as a common scenario among such bishop-seekers:

> The kind of thing which may happen is this: John Smith comes into contact with an *episcopus vagans*. He has certain social ambitions, and he has seen the social standing of the clergy. He therefore flatters the bishop, tells him that he wants to give his life to the service of God, and begins to serve the bishop's Mass. As soon as he has become efficient at the altar the bishop makes him a deacon, and then, when he has learned to say Mass, ordains him priest. John Smith has been made a priest solely on the merits of abeing able to say Mass with reasonable efficiency; he is uneducated, and his lack of cultural equipment may even be such that he finds difficulty in composing ordinary correspondence. Having been made a priest, he begins to work more on the bishop. He starts by telling him that, as he is head of an independent church, he ought to be an archbishop. But an archbishop must have suffragans, jurisdiction over whom justifies the claim to archiepiscopal status. John Smith and one of his fellow-priests are therefore "elected" by a synod of sycophants and consecrated. After the consecration the consecrator is elected archbishop. Thus matters continue for a few weeks until John Smith quarrels with his superior and proclaims himself independent. Whether he does that or not, the point is that the consecrator had some smattering at least of education, and knew matter, form and intention. John Smith's mind is a blank on such premises, though he may be able to chatter a jargon and deceive people as to his knowledge.[3]

* * *

A nationalist spirit motivated newly-arrived worshipers who had emigrated from Europe, primarily Eastern Europeans, into unfamiliar cities

---

3   Henry R.T. Brandreth, *Episcopi Vagantes and the Anglican Church* (London: Society for Performing Christian Knowledge, 1947), 3.

of the United States. Rather than integrate into the established parishes of an American diocese, these tight-knit ethnic clusters were willing to break communion with the universal church and the supreme pontiff, the pope in Rome, in order to remain tied to their faith communities they left behind. This loyalty to one's ethnic background and traditions created further microchurches derived from the Old Catholic Church, blending Eastern Orthodoxy and Roman Catholicism - although the two have been split since 1054. One of Earl James's consecrations, Carl Jerome Stanley of Kentucky, a man with a criminal record and key to exposing the New Orleans cabal of fake bishops who will assist in the assassination of President Kennedy and set up Oswald as a patsy, was so committed to unifying the two separated churches that he was invited to a session of the Second Vatican Council in 1964 as an ecumenical witness, a perplexing invitation indeed.[4]

We see an example of this fiery nationalist spirit in David Ferrie's hometown of Cleveland, Ohio. A wandering bishop, Joseph Rene Vilatte of the American Catholic Church, who was excommunicated from the Roman Catholic Church by Pope Leo XIII, wielded influence over confused congregations and impressionable young men doubting their vocations. J. Gordon Melton, in his *Encyclopedia of American Religions*, credits Vilatte for bringing the Old Catholic Church to America.

Cleveland priest Anton Francis Kolaszewski recruited Vilatte to consecrate the new Immaculate Heart of Mary Church in 1894 as an independent Catholic church for its Polish congregation. Vilatte agreed, promising a Catholicism free of "despotism." Quite simply, the ethnic Poles did not want to be part of a parish with a non-Polish pastor, and they found in Vilatte a prelate willing to sanctify the new church as they deemed acceptable. Kolaszewski was excommunicated by Cleveland's Catholic bishop, who warned the new church's parishioners not to go along with the schismatic behavior. In the end, Immaculate Heart of Mary parish assented to the Catholic bishop of Cleveland, and is still an active parish in the Cleveland diocese today. Vilatte also eventually reconciled with the Holy See in Rome before his death in 1929.

However, before his journey back to mother church, Vilatte became a bishop with the approval of Ignatius Peter III (Peter the Humble), patriarch of the Syriac Orthodox Church. Peter the Humble became interested in the Order of the Crown of Thorns, which claimed a medieval origin to 1239. Vilatte became Grand Master of the Order of the Crown of Thorns, a phony order heavily influenced on Gnosticism. As bishop, Vilatte con-

---

4   "Louisville Orthodox Prelate On Way To Vatican Council," *The Courier-Journal*, 23 Sept. 1964.

secrated men with ties to Gnostic churches in France. From the Greek word gnosis (knowing), Gnostics believed they were the privileged recipients of secret knowledge. Gnosticism was condemned as a heresy by the early Christian church.

Thomas Merton, the famed Trappist monk, wrote in his succinct style of his impressions of a wandering bishop he met at Gethsemani Abbey:

> The poor man, for some reason, had not lived as a good priest. In the end, his mistake had caught up with him. He had come into contact with some schismatics, in a sect known as "the old Catholics," and these people persuaded him to leave the Church and come over to them. And when he did so, they made him an archbishop. I suppose he enjoyed the dignity and the novelty of it for a while; but the whole thing was obviously silly. So he gave it up and came back. And now here he was in the monastery, serving Mass every morning for a young Trappist priest who scarcely had the oils of his ordination dry on his hands.[5]

Some were not so repentant. A former Franciscan who fell under Vilatte's influence was one Henry Carfora, born and raised a Catholic in Naples and ordained in the order of St. Francis of Assisi in 1901. His Franciscan superiors sent Carfora to work with the Italian immigrants in America. By decade's end, Carfora separated himself from the Catholic Church and established his own parish in Youngstown, Ohio. Here Carfora met Vilatte, who consecrated Carfora as a bishop in the Independent National Catholic Church in 1907. By the end of the 1910s, Carfora oversaw what he called the North American Old Roman Catholic Church. Prelates from  both the Roman or Episcopalian branches were welcomed.

In a 1968 letter to a Lutheran theology professor, Arthur C. Piepkorn, the metropolitan archbishop of the Old Roman Catholic Church (English Rite), Robert Alfred Burns, wrote, "You will be conscious of the fact that the late Pope Pius X publicly stated that 'Of all the Old Catholic Bodies

---

5   Thomas Merton, *Elected Silence: The Autobiography of Thomas Merton* (Berkeley: Hollis & Carter, 1949), 245.

in the United States, ONLY that under the jurisdiction of Carmel Henry Carfora can be said to possess VALID ORDERS and SACRAMENTS, since they have NEVER been guilty of preaching, teaching or entering into any heretical practices, or adhereing (sic) to any heretical doctrines."[6]

An especially unique individual was the Englishman William H.F. Brothers, a member of Old Catholic Benedictines living in Illinois. In 1916, Brothers was consecrated a bishop in the Czech Old Catholic Church by Bishop Rudolph de Landes Berghes. The next day, Brothers assisted de Landes Berghes in another consecration – that of Carmel Henry Carfora. Later, Bishop Brothers wound up in upstate New York, where he became known as Father Francis of Woodstock, the Hippie Priest. Bob Dylan counted him as a friend and confidant.

Both Vilatte and Carfora sought to expand independent Catholicism into Mexico. This initiative coincided with the launch of the anti-clerical Mexican Revolution. It was prescient thinking on the part of these wandering bishops to anticipate Mexico's fertile ground for enthusiastic converts and dissatisfied clerics at this time in its complicated history. Carfora consecrated former Catholic priest José Joaquín Pérez Budar, the founder and "patriarch" of the Mexican Catholic Apostolic Church in 1926, a movement which had the support of Mexico's then-president, Plutarco Elias Calles.

A health incident in 1953 forced Carfora to enter the Roman Catholic hospital in Galveston. He died in 1958, suffering and enduring persecution from fellow churchmen. But Carfora already established his foothold in Mexico, and his mission was inadvertently aided by the spirit of the Second Vatican Ecumenical Council (hereafter Vatican II) and its initiative to collaborate with developing nations. As the decades mounted, Supreme Primate Carfora seemed willing to consecrate anyone and everyone. "Carfora appears to have consecrated a multitude of strange people, so many, so strange, that a few years ago I refused to have anything more to do with any of them," the Archbishop of Caer-Glow, Monsignor Williams, complained in a letter.[7] Among these was Earl Anglin James, whom Carfora raised to the episcopacy on June 17, 1945. James's title was Bishop of Toronto for the North American Old Roman Catholic Church, although it was completely titular – James would never preside over liturgical events. Yet, from the Carfora line of succession, James could claim his sacred position of bishop can link all the way back to the Roman popes of the 17th century:

6   Burns to Piepkorn, 14 September 1968.
7   Peter Anson, *Bishops at Large* (Berkeley: Apocryphile Press, 1964), 432.

Earl Anglin James (1945)
Carmel Henry Carfora
De Landes Berghes
Arnold Harris Mathew
Gerardus Gul
Gaspard Johannes Rinkel
Herman Heykamp
Johannes van Santen
Johannes Bon
Willibrord van Os
Gijsbert de Jong
Johannes Jacobus van Rhijn
Adrian Broekman
Walter van Nieuwenhuisen
Johannes van Stiphout
Petrus Johannes Meindaerts
Dominique Marie Varlet
Jacques Goyon de Matignon
Jacques Benigne Bossuet
Charles Maurice Letellier
Antonio Cardinal Barberini
Alexander VII (Pope from 1655-1667)
Innocent X (Pope from 1644-1655)
Urban VIII (Pope from 1623-1644)
Gregory XV (Pope from 1621-1623)
Etc.

In turn, James consecrated Grant Timothy Billet on December 25, 1950. By 1964, when Billet consecrated Carl Jerome Stanley, there were two factions of the American Old Catholic Church (AOCC), both of interest to us: in the midwest, the Anglin James-Billet-Stanley line, of which Davd Ferrie, Jack Martin, Guy Banister and associated in New Orleans were aligned. The AOCC derived from a church called the Holy Orthodox Catholic Patriarchate of America, whose patriarch was Peter Zhurawetzky. Zhurawetzky was born in Galicia, Austria (now western Ukraine) and originally was ordained a priest in the Ukrainian Orthodox Church. He aligned himself with Orthodox clergy in America who refused to submit to Moscow. Zhurawetzky could not reconcile how the Orthodox Church could tolerate authority from the atheist Soviet politburo. As a bishop, the Polish Old Catholic Church fell under Zhurawetzky's jurisdiction. Writing about the Holy Orthodox Catholic Patriarchate of America,

Zhurawetzky remarked, "The aim of this Holy American Patriarchate of Eastern and Western tradition is to be a spring-board upon which all the independent groups of Catholics can unite to form a viable church with beliefs and principles of undivided Orthodoxy."[8]

Zhurawetzky collaborated with a priest in the Byelorussian Orthodox Church, Uladyslau Ryzy-Ryski, to forge the Byelorussian Catholic Church. Ryzy-Ryzski met Archbishop Walter Propheta of the AOCC. Eventually, Propheta and Zhurawetzky consecrated Ryzy-Ryzski as a bishop in the AOCC.

Walter Myron Propheta of New Jersey was a Ukrainian-born son of Archpriest Dimitray. Like his father, he joined the Ukrainian Orthodox priesthood, becoming the family's twelfth generation to carry on the legacy. Late in his ecclesiastical career, in the mid-1960s, Propheta abandoned the church of his ancestors for the Old Catholic Church. This rather casual transition from one church to the other is significant, given Propheta's long family lineage of Ukrainian Orthodox priests, a tradition that even continued with Propheta's son.

When Propheta's American Orthodox Catholic Church applied for a building loan in 1969, the application provided succinct insight into how the church viewed itself: "It is Orthodox but not Eastern. It is Catholic but not Papal." Loan consultant Abraham J. Isserman described it as "a national organization with international affiliations and overseas divisions with interracial communicants in both laity and clergy."[9]

Propheta attempted to assert his primacy over other bishops within the AOCC, requiring newly consecrated bishops to present their credentials directly to him. Like others in this world, Propheta was a rabid anti-communist, founder of the "Crusade Against Communism" movement.[10] He frequently appeared on radio and television speaking out against communist atrocities, such as the Katyn massacre, where the Soviet Union's NKVD executed 22,000 Polish soldiers and POWs, and the Vinnitsia massacre of 10,000 Ukrainians by the Soviet secret police.

Propheta also engaged in some racketeering activities. In March 1960, Propheta and Richard Brown, president of Local 522, Lumber Drivers and Handlers, distributed raffle tickets on behalf of Propheta's Cathedral Church of the Holy Resurrection at various New Jersey lumber yards

8   John Kersey, "Patriarchate," https://san-luigi.org/royal-office/royal-house/royal-belarus/patriarchate/.
9   "Project Proposed for City," *Asbury Park Press*, 21 January 1969.
10   "Forms Anti-Red Crusade; Jersey Pastor Raises Funds for Resistance With Movie," *New York Times*, 14 July 1954.

where Local 522 had contracts. While the tickets ostensibly were sold to aid Propheta's Ukrainian Greek Orthodox Church, persons identified with the Local 522 financially benefited in a backhand way.

Propheta's passion against the Red Menace was shared by leading American clerics of the time, such as Cardinal Richard Cushing of Boston and televangelist Bishop Fulton J. Sheen. Even parish priests framed their sermons to reference the red menace: "Our Christian culture is being threatened by Satan and his cohorts, the communists," Lyndon Johnson's unofficial spiritual director, Fr. Wunibald Schneider, preached in a Mass attended by Konrad Adenauer in Texas in 1961. But the most vocal *primus inter pares* of high-ranking prelates in America against Communism was Francis Spellman, cardinal archbishop of New York. Propheta knew both Cushing and Spellman, as  well as the New York archdiocese's vicar general and Spellman's successor, Terence Cooke. Propheta himself acknowledged that had Thomas Dewey won the 1948 election against incumbent President Harry Truman, Dewey intended to make Propheta White House chaplain. Propheta was also acquainted with FBI director J. Edgar Hoover, who recognized and admired Propheta's anti-communist initiative. Hoover was so involved in Propheta's work the FBI director personally installed him as "primate" of the AOCC at a Manhattan dinner.

Furthermore, Propheta's ties with the FBI are demonstrated by bishops presenting their credentials to Propheta, like Archbishop Stanley of Louisville and Earl Anglin James. These men were likewise vetted by the FBI. Propheta's highly probable role as an FBI informant would explain the shift from his family's long line of Ukrainian Orthodox priests.[11]

Another well-known anti-Communist cleric was demagogic Catholic priest Father Charles Coughlin, whose anti-Senitism ultimately proved his downfall. Coughlin, who achieved notoriety with radio broadcasts lambasting the Roosevelt administration and calling FDR a Jew, helped publicize *The Protocols of the Elders of Zion*, a forged document alleging

---

11   Email correspondence with Peter Levenda, 4/23/2023.

a longstanding Jewish conspiracy to achieve global domination from the hand of White Russian Boris Brasol (1885-1963). After a 1938 speech wherein he claimed "Nazism was conceived as a political defense mechanism against Jewish Communism," Coughlin echoed *Mein Kampf*'s central theme that Jewish bankers backed the Russian Revolution.[12]

Based in anti-Semite Henry Ford's Detroit, Coughlin ran the Christian Frontiers, as anti-black as it was anti-Jewish. A "lieutenant" of both Coughlin and Ford, Louisiana's white nationalist and religious militant Gerald L.K. Smith, will later prove to be an instrumental figure in our narrative.[13] The presence and influence of White Russians also greatly permeates our story.

* * *

It was not lost on American intelligence how much top-secret information flowed through the Vatican City State, the world's smallest sovereign state but ruled by a spiritual leader who shepherded nearly a billion souls in the Cold War period. No one knew the score of the world political game better than certain Vatican figures at the very top of the Church hierarchy. Again, this meant Cardinal Spellman, military vicar for the US Armed Forces. Spellman was also advisor to the American branch of the Sovereign Military Order of Malta (SMOM), the venerable Catholic chivalric order dating back to the Middle Ages, which counted among its knights former CIA directors William Casey and John McCone; President Nixon's final chief of staff, Alexander Haig; James Jesus Angleton, CIA's chief of counterintelligence; and former director of the Office of Strategic Services (OSS) under President Franklin Roosevelt, General "Wild Bill" Donovan, who yearned to create "shadow warfare magic."[14] Much of America's tilt towards a "national security state" can be attributed to Donovan, who was a proponent of assassination by clandestine means, if it meant security for the country.

Following the liberation of Rome from the Nazis, Pope Pius XII (Eugenio Pacelli, papal nuncio to Germany from 1917-1929) knighted Bill Donovan with the Grand Cross of the Order of St. Sylvester, a public gesture for decidedly clandestine operations. Among these efforts was Donovan's collaboration with Dominican priest Felix Morlion on his anti-communist apostolate, the Pro Deo Center of Information. Morlion was also a leader in Catholic Action Europe, a quasi-political movement that sought to bolster the Catholic presence under regimes hostile to the faith. Donovan helped

---

12   Charles Higham, *American Swastika* (Garden City: Doubleday, 1985), 71.
13   Glen Jeansonne, "Partisan Parson: An Oral History Account of the Louisiana Years of Gerald L.K. Smith," Louisiana History: *The Journal of the Louisiana Historical Association*, Vol. 23, No. 2 (Spring, 1982), 149-158.
14   Philip Taubman, "War By Other Means," *New York Times*, 21 August 1983.

relocate Fr. Morlion's Pro Deo headquarters from Lisbon to New York. There Fr. Morlion founded the American Council for International Promotion of Democracy Under God, a non-profit still registered in New York today. The Chairman of the Board was Henry Robinson Luce, founder of *Time, Life, Fortune, Sports Illustrated*, and husband of Catholic convert Clare Boothe Luce, President Eisenhower's ambassador to Italy.[15]

Luce was a powerful presence in the American press. Born in China into a family of missionaries, he was a Yale graduate and Skull and Bones member. Luce wrote a landmark *Life* editorial prior to the United States entry into World War II, "The American Century," the tone of which Walter A. McDougall called "brooding, even occult."[16] Luce felt Americans were living under a false sense of peace as the world burned around them, a mentality evoking the verse from the prophet Jeremiah: "they say 'Peace, Peace' when there is no peace" (Jer. 6:14).

Another board member was C.D. Jackson, formerly President Dwight Eisenhower's special assistant on psychological warfare and Time-Life's man in CIA's Operation Mockingbird, which aimed to exploit the news media for propagandistic purposes.[17] "*Life* magazine is always pulling chestnuts out of the fire for the CIA," Drew Pearson wrote.[18] Henry Luce and JFK did not see eye to eye on how to confront Fidel Castro in Cuba, so much so that Luce embarked on his own private war, purchasing communications equipment and life insurance for commandos of anti-Castro paramilitary group Alpha 66, as well as paying for their "exclusive stories – money often plowed back into the raids [on Cuba]."[19]

Both Luce and Jackson were also on the Board of Directors for the American Council for International Promotion of Democracy Under God. President Kennedy assassination researchers will recognize both Luce and Jackson from Time-Life's purchase of Abraham Zapruder's 8mm film recording of the assassination in Dealey Plaza the very weekend of the murder. Jackson was reportedly so horrified by the images of the Zapruder film he ordered it locked in the Time-Life vault. The 26-second film, which shows evidence of editing, would not be broadcast to the public until 1975.

Fr. Morlion ran his own university in Rome, the Pro Deo International University of Social Studies. Construction for the school was largely financed by the Kaufmann family of Pittsburgh. Pro Deo also involved it-

---

15   "Henry Robinson Luce Papers," Library of Congress, Box 52.
16   Walter A. McDougall, *The Tragedy of U.S. Foreign Policy* (New Haven: Yale UP, 2016), 205.
17   "Jackson, C.D. Papers, 1931-1967" Dwight D. Eisenhower Library, Box 71.
18   Quoted in Warren Hinckle and William Turner, *Deadly Secrets* (New York: Thunder's Mouth Press, 1992), 185.
19   Ibid., 187.

self in interfaith activities, such as a 1965 gathering with the aim to "establish unity" among differing faiths and backgrounds.[20] Its 1967 gathering concentrated on practically applying the themes in Pope Paul VI's economic encyclical, *Populorum Progressio* (On the Progression of Peoples). Such businessmen in attendance were U.S. Chamber of Commerce president and former governor of Texas, Allen Shivers; New Deal Democrat and president of Coca-Cola, James A. Farley, another board member for Morlion's American Council for International Promotion of Democracy under God; and Vermont C. Royster, editor of the *Wall Street Journal*. [21]

Perhaps Morlion's greatest ecumenical triumph was in shuttle diplomacy, assisting Pope John XXIII's mediation between Kruschev's Kremlin and the Kennedy White House during the Cuban Missile Crisis.[22]

But Pro Deo's ultimate goal went beyond combating the spread of communism or finding common ground among other religions. Fr. Morlion, through his apostolate and university, had greater ambitions. In anticipation of its 1963 summit in New York, Pro Deo published its fundamental principles, among them: "To widen political horizons in an international spirit resulting in a scientific activity which will be the precursor of a political unification of human society and will offset all nationalist doctrines."[23] Such language hearkens to a theme in *Populorum Progressio* that argued advancing human development must come from an effective world authority, such as the United Nations.[24] The United Nations, then, was a model example in advancing the worth and dignity of all people; in the spirit of unity, even Archbishop Walter M. Propheta was permitted use of the UN's private chapel when he saw fit.

If there was any doubt about Pro Deo's intelligence functions, its president was J. Peter Grace, a devout Catholic who ran the W.R. Grace Company, a massively successful manufacturing conglomerate, and who, according to Hugh Wilford in *The Mighty Wurlitzer: How the CIA Played America*, "was an officer in a number of CIA front organizations."[25] This tactic of employing religious organizations to combat communism was a natural successor to stratagems the OSS employed during World War II; the MILTON Project was such an operation, in which the OSS used the Church for intel against

---

20   "Interfaith Meeting Praised by Pontiff," *Chicago Tribune*, 30 April 1965.
21   "Farley Heads Study Group at Vatican," *Tampa Tribune*, 25 June 1967, 38. See also "To an interfaith session," *Kansas City Times*, 23 June 1967.
22   "Pope John Helped Ease Cuba Crisis, Editor Confirms" *Miami Herald*, 05 June 1971.
23   Michael Wilson, "God Centered Society Goal of Scholars of Many Lands," *Catholic Advocate*, 03 March 1963.
24   Pope Paul VI, *Populorum Progressio*, n.78.
25   Hugh Wilford, *The Mighty Wurlitzer: How the CIA Played America* (Cambridge: Harvard University Press, 2008), 187.

Nazi movements.[26] In his book *A Certain Arrogance: The Sacrifice of Lee Harvey Oswald and the Cold War Manipulation of Religious Groups by U.S. Intelligence*, George Michael Evica notes, "Over the years, Allen Dulles and the OSS/CIA used the Quakers, the Unitarians, the World Council of Churches and other religious groups as sources of intelligence and information."[27]

But why the interest in religious groups, aside from these churches and apostolates having a foothold in geographic territory of strategic importance to the United States? The sheer number of individuals we will meet in the pages ahead who come from families of ministers and preachers is so prominent their preoccupation with using religion to advance interests reveals how ingrained religion was instilled in them. Allen Dulles is a prime example, as the son of a Presbyterian minister and uncle to Jesuit Avery Dulles (though neither uncle nor father, John Foster Dulles, were too happy about the vocation), who later became a cardinal of the Catholic Church by Pope John Paul II.

Beyond tapping into religious emotivism for intelligence purposes, a common psychology among these religiously-raised intelligence operative emerges: a worldview shaped by spiritual notions of a Divine Creator, sin, the blood atonement of the Christ, the sacrificial lamb who gave his life for the many. These were men who knew both the Old and New Testament, who saw the battle between the free world and atheistic communism as an apocalyptic battle between good and evil, not unlike the ideas and imagery expressed in Milton's *Paradise Lost*. A sense of urgency had to be created to alert Americans that the Nazis may have been defeated in a "great crusade" against the Axis Powers, but an even greater, nihilistic and existential threat loomed: the specter of Communism. If there was no sense of paranoia or trepidation regarding the Red Menace threatening to uproot their daily lives, there would have been no Cold War.

A new worldview was forced upon the American populace in the post-World War II era. Great lengths were taken by the intelligence communities and their partners in the news media to depict that new world as unfamiliar, dangerous territory. As early as 1944, cartographer Wallace Atwood observed "a broad world-wide study of geography with a human point of view is sweeping over the country like a great tidal wave."[28] World maps and globes symbolizing unity and peace among peoples became

---

26   Records of the Office of Strategic Services (Record Group 226) 1940-1947, Box 51 [WN#01354] and 316 [WN#13103].

27   George Michael Evica, *A Certain Arrogance* (Trine Day: Walterville, OR, 2011), 72.

28   Quoted in Matthew Farish, *The Contours of America's Cold War* (Minneapolis: University of Minnesota Press, 2010), 11.

prominent logos for organizations such as the United Nations or the 1964 World's Fair Unisphere. Allen Dulles, FDR, George C. Marshall and others were obsessed with maps. This obsession was turned into a public relations mission: shift American thinking from its pre-war isolationist mentality to one of globalization. In a way, the Cold War was a new world war, "the entire planet became an American strategic environment."[29]

Moreover, it was preparation for the age of geopolitics, of the military-industrial complex, a world hegemony shaped by the interests of WASP businessmen as much as WASP politicians, although neither were opposed to collaborating with the Italian-Catholics in the Mafia, or the Asian drug lords. The old isolationism policy now became a policy of winning hearts and minds – nation-building – via federal quasi-charities like the Office of Inter-American Affairs, the Good Neighbor Commission, Peace Corps, Alliance for Progress, AID (Agency for International Development), and the CIA. "The perverse results often included the multiplication of enemies, alienation of friends, toleration of friendly dictatorships."[30]

So, in this new time, the whole world was in play, from the densely populated continents of Asia and South America, to the forsaken North Pole and Antarctica. Radar, aerial intelligence and space technology now came into focus. Spies and subterfuge replaced diplomacy. Paranoia loomed over suburbia, represented by atomic mushroom clouds and prospective alien invasions. Top secret missions like Admiral Richard Byrd's Antarctic explorations and the establishments of bases on the continent were the priorities known only to a privileged few. Byrd even found himself indebted to the intelligence community: "I wish still again to offer you my services," Byrd wrote to CIA director Dulles in 1954. "Of course, since I wrote you last I have been doing what I can to help."[31]

Anyone who was anyone did not go unnoticed by American intelligence. Most likely, anyone who was anyone probably worked – witting or unwitting – for the intelligence community in some capacity on their way to the top.

---

29   Ibid.
30   McDougall, 283
31   Letter to Allen Dulles from Admiral Byrd, June 8, 1954, Central Intelligence Agency, Approved for Release 2002/10/10, CIA-RDP80R01731R000400300007-2.

CHAPTER FOUR

PASS THE PLATE

For when they speak great swelling words of vanity,
they allure through the lusts of the flesh,
through much wantonness,
those that were clean
escaped from them who live in error.

– 2 Peter 2:18

Meanwhile, Earl Anglin James was busy cultivating his empire. His fingerprints are all over a ten year scam run by faux priests out of Hell's Kitchen until they were convicted in 1945. Posing as clerics, a trio of men panhandled New Yorkers year after year to support their "Community Mission," a furnished storefront replete with Bibles and comic books. But there never was any charity or community outreach. They pocketed nearly $500,000 in those ten years. The priests were Father Raymond Norman (aka the Professor), Father Lyman Appleby (alias Nick Parker), and Archbishop William F. Tyarks (Dutch Willie) – priests in the American Orthodox Catholic Church.[1] Indeed, it was the successor of Archbishop Vilatte who ordained Tyarks in 1916, Archbishop Frederick E.J. Lloyd.[2] In 1926, Tyarks and some other priests, including one Cyril John Clement Sherwood, formed the American Catholic Orthodox Church. As is the pattern, Sherwood eventually broke with Tyarks, forming the American Holy Orthodox Catholic Apostolic Eastern Church in 1932.

One of the men Sherwood will make bishop was George Augustine Hyde, a major figure in gay ministry and founder of the first openly gay congregation, in Atlanta in 1946 (the Eucharistic Catholic Church). By 1967, Hyde was "chancellor" of the North American Province of the Orthodox Catholic Church. He was also one of the three individuals mentioned by name in the will of David W. Ferrie.

Norman, Appleby, and Tyarks were indicted on three counts of grand larceny in the second degree, one count of conspiracy, and 46 felony

1   Dick Terry, "The Holy Men of Hell's Kitchen," *St. Louis Dispatch*, 29 April 1945.
2   "Independent and Old Catholic Churches," Encyclopedia.com

counts of fraudulently soliciting funds for charitable purposes. They passed off their legitimacy by waving around beautifully designed paperwork; clearly the craftsmanship of Earl Anglin James: "The letterhead was not only dignified but impressive. On one side it listed the Mission's 'staff.' On the other side were listed its sponsors. The staff consisted of a prominent physician, a prominent dentist, a registered nurse, a social visitor who was a well known New York social worker, a minister general, and a pastor. These people are real. You can find their names in the telephone book. But they were totally unaware of the 'honor' bestowed on them by the Mission. This list of sponsors, 23 of them, contained names like Ralph W. Budd, internationally known manufacturer; Jack Dempsey, Countess Bula de Montagny and Mrs. Oliver Harriman, all of them names designed to make you sit up and take notice. They were unaware of their status with the Mission."[3] In addition to the intricate letterhead, the name dropping without the individual's knowledge or consent is classic James.

What finally tipped them off? The funds were deposited directly in their own bank accounts. Even though it cost only about $12 at the time to incorporate a church in New York, the crooks never took the time to create a church account. After a three-and-a-half week trial, Tyarks was sentenced to 2 ½-5 years; Norman and Appleby got 5-10 years.[4]

* * *

In the fall of 1946 – a few months after James set a record for submitting 95 ideas in a contest to design the new flag of Canada – he was elected exarch of the Canadas by Mar Georgius (Hugh George de Willmott-Newman), with the title Archbishop and Primate of Acadia, and Exarch of the Catholicate of the West in Canada. He was now vested with the episcopal name Mar Laurentius.[5]

And he continued to bestow worthless degrees. Some of these recipients proudly parlayed their degrees into major career advancements, such as James T. Killeen of Galion, Ohio. Armed with his honorary doctorate and fellowship from National College, Killeen ran a number of chiropractic and naturopathy practices.[6] So did Richard Oliver Dortch, who claimed a B.S. from National College and opened the East Texas Chiropractic Clinic in 1948, which he ran for 43 years.[7]

3   "The Holy Men of Hell's Kitchen."
4   Phil Santora, "Phony Churches Take Hits Legits." *New York Daily News*, 04 January 1956.
5   Anson, 245-246.
6   "Chiropractor Opens Office Here Friday," *Galion Inquirer*, 03 March 1949.
7   Advertisement, *Longview News-Journal*, 21 June 1948.

James came under a certain amount of scrutiny in 1948 by the Foreign Exchange Control Board on suspicion of illegally dealing in foreign currency. He allegedly had a new wife, Olive Bannan, whom James married when she was 17, but reliable information on the relationship is scant.

On July 26, 1950, calling himself the Duke of Scala and Prince of Parma, James was charged with smuggling movie cameras and film equipment into Canada from Chicago. Further inquiries by the Royal Canadian Mountain Police determined this was an ongoing practice by James – one of his chief means of income. He would then attempt to sell the equipment on consignment at local camera shops, such as the one which usually had striptease photos developed.[8] He pleaded guilty that September. (When *Toronto Star* reporter Earl McRae interviewed James in 1968, he observed a dusty collection of photographic equipment.) In November of 1950, Warden Frank Sain of the House of Corrections in Chicago obtained an honorary degree in psychology from National College, evidently without any solicitation for it on his part. In turn, James added "Sheriff of Chicago" to his sprawling list of fraudulent titles, and was known to put police decals on his own car.[9]

James's smuggling practices continued as late as the 1960s. In the mid-1960s, the RCMP suspected that James was an arm of an international smuggling operation, spearheaded by an unmasked secretary general from an unknown nation. This man traveled to Hong Kong every year before delivering to James stolen immigration papers from Hong Kong that James then dispersed throughout Canada.

The Hong Kong smuggling scheme naturally raises other questions: to what extent was James involved in the movement of narcotics, money laundering, human smuggling or human trafficking? When Carlos Marcello illegally brought Italian and Sicilian immigrants into the United States from Canada, did James's forgery skills get people across the border on behalf of the Mafia? Where did he fit in organized crime's drug trade? Unfortunately, such questions might never be known, especially when most of James's paperwork was burned during a three month stint in a mental health facility in early 1963.

* * *

In 1950, at the consecration of Grant Timothy Billett, James had been assisted by an English priest, Charles Dennis Boltwood, who also would

---

8   "'Prince' Charged," *Chicago Sun-Times*, 26 July 1950. The author attempted to identify the Chicago camera store where James purchased his film equipment, but was unsuccessful.
9   RCMP Dossier on James, 187.

become a bishop in 1952 and affiliate himself with the Free Protestant Episcopal Church. On paper, Bishop Boltwood and Bishop Mar Laurentius – James – could be identical twins, if not doppelgangers. An Englishman, Boltwood grew up Anglican like James, and like James also embraced spiritualism and theosophy. Theosophy will return as a key factor in our journey, so it's important to note here the Anglican Church deemed Christianity and Theosophy irreconcilable, particularly Theosophy's belief in karma and reincarnation, two thoughts anathema in Christianity. The Vatican totally banned any association with the movement, as well as possessing or reading its literature.[10] Once James, and in turn Boltwood, drifted into official Spiritualism and Theosophy, they lost mainline recognition as legitimate clerics. They were now occultists, an exoteric portal with no restrictions to the bizarre. So while James remained the "bishop of Toronto" in the Old Catholic world, it was purely nominal. All that mattered was that he retained the power to consecrate new bishops – a power he held even if he himself had no personal investment in his office. This is one of the unfortunate consequences of valid ordination: "once possessing the powers of a bishop, always possessing the powers of a bishop."[11]

Boltwood was the founder of St. Andrew's Collegiate Church, and linked to James in one way by Willmott-Newman/Mar Georgius, who consecrated Boltwood as bishop in the Catholicate of the West. Boltwood also professed to be a Radionic Therapeutist and Psychologist, and regularly held clairvoyance séances and healing services. And just like James, Boltwood operated his own diploma mill, a correspondence college called St. Andrew's Collegiate College, which he continued to do even after the Registrar of Business Name prohibited Boltwood usage of it.[12] Eventually, Boltwood did change the name to St. Andrew Ecumenical College, which nevertheless was accused by the FTC of claiming to be a legitimate university, when it had no actual authority to confer degrees. This was corroborated by a report from the

10   Cf. Gillian McCann, *Vanguard of the New Age: The Toronto Theosophical Society, 1891-1945* (Montreal: McGill-Queen's University Press, 2012), 20.

11   *Episcopi Vagantes and the Anglican Church*, 20.

12   Pat Tyler, "He Gave Worthless Degrees," *Daily Herald*, 15 October 1954.

American Council of Education, which named two other degree mills along with St. Andrew's as being worth no more than the paper they're printed on: Minerva University and Phoenix University, both of Bari, Italy.[13] Phoenix University is the "institution" from which David Ferrie claimed his Ph.D. in hypnotherapy in 1957. In 1960, Dr. Filippo Donini, director of the Italian cultural office in New York, said neither "are not legally accepted by the Italian government, and the degrees granted by them have no validity according to Italian law."[14]

In time, Earl Anglin James became "Dean" of St. Andrew International Synod. "With Earl Anglin James in Canada as its supreme head, St. Andrew's Collegiate College could boast of an international group of eighteen patrons, each with impressive titles and degrees."[15] Perhaps the best known of these "patrons" – and whether they knew they were patrons or not is a wholly different matter – was California-based Dr. Charles Lathrup Warn, D. Litt., Ph.D, LL.D, known among various spiritualist and Masonic circles as a lecturer on end times prophecy, and author of two small books, *Today, As In The Days of Noah*, and *Thine Is Thy Kingdom*.

St. Andrew's sponsored an annual writing competition, its long-winded objective written by James: "We do not want theses which advance the benefits, so-called, of drugs, or any form of distorted conceptions proclaimed as benefits to mankind. The subjects in which we are interested are: science; biochemistry; homeopathy; naturopathy; biology; radiotherapy; psychiatry; psychology; chromotherapy; psycho-analysis; divine healing; metaphysics; psychotherapy; theology; philosophy; literature; arts and sciences; music."[16] James is describing elements of the German Lebensreform movement, which advocated alternative lifestyles as an antidote to urbanization and industrialization. "Theosophy," according to M. Dorothy Figueria, "provided a philosophical rationale [to the movement]."[17]

In 1952, Boltwood developed a chivalric order, The Ancient Order of Ursus, which occupied itself "preparing against the possibility of Atomic War and also against other world calamities."[18] Boltwood, James and Company prepared leaflets about "Spiritual Cataclysmic movements in the Heavens

---

13   "College Courses For 'Degrees,'" *Daily Telegraph*, 15 August 1960. See also Federal Trade Commission Deadlines, Volume 59, p. 53ff.

14   "Worthless Academic 'Honors' Being Sold," *Tampa Bay Times*, 11 Sept. 1960.

15   Anson, 247.

16   John Kersey, "Members of the San Luigi Orders: Primus Dr. Charles Boltwood," 18 September 2012, https://san-luigi.org/2012/09/18/members-of-the-san-luigi-orders-primus-dr-charles-boltwood/.

17   Nicholas Goodrick-Clarke, *The Occult Roots of Nazism* (London: IB Tauris, 1985, 2004), 22-23.

18   *Bucks Examiner*, 01 August 1952.

and on the Earth Planet."[19] The pamphlet, they hoped, "should be recognized as wholly Worthy and Beneficial to our Queen and to the Governments of the Commonwealth of Nations, and to the people in very truth." Most of this verbiage was likely derived from the writings of Dr. Charles Lathrup Warn.

* * *

The origins of the diploma mill business in the United States is due in large part to Helmuth P. Haller. Haller was actually put on trial for his racketeering and convicted of mail fraud in 1927. He was sentenced to a two year prison term. Haller, self-styled bishop of the Theomontism Church, peddled diplomas-for-sale from his phony school, Oriental University. The case helped codify an accreditation system to formally recognize colleges and universities. But the diploma mills only temporarily ground to a halt; learning their lessons from the consequences of the Haller case, they soon started churning again. Thus, in the morality lesson of "Bishop" Helmuth Haller, the esoteric world of the wandering bishops and the phony degree racket became inextricably linked.[20] Both are on the fringes of legitimacy and official recognition in their respective fields. One ordains priests and bishops as the other confers doctorates and fellowships. People like Earl Anglin James and Charles D. Boltwood were the bridge to both. A final example of this interconnectivity is the president and chancellor of the phony "Indiana Northern University," the Most Rev. Dr. Gordon A. DaCosta, who opened the college on a dairy farm in 1963. DaCosta emerged from Illinois obscurity in the mid-1940s to command the Illinois Civil Air Patrol, without any relevant experience, until he was deposed in 1949 for mishandling federal funds.[21] He then collected a string of initials after his name and began pumping out degrees to anyone willing to pay for them. Sidestepping accreditation issues by creating his own accrediting commission, DaCosta recognized likeminded diploma factories, such as Philathea Bible College of London, Ontario, whose president was another doppelganger, the Most Rev. Dr. Benjamin C. Eckardt, LL.B, LL.D, Ed.D, D.D, the archbishop of Ontario in Charles D. Boltwood's Free Protestant Episcopal Church. In 1971, DaCosta would become a bishop in the same church. By 1973, DaCosta was out. He had set up his own – the Anglican Church of North America.

After founding the Anglican Church of North America, DaCosta was consecrated into the American Orthodox Catholic Church by Robert S.

---

19   Anson, *Bishops at Large* (Berkeley: Apocryphile Press, 1964, 2006), 257.
20   See Bender and David, "Danger: Will External Degrees Degree Mills? A Challenge to Agencies," FSU Dept of Education, Jul. 1972.
21   Kemper Diehl, "University Draws Official Ire," *Express and News*, 24 June 1973.

Zeiger, whose associate and colleague in the American Orthodox Catholic Church was Bishop Carl Jerome Stanley. Stanley was consecrated a bishop by Earl Anglin James.

It should be noted that the former Attorney General of New York, Louis Lefkowitz, looked into Philathea and other institutions when it became clear "doctoral degree graduates" were practicing psychotherapy without a license. Lefkowitz found women were "encouraged to have sexual relations with their 'therapists.'"[22]

* * *

For certain crafty individuals the degree-by-mail and storefront churches were ripe for intelligence gathering in their own obtuse way. The networking possibilities with people of all walks of life were endless. As such, a quid-pro-quo arrangement seemed at play among the "chancellors" and "presidents" of these places. Eckardt confirms just as much: "As for honorary degrees, we grant them to people who have helped us. But they're only theological degrees."[23] Of course, we see this quid pro quo strategy in Earl Anglin James's playbook: recall House of Corrections Warden Sain's honorary degree in psychology from the National College. When James was fined $500 for impersonating a police officer in 1956, he claimed not to be impersonating an officer but that he was a prison chaplain. Sain's successor, Warden Jack Johnson, denied James was ever a chaplain, which was also corroborated by Cook County sheriff, Elmer Walsh.[24] However, a letter from the Chicago Special Agent in Charge (who succeeded Guy Banister in that role) to J. Edgar Hoover, states that Warden Sain admitted making James a chaplain of Cook County Jail, but without any salary.

This trade-off can also be seen on other occasions, such as in 1945 when Margaret Schramm Holten was awarded an LL.D degree and fellowship from the National College and in turn a profile on Schramm Holten was written for the *Schramm Family Society News*, written by none other than "The Hon. Dr. Earl A. James, biographer of interesting personalities."[25]

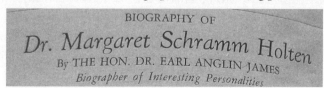

BIOGRAPHY OF

Dr. Margaret Schramm Holten

By THE HON. DR. EARL ANGLIN JAMES

Biographer of Interesting Personalities

---

22   John Wildgust, "'College' Called Diploma Mill," *Kingston Whig-Standard*, 16 December 1972.

23   "There are no restraints against granting degrees," *Sault Star*, 26 July 1972.

24   "A Renegade Bishop Seeks $150,000," *Daily Telegram*, 10 June 1966.

25   Schramm Family Society News (Yucaipa, California). James contributed a number of bi-

James claimed a Bachelor of Divinity degree from Trinity Southern Bible College and Seminary in Mullins, South Carolina. In turn, its president, a Seventh-day Adventist named A.D. Shoemaker, received a law degree from the National College. Shoemaker was also inducted into the Order of Legion of Honor, sealed with the coat of arms of Togoland's Fio Agbano II, one of James's favorite go-to monarchy for pseudo-prestigious titles.

Sir Sidney Lawrence, a James-like fraudster out of the U.K. whose main teaching tract was in hypnosis, received an immense document designed by James which bestowed upon Lawrence the title "Knight of His Majesty's Royal House" – as in the royal house of Fio Agbano II of Togoland. Lawrence's particular racket was the International Hypnotists Association, yet another correspondence-by-mail outfit. And sure enough, James is listed as "dean" of the International Hypnotists Association.

"I have never met Mr. James," Lawrence told Ross Richards of London's *Sunday Pictorial*, "but I understand he has done a great deal of good." And, as expected, Lawrence obtained his own degrees from National College of Canada,[26] and was fond to stamp his correspondences as "Hon. Attorney General U.S.A." Lawrence was also friends with an auto mechanic we will encounter numerous times ahead: "Archbishop" Charles Brearley of Sheffield, England.

The *Sunday Pictorial* piece eviscerates "Sir" Sidney Lawrence, accusing the man of dishing out degrees to anyone willing to pay for them, including would-be rapists, perverts, or just plain fools. "There's no law against selling knives," was Lawrence's reply. And individuals continued to pay, keeping conmen like Earl Anglin James alive and well. But if things got too hot, they could slip behind their priestly collars or myriad of degrees. James, forger that he was, also went under at least one false identity, E.A. Jones.[27] Survivors like James were able to dodge getting shut down for good by thriving in the gray zone between what was legal and what was not.

And he was also quite literally familiar with the art of slipping a tail, telling Earl McRae in his 1968 interview that the elevators in Toronto's Eaton's department store was "the best place to lose somebody."[28]

ographies to the family's histories.
26   Ross Richards, "The Dopiest Diploma," *Sunday Pictorial*, 02 December 1956.
27   HSCA Letter to Attorney General Griffin B. Bell, 7 March 1978. NARA Record Number: 124-10182-10375.
28   McRae, "The Garrison Probe."

In 1956, for having "discovered the fundamentals of Peace amongst various races whose Creeds differ, namely – accepting the One Harmonizing Face of One Great Spirit," Earl Anglin James, "Canadian philanthropist," was "nominated" for the Nobel Peace Prize.[29] He was ostensibly nominated by two men, Alceste Barba, Italian professor at an Italian diploma mill, and Jose Vibora, professor at Andes University in Havana, Cuba, another phony school. Needless to say, he didn't win.

---

29   Nobel Prize Nomination Archives, https://www.nobelprize.org/nomination/archive/show_people.php?id=4536.

THE SOVEREIGN GREEK ORDER OF ST. DENNIS OF ZANTE

1 9 6 4

Activities of 1963
Published by
The Chapel of the Order of St. Dennis of Zante

CHAPTER FIVE

KNIGHTS OF THE CHURCH

Cursed be anyone who takes a bribe to shed innocent blood.
And all the people shall say, "Amen."
                                        – Deuteronomy 27:25

As the 1950s closed, those in the diploma mill/clergy-making business seemed poised to get their comeuppance when U.S. Secretary of Health, Education, and Welfare, Arthur S. Flemming, announced his war on diploma mills on October 30, 1959. But *Sir* Earl James still found one more improbable feather to add to his cap. On the floor of the U.S. House of Representatives on August 23, 1960, Rep. Robert Barry (R-NY) inserted into the Congressional Record highlights of the Eloy Alfaro International Foundation of the Republic of Panama award ceremony held at the Astor Hotel in New York. The man of honor was "the Right Honorable Earl Anglin James, D.D., Kt., Abp., of Toronto, Canada." General Alfaro was the former president of Ecuador and leader of the Liberal Party's opposition to pro-Catholic president Gabriel Garcia Moreno – and who was ultimately killed by a pro-Catholic mob.

The award ceremony was overseen by the foundation's secretary general, Vienna-born psychiatrist Dr. Herbert Holt, who trained clergy in psychotherapy and authored the book *Free To Be Good or Bad.* The award of the Grand Cross and diploma were conferred on James by longtime insurance broker "Dr." Herman A. Bayern, "American provost" of the Eloy Alfaro Foundation and, unsurprisingly, a veteran of diploma mills, billing himself "professor of economics" at London, Ontario's Philathea College, the diploma mill we previously encountered which  Eloy Alfaro Award medal considered its campus a room in an abandoned building. Tracing the history of the Foundation, it appears that at the end of its run, about 1970, the entire operation seemed to be run by those associated with Philathea.

That such a proceeding would merit enough relevancy, let alone legitimacy, to be part of the Congressional Record is astounding. James's eight-paragraph acceptance speech is also included in the Congressional Record. Its content is typically ambiguous, with emphasis on ecumenism, peace, unity and goodwill. "I shall be glad to continue my efforts of world peace throughout the civilized world through prayer to the Great Spirit," James said in the speech.[1]

The three grandsons of Alfaro ostensibly launched the foundation in 1949. That's the official public relations statement. However, Foundation correspondences reveal an internal war between the Philathea contingent and the original founders. And this discord and strife is a revelatory clue for us: we are about to leap from the idiosyncratic world of the phony churches and colleges racket to interests of the State Department, CIA fronts, and the connection with the likes of David Ferrie and his brother bishops in New Orleans.

What the Eloy Alfaro International Foundation (hereafter EAIF) amounts to, ultimately, is Pan-American propaganda. Most of the recipients during the foundation's documented existence (c. 1950-mid-1970s) were government or military-connected individuals cited for their work in inter-American humanitarian efforts and religious service. Its brainchild in America was Dr. A. Curtis Wilgus, a prolific researcher in Latin American affairs at the University of Florida, where he oversaw the annual Caribbean Conference and Inter-American Studies while also running the private Inter-American Center/Pan American Foundation research institute. Although the foundation claimed to have "neither political nor lucrative purposes,"[2] its titular president was a living legend in his time, the Cuban Dr. Emeterio S. Santovenia.

When Earl Anglin James accepted the award in 1960, the aged Santovenia was living among the anti-Castro Cuban exiles in Miami. A native of Havana, Santovenia was both a lawyer and a prolific historian of Cuba and the wider Caribbean. He also became quite political, so much so that soon after seizing power, Fidel Castro had the bookish, 60-something Santovenia imprisoned. Santovenia's political affiliation was, for all intents and purposes, a Cuban terrorist organization. It was called ABC, "a secret organization that employed terrorist means to bring about the

---

1   "Eloy Alfaro Award: Extension of Remarks of Hon. Robert R. Barry," U.S. House of Representatives, August 23, 1960.
2   *Star & Herald* (Panama City, FL), 10 September 1949, as cited in "Presentation of Bust of Abraham Lincoln by Eloy Alfaro International Foundation: Extension of Remarks by Hon. Clyde Doyle of California," Appendix to the Congressional Record, 20 February 1950, A1238-A1239.

downfall of [Gerardo] Machado," Cuban's president from 1925-1933.[3] Under pressure by the U.S. government to abdicate, Machado complied, living in exile in Miami Beach until his death in 1939. Santovenia joined the subsequent coalition government as Presidential Secretary, representing ABC. During this brief period, Santovenia wrote a biography on Eloy Alfaro while at the same time networking with U.S. politicians. His interest in Cuba-U.S. relations deepened as a result.[4] However, an ABC political march turned violent and deadly. Santovenia resigned his post.[5] Now in opposition to the current government, Santovenia was a dissident and wanted for capture. He fled to Miami. After returning to Havana, he became head of the ABC party in the province of Pinar del Rio. He rose to become a senator in 1940, during the presidency of Fulgencio Batista, serving two terms while also for a time the Minister of State.

Santovenia thrived under the presidency of Carlos Manuel Prío Socarrás, his accomplishments recognized as far as France. The year EAIF was established, 1949, Santovenia gave the commencement address at the University of Florida.[6] When Fulgencio Batista's coup toppled Prio's government, Santovenia was called on by the deposed president and his cabinet members seeking asylum; Santovenia negotiated their safe departure out of the country and into exile. Socarrás will return later as an instrumental figure in pre-Castro gunrunning to Cuba. When Castro pushed the Batista regime out in January 1959, Santovenia was labeled "a collaborator of the despot Batista," and imprisoned for eight months at the age of 69.[7] When he was released, Santovenia and his family settled in Miami, relying on help from the Cuban Refugee Center and writing for Spanish-language exile newspapers in Miami. He lingered nearly another ten years, dying in 1968.

If Santovenia was the nominal head of the EAIF, A. Curtis Wilgus and his wife, Karna, kept the operation running in Florida. But their vision for the foundation clashed with the Philathea College-affiliated New Yorkers: Bayern, Holt, Civil Air Patrol veteran Dr. Lester Beecher, and John Keesing. Bayern especially pestered the grandsons of Eloy Alfaro. A rabid anti-communist, Bayern wrote to Olmeda Alfaro in September 1960:

> Certainly, if General Alfaro were alive today, he would do something about Castro. If your father were here, we would try to do

3   Antonio De La Cova, "Emeterio S. Santovenia." On early life, see pp. 1-7; on ABC, 9ff.
4   Ibid., 11.
5   Ibid., 10.
6   Ibid., 14.
7   Ibid., 16.

what we did in Guatemala in 1954. At any rate, we are here, and we must do something about meeting the menace of the Communist Internacional [sic] Conspiracy [n]ow or we will be lost if they get a firm foothole in this Hemisphere.[8]

It appears Bayern eventually overwhelmed Wilgus and Santovenia, wresting the foundation into his image and likeness. Hence, the award to Earl Anglin James in 1960.

* * *

As for Wilgus and his wife, they lived and breathed all things Latin American, from university courses and institutes to associations with the Organization of American States and the American Peace Society. Wilgus often utilized his Masonic connections to promote and expand his work.[9] "The biggest problem in Latin America today is the Russians in Cuba," he said in November 1963, in language much more tempered than Bayern. "If we could solve that, a lot of other things would be fairly simple."[10] In February 1967, it came out that Wilgus's Pan American Foundation was subsidized by the CIA. To Wilgus, the revelation was "a surprise to me," suggesting he was an unwitting participant, if the surprise was genuine.[11] However, both Wilgus and his wife are identified in CIA files with Project DTEMBARGO, the Agency's cryptonym for the Pan American Foundation, an acknowledged proprietary of the CIA's Western Hemisphere Division (WHD).[12] Furthermore, two 1961 memos from J.C. King, Chief of WHD, cite DTEMBARGO as the cover for CIA contract agent Henry Preston Lopez (using the alias Edward G. Tichborn), who in 1959-1960 participated in CIA's Operation AMPATROL, in which he was hired by the Agency as a "political organizer to bring together the most promising anti-Castro groups."[13]

It is worthwhile to note that it was King, who in a December 1959 letter to CIA director Allen Dulles, recommended Castro be assassinated: "Thorough consideration be given to the elimination of Fidel Castro.

---

8   Quoted in letter from Olmedo Alfaro to A. Curtis Wilgus, September 24, 1960.
9   See Wilgus letter to John M. Keesing, January 23, 1961.
10   *Gainesville Sun*, 10 November 1963.
11   "CIA Funds 'Surprise' Wilgus," *Tampa Tribune*, 2 March 1967.
12   NARA 104-10112-10090, CIA, 27 June 1958. According to NARA NARA Record Number: 157-10014-10144 re: DTEMBARGO: "This foundation was established in 1938 without Agency support. After a long period of inactivity, the Agency took over the entity in 1953 and used it to support a publication produced at a U.S. University and aimed at Latin America. In 1967, the Agency withdrew its support from the foundation, and gave the office furnishings to the witting directors of the foundation with the stipulation that the furnishings would be turned over to the university."
13   "Cryptonym: AMPATROL," https://www.maryferrell.org/php/cryptdb.php?id=AMPA-TROL. See also NARA 104-0174-10061.

None of those close to Fidel, such as his brother Raul or his companion Che Guevara, have the same mesmeric appeal to the masses. Many informed people believe that the disappearance of Fidel would greatly accelerate the fall of the present government."[14] Richard Bissell, Deputy Director of Plans, identified King's recommendation as the first seed of "the gambling syndicate project," later known as ZRRIFLE, and ultimately, Operation Mongoose.[15] The CIA ventured to solicit the assistance of "the U.S. gambling syndicate that was active in Cuba" to kill Castro, who booted them out of their lucrative Havana casinos shortly after assuming power. This "gambling syndicate" was composed of Mafia don Santos Trafficante, Chicago boss Sam Giancana, New Orleans Mafia chieftain Carlos Marcello, and Meyer Lansky.

Strategically, the word "assassination" was purposefully avoided in this phase of planning.[16] The intent was to at least undermine Castro's legitimacy in the eyes of Cubans and destabilize the region. When briefed by Bissell and Sheffield Edwards, there was "no opposition" from Dulles, who was joined in the meeting by deputy director General Charles P. Cabell.[17] Once again, the U.S. intelligence community reveals its enduring partnership with organized crime – as well as its penchant for assassination. A 1949 CIA document asks, "Let's get into the technology of assassination, figure most effective ways to kill – like Empress Agrippina – do you want your people to be able to get out of the room? Do you want it traced?"[18]

According to a 1966 document only fully released by the National Archives in 2017, CIA cut-out Robert A. Maheu, who like Guy Banister was an ex-FBI man from Chicago now running a detective firm, Robert A. Maheu and Associates, was assigned to meet with Mafia don Johnny Roselli in Las Vegas. Part of the document goes on to state:

> 6. Maheu was asked to approach Roselli, who knew Maheu as a personal relations executive handling domestic and foreign accounts, and tell him that he had recently been retained by a client who represented several international business firms which were suffering heavy financial losses in Cuba as a result of Castro's action. They were convinced that Castro's removal was the answer to their problem and we re willing to pay a price of $150,000 for its successful accomplishment. It was to be made clear to Roselli that

---

14   HSCA, IV, 156.
15   "Plots to Assassinate Castro," NARA Record Number 104-10061-10080, 14.
16   Ibid.
17   Ibid., 18.
18   Cited in H.P. Albarelli, *Coup in Dallas* (New York: Skyhorse Publishing, 2021), 124 (digital version, scribd.com).

the U. S. Government was not, and should not, become aware of this operation.

7. The pitch was made to Roselli on 14 September 1960 at the Hilton Plaza Hotel, New York City. His initial reaction was to avoid getting involved but, through Maheu's persuasion, he agreed to introduce him to a friend, Sam Gold, who knew the "Cuban crowd." Roselli made it clear he did not want any money for his part and believed Sam would feel the same way. Neither of these individuals was ever paid out of Agency funds.

8. During the week of 25 September, Maheu was introduced to Sam who was staying at the Fontainebleau Hotel, Miami Beach. His initial impression of Sam was that of a hard, uncouth individual who looked and acted like a common run-of-the-mill hoodlum. However, his living ac:commodations at the hotel belied this, as did the fact that Maheu learned Sam was under periodic surveillance by the FBI. It was several weeks after his meeting with Sam and Joe, who was identified to him as a courier operating between Havana and Miami, that he saw photographs of both of these individuals in the Sunday supplemental "Parade." They were identified as Memo Salvatore Giancana and Santos Trafficante, respectively. Both were on the list of the Attorney General's ten most-wanted men. The former was described as the Chicago chieftain of the Cosa Nostra and successor to Al Capone, and the latter, the Casa Nostra boss of Cuban operations. Maheu called this office immediately upon ascertaining this information.[19]

Even biochemist mind control mastermind Dr. Sidney Gottlieb was brought in at a point to concoct fantastic schemes that might eliminate Castro. Eventually, William Harvey assumed control of ZRRIFLE in November 1961.[20] Harvey preferred to call it "Executive Action Capability." *Bloody Treason* author Noel Twyman concluded that "Harvey's conceptual notes for ZRRIFLE are a blueprint for the JFK assassination plot, both in concept and in detail."[21]

DTEMBARGO factors into one other noteworthy cover. Donald Soldini, a young man from Staten Island, had joined the Castro barbudos fighting under Raul Castro. After the revolution, Soldini was assigned to work in the presidential palace, hoping Fidel might honor his promise to

19   NARA Record Number 178-10002-10297.
20   Harvey appears to be using an alias in his dealings with Roselli. See NARA document 104-10133-10341: "It is not known whether Roselli ever became aware of Harvey's true name."
21   Noel Twyman, *Bloody Treason – The Assassination of John F. Kennedy* (Rancho Santa Fe, CA: Laurel Publishing, 1997), 424.

send the young man to the University of Havana. But Soldini found himself imprisoned for ostensibly stealing presidential stationery. By the fall of 1963, he was free and now a student at the University of Mexico. There he attracted CIA's attention as a possible contributor to the journal publication that DTEMBARGO represented.[22]

What are we to make of this? We have Earl Anglin James accepting an honor in the summer of 1960 by a foundation whose president was an anti-Castro Cuban exile (Emeterio Santovenia), whose American director (A. Curtis Wilgus) ran Inter-American/Pan American programs subsidized by the CIA – particularly its plots to assassinate Fidel Castro – and whose "provost" (Herman Bayern) was a seasoned diploma mill veteran with a militaristic attitude towards ousting Castro.

Furthermore, we gain still deeper context by analyzing an EAIF ceremony honoring recipient Phoebe Morse in 1962. The Master of Ceremonies was fervent anti-communist and Havana native Dr. Marcos A. Kohly, national director of the Organization of American States (OAS) and former Cuban ambassador to Mexico. "Show me a country that has no spiritual life and you show me a country that is ready for Communism," he once said. "We have much to worry about as Communism is less than an hour from our shores." The main topic of that particular speech was about the role of women in the Alliance for Progress, the Kennedy Administration's programme for Latin and South America.[23]

Avellanal

In 1945, Kohly accepted a degree from a diploma mill – José Luis Avellanal's Southern University for the degree of Doctor of Social Sciences and Public Law. Avellanal was yet another Earl Anglin James doppelganger: he often roamed the city of Tampa in the uniform of a Mexican lieutenant; he believed he could raise the dead; he insisted he was a medical doctor.[24] Avellanal also founded Tampa's Pan-American Federation and Cuban Legion of Honor.

22   NARA Record Number 104-10100-10314.
23   Rose Bobroff, "Kissimmee BPW Clubwomen Hear OAS Director Laud Spiritual Life," *Orlando Sentinel*, 20 June 1962.
24   Gill Gott, "The Legend of José Luis Avellanal," *The Florida Archivist* (Vol. 32, No. 4, Fall 2016), 5.

But Avellanal was compelled by a Jacksonville circuit judge to cease giving out degrees and to dissolve the university's charter. Charges came after recipients paid for medical degrees and attempted to practice medicine.[25]

How might have James positioned himself to become an EAIF award recipient – its relevancy and legitimacy notwithstanding?

* * *

Here we arrive at a third element: counterfeit chivalric orders, completing an increasingly darker and sinister triangle. Like the phony colleges and churches, these orders were fronts. Behind the veneer lurked an abiding allegiance to occultism, the same cultish ideology that influenced the architects of Nazism.

By the 19th century, Gnostics drew on elements, for instance, of Eastern/Oriental Christianity and from heretical movements like Catharism and divination. Gnostics mingled with Rosicrucians and Freemasons, and identified with the monastic military order from the Middle Ages, the Knights Templar, "wandering knights" whose success and eventual suppression bore many legends. As the Templars supposedly safeguarded esoteric secrets such as the treasure of Solomon or the Holy Grail, the Gnostics believed they were the contemporary custodians of the Templar tradition. Theosophy, based on the writings of Russian Helena Blavatsky, was another movement that attracted these same devotees to occultism. Many in the independent Catholic movement, like James, were shaped by this cabbalistic thinking. We saw this when James integrated himself with the Metaphysical Spiritualist Church and the Catholicate of the West, each underpinned less by Christian teaching than by occultism.

In effect, all of these facets fit under the umbrella of what Blavatsky deemed the "great white brotherhood," or the "Great White Lodge."

At the dawn of the 20th century, anti-Bolshevik and anti-Semitc ideologies attracted White Russian nationalists who identified not with Marxism-Leninism but with the dying Russian monarchy. This ideology spread to Germany and Austria, where the Habsburgs ruled in their final years of dominance. There, Adolf Hitler and his like-minded cronies found an occultic basis for National Socialism.

In the decades ahead, this ideology shaped the architects of National Socialism. *The Protocols of the Elders of Zion*, which spouted diatribes of a Jewish conspiracy to take over the world ("Jewry is enslaving all Christian

---

25   *Tampa Tribune*, 17 January 1947.

people," is an example of the document's rhetoric.) As we will see, this racist and Aryan worldview mixed with occultism shaped the Grand Priory of America of the Sovereign Order of St. John of Jerusalem (the Shickshinny Knights), a pseudo-chivalric order which consisted of bigots and racists – including those who plotted to destroy the Kennedy dynasty.

As discussed earlier, the most probable conduit that enabled James to claim the EAIF award is Herman Bayern. Bayern, a longtime New York insurance broker, recommended Congressman John Wydler (R-NY) to be decorated by the Sovereign Order of St. Dennis of Zante in 1974. Wydler recounted the lengthy history of the obscure order before the House of Representatives. Its Prince Grand Master was a Greek-born former band leader in the 1920s and 30s, Perry Voultsos, who had now refashioned himself as Count Dr. Pericles Voultsos-Vourtzis. Voultsos claimed, among other things, such distinctions as honorary attorney general of Louisiana – a title James himself also held – honorary consul of Grenada; goodwill

A typical pseudo-knighting ceremony. Here, Pericles Voultsos of the Greek Order of St. Dennis of Zante, right, knights an unsuspecting gentleman

59

ambassador to Greece on behalf of Governor Preston Smith of Texas; and personal ambassador to the United States of King Ntare V of Burundi. Voultsos was also an alum of a number of diploma mills, namely Calvin Coolidge College, an unaccredited outfit located on Beacon Hill in Boston, a location that served as a haven for politics, religion, and education.

Voultsos was a U.S. lay representative of the Old Holy Catholic Church (OHCC), under the leadership of Archbishop Charles Brearley of Sheffield, England – the auto mechanic we met earlier. Like James, Brearley ran an establishment that distributed degrees, the Ministerial Training College. He was active in numerous chivalric orders, and steered OHCC in a New Age direction at the end of the 1950s. Brearley also advocated British (or Anglo) Israelism, which championed the white supremacist notion that the British are the descendants of the Ten Lost Tribes of Israel.[26] This will not be the last time we hear of this idea.

Brearley was a member of the Sovereign Order of Cyprus, a dubious group not to be confused with the genuine Sovereign Military Order of Malta, but one which claimed to be founded in 1192 by Guy de Lusignan, crusader king of Jerusalem and then of Cyprus. Among those counted as members with Brearley was General James Doolittle (who donated his Order of Cyprus medal to the Smithsonian). Its grand chancellor was Michel Paul Pierre Count de Valitch.[27] In 1968, Count de Valitch was consecrated a bishop in Archbishop Walter Propheta's American Orthodox Catholic Church, essentially making Valitch's bogus chivalric knights the official order of the AOCC.[28] The *Baltimore Sun* reported in 1983 that Valitch ran "two tax-exempt knighting operations" out of his New York apartment. The article goes on to mention the number of people mistakenly taken in by Valitch as a legitimate prelate of the Roman Catholic Church, and the Order of Cyprus as an authentic Catholic order. It was a situation that "deeply troubled" the Roman Catholic Archdiocese of New York. Indeed, newspaper reporters covering various investiture ceremonies of the Sovereign Order of Cyprus routinely mistook it as the Order of Malta, the legitimate Catholic body approved by the Holy See.

In 1949 and again in 1952, Earl Anglin James unsuccessfully sought formal recognition from the Canadian government as the minister of Thomond, an ancient – and long defunct – principality on the west coast

---

26   David Baron, *The History of the Ten "Lost" Tribes: Anglo-Israelism Examined* (London: Morgan & Scott, 1915), 7.

27   Congressional Record – House, 14 June 1967, 15886.

28   For further explication, see Levenda, *Sinister Forces, Book One: The Nine* (Walterville, OR: TrineDay, 2011), 283.

of Ireland. The last independent prince died in 1539, after which his brother surrendered all claims to the territory to King Henry VIII. The last Earl of Thomond died in the 18th century.

In his attempts at validation, James was also referring to himself at this time as the Archbishop of the Western Orthodox Church (another name for the Catholicate of the West), and professed the principality was recognized by nations that included the United States and France. Canadian authorities dismissed it all as "elaborate nonsense," and determined James met a like-minded imposter, Raymond Moulton O'Brien, a mentally unstable degenerate "who arrived in Ireland at the beginning of the Second

World War, claiming he was Earl of Thomond and "The O'Brien" and supported by a Mexican court judgment and newspaper reports. He called himself Prince on his children's birth certificates, faked a court case of slander against him, faked a chivalric order, attempted to get postage stamps issued for the principality of Thomond, claimed he had an embassy in Dublin, and had a report in a French newspaper state that the principality was an independent state with its own currency."[29] James pestered the Irish consulate in Chicago to announce himself as O'Brien's envoy to the U.S., Mexico and Canada.

O'Brien

O'Brien, who was born in 1905 and raised in the U.S., was actually acknowledged by the British Crown as the rightful Earl of Thomond in 1936, according to the *New York Times*. O'Brien and his wife, "the former Vassilia Comtesse Guliaris de Zante of Greece," presented themselves at the coronation of King Edward VIII as the Earl and Countess of Thomond. Nevertheless, both the *Times* and the Crown were duped by the false story of the imposter. In-

---

29   Catherine Nash, *Of Irish Descent* (Syracuse, NY: Syracuse UP, 2008), 293n54.

stead, O'Brien was a "compulsive child molester, most of whose time was spent in the parks, cinemas and buses of Dublin in search of the children of both sexes upon whom to prey."[30] O'Brien spent his final years committed to a psychiatric institution.

The political interests and ideologies of Raymond Moulton O'Brien, a "Manhattan oilman,"[31] open a wider door into an underground network of fascist white supremacists that leads directly to the kill zone of Dealey Plaza on November 22, 1963.

---

30   R.M. Douglas, *Architects of the Resurrection* (Manchester: Manchester UP, 2009), 281.
31   *Time*, 12 October 1936.

Chapter Six

Whither Thou Goest?

I will go, and where thou lodgest, I will lodge.
Thy people shall be my people, and thy God my God
— Ruth, 1:16

In 1951, Raymond O'Brien launched the United Christian Nationalist Party in Ireland, borrowing its objective from the Christian Nationalist Crusade, a quasi-political party from St. Louis, Missouri. In reality, the Christian Nationalist Crusade was a platform for antisemitic publications like *The International Jew* and *The Protocols of the Elders of Zion*, as well as a vehicle for promoting segregation. Its founder was Gerald L.K. Smith, another believer that Jesus was a Gentile. Smith, a former aide to Louisiana senator Huey Long in the 1930s, sent an appeal letter to benefactors in the summer of 1960 that read in part:

> [Y]ou and I must make a choice between Kennedy and Nixon. There is no difficulty as far as I am concerned even though Nixon might repudiate me in public for my alleged anti-Semitism. Nixon is under the influence of great Christian men, and he has a noble Christian background. He may say some things in the campaign with which you and I do not agree, and if he says things to test my patience, I will say within my soul, "We dare not have Kennedy."[1]

There is no evidence Smith and O'Brien actually met, which did little to deter O'Brien from his comments and beliefs.

"[T]o protect Ireland from the encroachment of Bolshevism, [O'Brien] set up a paramilitary organization nicknamed 'the Black Eagles,' which would fight 'in the spirit of the Crusaders.'"[2] Advertisements around Dublin for this security arm of the United Christian Nationalist Party caught the attention of Colonel Dan Brien of Irish military intelligence. He con-

---

1   Gerald L.K. Smith, "I Took My Life in My Hands," 11 July 1960, Papers of John F. Kennedy. Pre-Presidential Papers. Presidential Campaign Files, 1960.
2   Jérôme aan de Wiel, "The Principality of Thomond and His Royal Highness Raymond Moulton Seaghan O'Brien, 1936-1963; Ireland's Greatest Diplomatic Farce," *North Munster Antiquarian Journal*, Volume 47, 2007, 105.

cluded it had "all the hallmarks of [an] orthodox Fascist movement."[3] At the same time, as R.M. Douglas noted, both failed to ignite much of a following as effective domestic subversive groups.

O'Brien and James might seem like small fish, but too often historic events are defined by those ignored as public nuisances before it was too late: consider the behaviors of Charles Whitman, Timothy McVeigh or Dylann Roof leading up to their murderous actions. Moreover, the relationship between O'Brien and James cannot be ignored due to the similar fascist ideology advocated by another ancillary network of Earl Anglin James: the New Orleans cabal of bishops under Guy Banister.

Viewers of *JFK* will remember Jack Lemmon's memorable turn as the bumbling drunk Jack Martin, particularly when he is pistol-whipped by his employer, Guy Banister (Ed Asner in the film) in Banister's New Orleans

Banister

office. It was the night of the Dallas assassination, the two had been drinking, and Martin insinuated Banister had foreknowledge of the shooting. But movies are limited by their own thematic agendas; both men were more complex than *JFK*, for all its bravura, could afford. Banister was a Caldwell Parish native in rural northern Louisiana. His father was the parish's deputy sheriff, who died of an accidental drowning on Halloween night in 1940.[4] Banister joined the nearby Monroe Police Department before becoming an FBI special agent in 1934. By 1954, he was Chicago's FBI agent-in-charge where he retired from the FBI at age 53. The reason for Banister's retirement deserves further scrutiny. In a complaint to director J. Edgar Hoover, Banister wrote, "Twenty years ago the FBI leadership had divorced the field investigators and the two have been living in adultery ever since."[5] After that, Banister was told he was getting transferred from Chicago to Hawaii. Banister retired instead and moved back to Louisiana.

Banister became assistant superintendent of the New Orleans PD – the third ranking officer on the force – in 1955. He drew the ire of officers when he conducted an internal investigation of suspected grafting and illegal lottery operations. And he drew the ire of boxing promoters for cracking down on racketeering. In March 1956, a voodoo curse was put on Chief Banister and a shoebox bomb intended for the New Orleans Police

3   Ibid.

4   "Banister's Death Held in Accident," *Monroe News-Star*, 1 Nov. 1940.

5   "Hearings, Reports and Prints of the Senate Committee on Government Operations," 1975, 517.

Department went off at the post office.[6] That same month, he undertook an investigation of possible Communist activity in New Orleans, attempting to recruit former Communist spy-turned FBI star informant and converted Roman Catholic Elizabeth Bentley to assist. Bentley declined.

Banister himself is typically portrayed as the ideal anti-communist crusader. But there is another factor beyond Communism that motivated those thoughts and actions of crusaders like Banister, an issue much closer to home than Marxism: civil rights, and the ramifications of the Supreme Court's 1954 ruling on *Brown v. Board of Education of Topeka* that deemed segregation in public schools unconstitutional. Speaking at a rally in Northern Louisiana in 1957, state Attorney General Jack Gremillion "asserted that Communism is behind the integration movement."[7] The rally was sponsored by the White Citizens Council of Claiborne Parish. Guy Banister himself was deeply bonded with the Greater New Orleans Chapter of that racist group. Furthermore, Banister testified before the Louisiana Joint Legislature Committee on Subversion in Racial Unrest; that hearing concluded integration was Communist-backed.[8]

Banister was suspended from the New Orleans Police Department for allegedly pulling his gun on a bartender during a fight during the Mardi Gras of 1957; Banister had been drinking. When he was demoted from assistant superintendent, Banister refused the lower job offered him, and was duly fired in June 1957. He became president and publisher of a weekly newspaper, the *West Bank Herald*, writing a short-lived column, "Behind the Scenes with Guy Banister," mostly fire and brimstone pieces on Communism. The address for his investigative firm, Guy Banister Associates, Inc., was 434 Balter Building. Bluford Balter was a co-owner of the *West Bank Herald*; he was also one of the heads of the New Orleans American Nazi Party. It was not uncommon for Klansmen, Minutemen, White Citizens Council members and other fascist sympathizers coming and going out of the Balter Building, making it "the center of radical right-wing activity in New Orleans in the 1950s and 1960s."[9]

* * *

Jack Martin was born Edward Stewart Suggs in Dallas about 1906. He was a Navy veteran of Pearl Harbor, and loyal to the American Legion and VFW when out of service. He also worked in law enforcement. In 1952,

6   "Police Official Under Threat," *Town Talk*, 13 March 1956, 16.
7   "Gremillion Smacks Civil Rights Bill in Congress," *Shreveport Journal*, 02 April 1957.
8   Jeffrey Caufield, *General Walker and the Murder of President Kennedy* (Clearwater: Moreland Press, 2015), 168.
9   Ibid., 71.

Suggs was connected to a murder plot to blow up the sheriff of Houston. By then, he was wanted on a murder charge out of Dallas – a back alley abortion, resulting in the woman's death – though that evidently was dropped.[10] He was a slippery character, one didn't know quite what to think of him or what he said. When Suggs went to work for Banister he was under the alias Jack Stewart Martin. As in Bishop Jack Martin, a Freemason who sat in Lodge with Carlos Marcello and Thomas Jude Baumler, another one of Banister's investigators who later became the lawyer who incorporated the Process Church of the Final Judgement.

Martin was heavily involved in independent Catholic church affairs. Largely based on Martin's recommendation, Archbishop Carl Stanley

Martin

consecrated David Ferrie as bishop in the Old Catholic Church in November 1961. Martin served as co-consecrator. At long last David Ferrie achieved the clerical role he long sought. However, the ceremony and honors were completely hollow, even if great pains were taken to authenticate the so-called apostolic lines of succession. The formal name of the church was the Église Catholique Apostolique Primitive d'Antioche Orthodoxe et de Tradition Syro-Byzantine (the Primitive Catholic Apostolic Orthodox Church of Antioch of the Syro-Byzantine Tradition). This is another revealing clue to the loyalties and ideologies that influenced both Carl Jerome Stanley and the New Orleans cabal. Ultimately, the assassination of Robert F. Kennedy will reveal the extent of these influences on this church.

The Primitive Catholic Apostolic Orthodox Church of Antioch of the Syro-Byzantine Tradition fell broadly under the umbrella of Christian Universalism, or the Universalist Church, and specifically was a faction of the Catholicate of the West, founded in 1944, which included Earl Anglin James as exarch of the Canadas. Its makeup was a constellation of individuals from different microchurches – the influence of its universalist origins – but rooted in one common interest: occultism. Its first Catholicos, Hugh George de Willmott-Newman, was not invited to participate in Vatican II, while Stanley, as we pointed out, did receive an invitation.[11]

Willmott-Newman was consecrated by William Bernard Crow. Both Crow and Willmott-Newman established a correspondence with occult-

---

10   "4 To Testify on Plot on Sheriff Kern," *Austin American*, 26 October 1952, 52. See also 10/30/61 FBI file on Ferrie, p. 10.

11   Alan Gill, "Patriarch keeps it a family affair," *Sydney Morning Dispatch*, 09 January 1987.

ist Aleister Crowley. William Bernard Crow was also an occultist, a priest in the Liberal Catholic Church who composed a Mass ("Mass of the Planets"), and founded the Order of the Holy Wisdom, the purpose of which was to "teach the 'Orthodox Catholic Faith' to occultists in their own vernacular. According to one of [its] fliers, the church incorporated the traditions of the Hindus, kabbalists, gnostics, Zoroastrians, Rosicrucians, Druids, Buddhists, and Sufis."[12] Furthermore, the Order of Holy Wisdom considered itself "an order within the Universal Church…"

> [The Universal Church] seeks to reproduce, as fully as possible within its own sphere, for the benefit of its members and humanity in general, the deep spiritual experience enshrined in ritual and symbols. It is particularly concerned with cosmic symbolism. It endeavors to teach the doctrines and practices of the Ancient Wisdom Religion, and to preserve such knowledge of value which has largely disappeared in the historical development of outer institutions. Being absolutely universal (that is truly Orthodox and Catholic) it has access to the divine wisdom of Theosophy, embodied in the symbols of all nations.[13]

There is, of course, much to say about Aleister Crowley, but for our purposes it is important to note he was the author of the "Gnostic Mass," the semi-religious ritual for the Ordo Templi Orientis (Order of the Templars of the East), the Masonic sex magick cult Crowley oversaw in the early 20th century. Crowley's various communes were purportedly laden with drug use. And while he claimed never to perform a Black Mass, Crowley was deeply familiar with its proceedings. Crowley's own definition of a Black Mass is as follows:

> The celebrant must be a priest, for the whole idea of the practice is to profane the Sacrament of the Eucharist. Therefore you must believe in the truth of the cult and the efficacy of its ritual. A renegade priest gathers about him a congregation of sensation-hunters and religious fanatics; then only can the ceremonies of profanation be extended black magical effect.
>
> …
>
> The ceremony is a parody of the orthodox Mass, with blasphemous interpolations. The priest must be careful, however, to conse-

---

12   Richard Kaczynski, *Perdurabo: The Life of Aleister Crowley* (Berkeley: North Atlantic Books, 2010), 528.
13   Cited in John Kersey, "Ancient Orthodox Catholic Church and Order of Holy Wisdom – clarification," https://san-luigi.org/churches/catholicate-of-the-west/mission/ancient-orthodox-catholic-church-and-order-of-holy-wisdom-clarification/.

crate the Host in the orthodox manner. The wine has been adulter-
ated with magical drugs like deadly nightshade and vervain, but the
priest must convert it into the blood of Christ. The dreadful basis
of the Mass is that the bread and wine have imprisoned the Deity.
Then they are subjected to terrible profanations.[14]

That Crowley emerges as a link is both startling and unsurprising:
when Perry Russo, DA Jim Garrison's chief witness in the Clay Shaw-con-
spiracy trial, talked about David Ferrie performing private Masses in
makeshift vestments, we are no longer inclined to as easily dismiss such
behavior as idiosyncratic, but rather as perpetuating the occultic practices
of his spiritual forebears. Peter Levenda elaborates:

> The Black Mass which Ferrie was accused of performing is a rit-
> ual that mocks those of the Catholic Church; essentially, it is an
> attempt at organized blasphemy, an attack of rebellion, political as
> well as theological. It is also designed to attract demonic influenc-
> es, evil spirits and the souls of the angry dead. Yet, this ritual carries
> very little weight if performed by a lay-person. It is potentially quite
> powerful, however, if performed by an ordained priest.[15]

Another Crowley acolyte, George Winslow Plummer, was a member
of the Ordo Templi Orientis and founded the First Rosicrucian Church of
America. After his death, his widow married S.W. de Witow of the Holy
Orthodox Church. de Witow consecrated Walter Propheta of the American
Orthodox Catholic Church, of which Carl Jerome Stanley was archbishop.

Upon Ferrie's consecration, his full name on the consecration certificate is Francis Maria D.W. Ferrie, O.S.J. Typically, O.S.J. refers to the
Order of St. John, a quasi-chivalric order. For ecclesiastical names, however, post-nominal letters indicate a religious order. O.S.J. might refer to
the "Orthodox Society of Jesus," created by Archbishop Stanley as a New
Orleans-based order for military veterans – not to be confused with the
Society of Jesus, the Jesuits.

Archbishop Stanley told Louisville Police homicide detective Herman
Mitchell that Martin wanted to become a bishop in order to be able to
enter Cuba.[16] This claim suggests that possession of a fake passport was a
chief perk in this racket. The reason Stanley was identified as the conse-
crating bishop, most likely, was his association with both the Shickshinny
Knights (explored in the next chapter) and Propheta's storefront church

---

14   Aleister Crowley, "Black Magic Is Not Myth," *Sunday Dispatch*, 2 July 1933.
15   Levenda, *Sinister Forces, Book One, The Nine*, 287.
16   NARA Record Number: 1994.05.06.08:44:58:780005.

for the FBI. Martin also was able to get a string of Banister investigators ordained to the bishopric, including Banister himself. But in early 1962, Stanley discovered the ruse, and issued a "bull of excommunication," signed by Stanley (as "Christopher Maria"), "Archbishop-Primate of N.A. Byzantine Primtive (sic) Orthodox Church, and the Holy Catholic Apostolic Church of N.A." The bull declared anathema a slew of bishops:

> ...for the reason that the (sic) had attempted to receive Holy Consecration to the episcopate in violation of all the Ancient and Sacred Canons of the Church since they made false and lying claims and statements in order to fraudulently obtain Sacred Consecration and we warn all bishops and relates (sic) everywhere to declare them frauds and to turn them out: Jack J.S. Martin, Victor H. Schiro, Guy W. Banister, Thomas Dooling, William G. Bell, Jr., George E. Grienen, and Thomas Bechman (sic). Amen.

Ferrie, however, is not included in this particular bull, although it is generally thought Stanley also defrocked Ferrie in early 1962, presumably on account of his homsexuality. However, Peter Levenda found that laughable: "[I]t is doubted that [Ferrie] was ever removed at all, for any reason. If he was, he would have been the first (and probably only) person ever kicked out of the wandering bishops' club."[17] When Ferrie, Martin and Stanley met in Louisville in November 1961 – according to Stanley's

statement made the day after Ferrie's death in 1967 to Detective Mitchell – while the three were "drinking and 'hitting the bars' [Ferrie and Martin] told Stanley that Ferrie had been involved in a plot against President Kennedy" two full years before the president's eventual murder.[18] Stanley also relayed, per Martin, that Lee Oswald and Ferrie were "buddies."

New Orleans DA Jim Garrison and others have questioned the accuracy of Stanley's statements, writing him off as a rambling, mentally unstable conman. Indeed, this participant in Vatican II had a lengthy rap sheet all over the United States dating back to the 1920s, mostly for grand theft auto and sending obscene letters through USPS. Stanley also managed to secure Canadian citizenship. There, he associated directly with Earl Anglin James.[19]

Other boy bishops connected with Ferrie and Martin were men such as Thomas Edward Beckham, Thomas Jude Baumler, Raymond Broshears – all men of dubious repute and with criminal records. Like Earl Anglin James, theology and the word of God were not necessarily foremost on their minds, if at all. It was as if another motive drove them to seek the bishop's miter. Telling is an exchange between Jim Garrison and Thomas Beckham during Beckham's grand jury testimony in 1968:

> **Garrison:** Well, suppose you tell me the name of the church you belong to?
>
> **Beckham:** I got the papers at home, I can show you the papers, but I don't have them with me .
>
> **Garrison:** Well, tell me what you recall that is on the paper?
>
> **Beckham:**. Let me see if I can recall what is on the paper. I don't know, it says that I am an ordained priest within the Holy APOLO-TOTIC, or something like that.
>
> **Garrison:** Are you trying to tell me you don't know what church you are a priest in?
>
> **Beckham:**. No, because I wasn't even interested in that, I never even messed with it.
>
> **Garrison:**. Were you wearing the habit?
>
> **Beckham:** At that time, yes.
>
> **Garrison:** While you were wearing the habit what church did you think you belonged to?
>
> **Beckham:** That's a good question. Ask Mr. Martin. I don't know myself.

---

18   Ibid.
19   2005 email from Colin Guthrie to Peter Levenda; shared with the author, April 2023.

Garrison: I am asking you.

Beckham: I don't know.

Garrison: Were you aware that was the same church in which David Ferrie was a priest?

Beckham: No, not until a news service ... that's what I said ... not until a news service ... then after I read your article I figured that you and Martin were working together and you set up a frame.

Garrison: I am not interested in what you figured, your answer is 'no', is that correct?

Beckham: Which was it, which part. Will you read it back?

Garrison: Are you aware that was the same church in which DavidFerrie was a priest?

Beckham: I know now ... the news service ...

Garrison: You know now – you did not know it then?

Beckham: No.

Garrison: Were you ordained in any way?

Beckham: How do you mean – God ordains, man doesn't ordain ... Ireceived papers...

Garrison: We don't understand things like that. Will you explain, were you ordained by any men?

Beckham: Can I explain it...

Garrison:. No, just answer it.

Beckham: I can't answer it that way.

Garrison: Then answer the best way you can, but cut it down to five minutes.

Beckham: According to Christianity and the National Council of-Christian Churches, ordination is exposed by God, the only person that can ordain. Certain churches set up councils for ordination, or licensing of ministers. Some states recognize only ordination ministers to perform marriages or to preach funerals. Others who are licensed are not allowed they are to act more or less as a deacon, that's one step to work up to ordination. I received papers stating that I was ordained. Now if that constitutes ordination I was ordained I don't think it does.

Garrison: Who handed you the papers?

Beckham:. They were not handed to me, they were mailed to me.

Garrison: How did you get them in your hand?

Beckham:. Through the mailman.

Garrison: All right, you got them through the mailman. What did these papers say? Did they say you were a priest?

Beckham: Yes.

Garrison: How much did they cost you?

Beckham:. If you total up what I gave Martin all along, I don't know. I see now what they cost me.

Garrison: You do not recall how much they cost you?

Beckham: They didn't cost me.

Garrison: Have you ever heard of the Archbishop Christopher Maria?

Beckham: Is that a ship or a person?

Garrison: Just answer me without being cute.

Beckham: I don't know.

Garrison: Have you ever heard of Bishop Hyde?

Beckham: Sounds familiar, but I don't know.

Garrison: How about Bishop Stanley?

Beckham: No ... could that be Earl Stanley James ... or Stanley Earl James, something like that? If I am not mistaken ...

Garrison:. Have you ever heard of Bishop James of Canada?

Beckham: Yes.

Garrison: Where did you know him from?

Beckham: I don't know him, that's the guy whose signature is on the papers .

Garrison: Is that where you heard from him?

Beckham: Yes, his signature is on them papers.

Garrison: Are you aware that he was a friend of David Ferrie?

Beckham:. I am aware that he was a friend of Jack Martin.

Garrison: Are you aware that he was a friend of David Ferrie?

Beckham: No. I don't know if he knows Ferrie.

Garrison: Have you ever heard of the Twentieth Century Reformation Church? Dr. McIntyre's church?

Beckham: No. Carl McIntyre, I have heard over and over … every newsman has been asking me…

Garrison: Have you ever heard of him independently of the newsmen?

Beckham: What do you mean independently?

Garrison: Until the newsmen asked you, had you ever heard of him?

Beckham: I can't answer that because I don't know. It's a familiar sounding name.

Garrison:. Have you ever heard of a member of that church named Eugene Bradley?

Beckham: I don't think so.[20]

Thomas Edward Beckham, behind him are "degrees" – the craftsmanship of Earl Anglin James

Beckham's ignorance on anything having to do with the ministerial life is beyond the pale. In a scenario evoking the fraudsters of Hell's Kitchen we met earlier, Beckham blithely follows what Jack Martin tells him to do once Martin "ordains" him to the priesthood by conferring a forged letter upon his person and sending him on a mission – to open a place for the poor.

Beckham: In the meantime he [Martin] gives me a letter with all this fancy stuff on it, signed, that I was a minister. In the meantime

20 Orleans Parish Grand Jury Testimony of Thomas Edward Beckham, 15 February 1968, 25-29.

73

I went down to South Rampart Street and I contacted a Jewish guy who had a building, it was empty, it was next to a clothing store, I contacted him and I said "Sir, you are not using the building and I am going to open up a mission in it for men to go to, then I figured it out I would call all the hotels and all the food left over I would get it and give these men, I wouldn't have to buy no food, and some bread company would give me the old bread, so the guy agreed to it, and I said after I get the church going and people start coming in, I will have a church, so no use let this building going to waste. So I told the man I didn't want to take up an offering, if they wanted to give it, fine, but he couldn't count on me right away. So the guy agreed to it, well I had a sign company, which I doubt to this day has ever been paid, to put … this was some kind of a mission order. Jack told me what to put, so 1 put UCMF, United Catholic Mission Fathers, is what it stood for, this was a mission, and came through a guy named Earl Stanley James [sic], if I am not mistaken, I have it on paper.[21]

A few exchanges later, Garrison touches on the issuances of false degrees:

Garrison: Do you hold a PhD?

Beckham: I hold a PhD in Criminology, which is awarded.

Garrison: What university did you obtain a PhD from?

Beckham: Well, I have one from Brackenridge Forest, which is in England, which was awarded.

Garrison: How long did you attend that college?

Beckham: I stated it was an award. Most PhD's are granted to you in recognition as an award. I would say there are only about seven colleges in the U. S. that grants Doctor's degrees.

Garrison: Why did they give you a PhD?

Beckham: This was awarded to me. It's an award. Somebody will probably give you an award before it's over with, a PhD.

Garrison: Why did they give you this award?

Beckham: I knew Dr. Crisman and Dr. Crisman got it for me. I've got several awards…

Garrison: Dr. Crisman got it for you?

Beckham: Yes sir.

Garrison: Do you know where he got his PhD?

---

21   Ibid., 17.

Beckham: No sir. He attended the University of Washington and another college … he's got a secondary teaching certificate, you can check on it …[22]

Beckham was referring to Fred L. Crisman, ostensibly a high school journalism instructor at White River High in Buckley, Washington. He was also a pilot during World War II who spun fantastic tales that made him a legend with fans of the paranormal. A favorite yarn Crisman spun saw him getting shot down in Burma on his last mission, battling subterranean beasts in a cave while shooting his way out with a submachine gun; the account landed in *Amazing Stories* in 1946. In 1947, Crisman found himself in an even more amazing story: "The Maury Island UFO Incident" of June 21, 1947, in which Crisman, Harold A. Dahl, Dahl's son, and their dog encountered four to six flying donut-shaped spacecraft overhead in the Puget Sound off Maury Island, Washington. One of the crafts was malfunctioning; it emitted waste of some kind, killing the dog. As such, it is the first modern UFO sighting in the United States.

And perhaps even more bizarre than the story itself is the FBI agent who recovered a piece of the purported saucer: *Guy Banister*.

In any case, Garrison attempted to link Beckham with two radical-right individuals, Reverend Carl McIntire and Edgar Eugene Bradley. McIntire, a Princeton graduate who ran a Bible school, Shelton College (which eventually lost its accreditation), began his career as a minister in the Presbyterian Church. An outspoken fundamentalist and opponent of "godless communism," McIntire formed the American Council of Christian Churches (ACCC) in 1941 as a conservative alternative to the National Council of Christian Churches. He was also unabashedly anti-Catholic. "The Catholic Church is the harlot church and bride of the anti-Christ," he said.[23] Banister attended one of his meetings in New Orleans.

Edgar Eugene Bradley worked part-time for McIntire on the ACCC's Laymen's Commission. Bradley became of interest to Garrison based on an affidavit from Dallas County deputy sheriff Roger Craig who stated Bradley was in front of the Texas School Book Depository on November 22, 1963 impersonating a Secret Service agent. Edgar Eugene Bradley was a California right-wing preacher. Governor Ronald Reagan refused to extradite Bradley to New Orleans on a supposed lack of evidence that Bradley was in Dallas on November 22, despite the Craig affidavit.[24] According to Jeffrey Caufield,

---

22   Ibid., 30.
23   NARA, 124-10020-10204.
24   Caufield, 233.

Bradley's wife told neighbor Margaret McLeigh on the day of the assassination, "I've prayed every night, every night of my life that he'd [the president] be shot and killed." She stated, "You know Gene [Bradley] is right down there in it. He's right down in there. I'll be hearing from him any minute." When Bradley returned home from his alleged trip to El Paso on November 30, 1963, the neighbor asked him "Well, if I know you, you pulled the trigger." Embarrassed, he said, "Well, not exactly but I damn sure as well know who did."[25]

Caufield also wrote that Bradley reportedly had blueprints of the storm drain in Dealey Plaza – a sniper location that has been discussed elsewhere in the JFK assassination literature. Caufield further states Bradley beat his son with a strap when his son defended the slain president. If Bradley indeed was present at the kill zone, he was not the only member of the radical right roaming around Dealey Plaza. He was likely joined on site by white supremacist Joseph Milteer.

Bradley and Milteer were disciples of another white supremacist, the Southern California-based Reverend Wesley Swift. Swift became the leading proponent of Christian Identity theology, a racist and anti-Semitic ideology championed by those in Guy Banister's circle and factions of Old Catholics. Christian Identity stated those of Germanic and Celtic blood were the true Chosen People, the real descendants of the ancient Israelites. To them, the Jews were not only the offspring of Cain, murderous son of Adam and Eve, they were the spawn of the serpent, and should thus be enslaved with other non-whites. Swift pushed this worldview through his church, the Anglo-Saxon Christian congregation, renamed the Church of Jesus Christ Christian. Earlier, he studied scripture at L.I.F.E. Bible College at the Angelus Temple in the Echo Park neighborhood of Los Angeles. Swift was a speaker and member of the racist White Citizens' Council, was chaplain of the Ku Klux Klan's Christian Knights of the Invisible Empire, and was a KKK rifle instructor. Swift was also regarded among his acolytes as a gifted prophet. "Swift had prophesied the assassination of President Kennedy in 1960. Moreover, members of Swift's church notified the FBI on several occasions that Swift stated in 1960 that Kennedy would not finish his term in office. On the first Sunday of January 1963, when he gave his annual prophecy, Swift proclaimed that something would happen to President Kennedy. An informant told the FBI that he heard Swift say on a tape

---

25   Ibid., 235.

recording six weeks before the assassination 'Kennedy was entering a critical period.'"[26]

Joseph Milteer also accurately predicted how the assassination would go down in Dealey Plaza only weeks earlier. William "Willie" Augustus Somersett had been an FBI informant in Miami since 1949. Jeffrey Caufield cited him as "an unsung hero in his efforts against the terrorist campaign of racial violence in the South in the 1950s and 1960s. His work likely prevented untold numbers of bombings, burnings, and murders."[27] Somersett observed the intensity over Catholic school integration in the Archdiocese of New Orleans when he was sent there by the FBI in November 1960. He joined the Citizens' Council and surely rubbed elbows or was a handshake away from Guy Banister, David Ferrie, Delphine Roberts, Leander Perez, and Jackson Ricau. The latter three were excommunicated by the archbishop for opposing integration. Roberts was also the secretary and mistress of Banister.

Those on the far-right on whom Somersett informed for the FBI were interested in what also occupied Wesley Swift: the formation of a new party, neither Republican nor Democrat, but one that would unabashedly return America to its true roots: a segregated country geared to its white, Anglo-Saxon, Protestant population. Also sharing that view, Joseph Milteer, a far-right, unemployed political activist from Georgia who supported the Constitution Party. When he met Willie Somersett in Miami in October 1963, Milteer was planning a Constitution Party assembly in Indianapolis, in order to "put an end to the Kennedy, Khrushchev and King dictatorship."[28] A further meeting between Somersett and Milteer was set for November 9, 1963. The FBI planted a tape recorder in Somersett's closet, hoping to glean some knowledge from Milteer about the September 15 bombing in Birmingham that killed four black children. JFK was also scheduled to visit Miami on November 18. Somersett was to guide the conversation towards these topics. At last, they get to talking about the president:

> **Somersett:** I think Kennedy is coming here on the 18th, or something like that to make some kind of a speech, I don't know what it is, but I imagine it will be on TV, and you can be on the look for that, I think it is the 18th that he is supposed to be here. I don't know what it is supposed to be about.

26   Caufield, 163.
27   Caufield, 94.
28   Ibid., 97.

Milteer: You can bet bottom dollar he is going to have a lot to say about the Cubans, there are so many of them here.

Somersett: Yeah, well he will have a thousand bodyguards, don't worry about that.

Milteer: The more bodyguards he has the easier it is to get him.

Somersett: What?

Milteer: The more bodyguards he has, the easier it is to get to him.

Somersett: Well how in the hell do you figure would be the best way to get him?

Milteer: From an office building with a high-powered rifle, how many people *[room noise – tape not intelligible]* does he have going around who look just like him? Do you know about that?

Somersett: No, I never heard that he had anybody.

Milteer: He has got them.

Somersett: He has?

Milteer: He had about fifteen. Whenever he goes anyplace they *[not intelligible]* he knows he is a marked man.

Somersett: You think he is a marked man?

Milteer: Sure he does.

Somersett: They are really going to try and kill him?

Milteer: Oh, yeah, it's in the working.

A few moments later in the conversation:

Somersett: Boy, if that Kennedy gets shot, we got to know where we are at. Because you know that will be a real shake, if they do that.

Milteer: They wouldn't leave any stone unturned there's no way. They will pick up somebody within hours afterwards, if anything like that would happen just to throw the public off.

Somersett: Oh, somebody is going to have to go to jail, if he gets killed.[29]

In the same conversation, Milteer also mentions the weapon could be disassembled with relative ease. Milteer was right on these four essential points that became the cornerstone for the case of the government against accused assassin Lee Harvey Oswald: that he fired upon the president from an office building with a high-powered weapon, which could be

---

29   Cited in Caufield, 103-105.

disassembled and transported without causing suspicion, and that he was picked up within hours of the
shooting "just to throw the public off," a statement
corroborated later when J. Edgar Hoover fretted:
"The thing I am concerned about is having something issued so that we can convince the public that
Oswald is the real assassin."

Within a few weeks of the assassination, the FBI
issued its report condemning Lee Harvey Oswald as
the president's killer.

Milteer

Moreover, Willie Somersett received a call from Joseph Milteer two
hours before the president was gunned down: "Well you won't be seeing
your friend Kennedy down there in Miami no more," and then hung up.[30]

The next day, Somersett met Milteer at the Jacksonville, Florida train
station where he drove Milteer to a meeting with Klansmen in South Carolina. According to Somersett, Milteer was "very jubilant" as he shook
Somersett's hand. "Well, I told you so, it happened like I told you didn't
it? It happened from a window with a high-power rifle." Quite satisfied,
Milteer added, "Everything ran true to form."[31] Moreover, Milteer named
Theodore "Ted" Jackman, R.E. Davis, and Dallas police officer Jefferson
Davis "J.D." Tippit as the actual assassins of the president, positioned at
three different locations in Dealey Plaza. Tippit, was the officer allegedly

Milteer in Dallas, 11/22/63???

---

30   Quoted in Caufield, 127.
31   Donald E. Wilkes, Jr., "The Georgian Who Knew a Sniper Would Kill JFK," *Popular Media*,
University of Georgia School of Law, 2013, 178. See also Caufield, 534; Don Adams, *From an Office
Building with a High-Powered Rifle* (Walterville, OR: TrineDay, 2012).

killed by Lee Oswald shortly before his arrest. Tippit moonlighted at Austin's Barbeque on the weekends. Austin's Barbeque was the meeting place for the John Birch Society.[32] We will return to Jackman and Davis.

However, Milteer was not interested in dwelling too long on the mechanics of the assassination with Somersett, but rather was looking ahead to the next phase of the plan: blaming the assassination on the Jews. Such was the purpose of the meeting with the Klan, to push a message that the Jews were responsible. "Notice to all Christians," he drafted on hotel stationary, "The Zionist Jews killed Christ 2,000 years ago and on November 22, 1963 the Jews killed President Kennedy – You Jews killed the president. Now we are going to kill you. – The International Underground." The final draft read: "It now becomes the solemn duty of every true red-blooded American to seek, find, expel, drive out from our country every traitor be he Zionist Jew, Communist, or what have you. - International Underground."[33]

And so, when Jack Ruby descended on the scene as the murderer of Lee Oswald – a silencing which certainly did not come as a surprise to Joseph Milteer – Ruby's later fixation about Nazism, a government overthrow, and fear of a progrom against the Jews (Ruby, born Jack Rubenstein, was himself Jewish), could not be dismissed as the ramblings of a madman. As we will later explore, Jack Ruby did not appear out of thin air.

---

32   Caufield, 486.
33   Ibid., 535

CHAPTER SEVEN

KILLING KINGS

In his days Pharaoh Neco king of Egypt went up to the king of Assyria to the river Euphrates. And King Josiah went to meet him, and when Pharaoh Neco saw him he killed him at Megiddo.

– 2 Kings 23:29

David Ferrie also stated three men were involved in the shooting. He told this to Navy veteran Raymond Broshears, allegedly David Ferrie's roommate for a short time in 1965. Broshears formed the Lavender Panthers, "a group with martial arts abilities organized to prevent harrassment of gays," and one that subscribed to Arianism – "that the Logos (Word) incarnate in Jesus was not co-eternal with God, but rather was God's first creation – a theology condemned as heresy by the Council of Nicea in 325."[1] David Ferrie introduced Broshears to the Orthodox Old Catholic Church of North America.

Broshears testified that Ferrie was unquestionably linked to the assassination of the president. "David admitted being involved with the assassins," Broshears said in a television interview for a Los Angeles talk show.[2] Broshears told Garrison's office and later Dick Russell that Ferrie's job was to fly two assassins out of Texas to Mexico, who would then be flown to South Africa. Broshears further told Russell: "Ferrie was extremely angry with President Kennedy for selling out the country to the Communists. [Ferrie and Broshears] agreed that Kennedy was not telling the truth to the media about Cuba."[3]

In his House Select Committee on Assassinations testimony, Broshears touched on the phenomenon of the diploma mill. He mentioned how many FBI men in agencies offices flung across the country – such as the San Jose field office – all had ordination papers. This was also the case for the Secret Service as well, he said. Why? One reason, not of little importance for young men at the time, was that a member of the clergy, or a

---

1   Alan M. Bain, et al, *Independent Bishops: An International Directory* (Burlington: Apogee Books, 1990), 61.

2   Stephen Jaffe, "Broshears: Ferrie was involved," *LA Free Press*, 9 Aug. 1968.

3   Caufield, 586.

seminarian, was automatically exempt from a draft. "Young men – hippies – started coming to me asking to be student ministers, I later learned, for their only purpose, for being ministers was to escape the draft," Broshears said.

Broshears is a figure who has been dismissed as an unreliable spinster of tall tales. But further investigation into his claims piece into the larger picture. Broshears noted Ferrie implicated Kent Courtney, John Birch Society leader, as "involved in the assassination," along with Minuteman Rich Lauchli, a Southern gunrunner.[4] According to Daniel Levitas, "Both the [John] Birch Society and the Minutemen were fueled by the same potent mixture of anti-Semitism, anticommunism, and conspiracy-mongering that had dominated the radical right during World War II and the McCarthy era."[5] More to the point, Frank Ellsworth, an ATF agent (Alcohol, Tobacco, Firearms), is quoted in an April 16, 1964 Warren Commission file as saying: "An organization known as the Minutemen is the right-wing group in Dallas most likely to have been associated with any effort to assassinate the President. The Minutemen are closely tied to General Walker and H.L. Hunt."[6]

Both Walker and Hunt will re-emerge in the pages ahead. Both harnessed modern communications to reach large conservative audiences. Hunt was especially keen to the power of radio and its ability to influence swaths of the American right: Hunt funded "one of the three most influential conservative programs of the 1960s – the Facts Forum."[7] The power of conservative broadcasters and programs was not lost on the Kennedy Administration, which waged war "to mute the Radio Right using federal regulatory power" by way of the IRS and FCC.[8] Hunt, who sponsored another popular program, Life Line, was a prime target for Attorney General Robert Kennedy's Justice Department, because JFK was "frustrated that rich conservatives had their already light tax burdens made even lighter by deductions for their contributions to 'ultra-right' broadcasters."[9] It is likely no coincidence that Hunt and major conservative broadcasters Rev. McIntire and Rev. Billy James Hargis all rise as influential figures fomenting radical right-wing animosity towards the Kennedy presidency, as we will see.

* * *

---

4   Caufield, 581.

5   Daniel Levitas, *The Terrorist Next Door: The Militia Movement and the Radical Right* (New York: Thomas Dunne Books, 2002), 73.

6   Dick Russell, *The Man Who Knew Too Much* (New York: Carrol & Graf, 1992, 2003), 357.

7   Paul Matzko, *The Radio Right* (Oxford: Oxford UP, 2020), 10-11.

8   Ibid., 6.

9   Ibid., 101.

An individual who bridged the radical right with the fringe bishops was Frederick Charles King, Titular Archbishop-Primate of the Old Roman Catholic Church of California. A New Orleans native and baptized Catholic, King racked up degrees from respectable schools such as Tulane, St. Louis University, and the University of Southern California – until his PhD from St. Andrew's Collegiate Church, whose dean was Earl Anglin James. A bit-part player in low-budget Hollywood and Mexican westerns and swashbucklers, King found an outlet for his spiritual wandering in Bishop Boltwood's Free Protestant Episcopal Church

Bishop Frederick Charles King

and the Old Roman Catholic Church.[10] He was consecrated bishop by Homer Ferdinand Francis Roebke, who was consecrated by both Archbishop Propheta and Archbishop Carl Jerome Stanley. Indeed, King was a priest in Stanley's Orthodox Society of Jesus – of which David Ferrie was a member. King was first made a bishop by the regionary bishop of the Americas in the Western Orthodox Catholic Church/Catholicate of the West.

King amassed a number of pseudo-princely titles: Marquis de St. Laurent, Prince of Vilna and All of Byelorussia, and Duke of Serbia, Duke of Bosnia, and Duke of the Holy Roman Emperor.

Like most in this world, King was a patriotic anti-communist. And he was a John Birch Society member, at one point head of its Hollywood chapter. He launched an initiative called the Bishop King Crusade, a "Christian, Anti-Communism, Anti-Socialism, educational program designed to awaken and educate the American people concerning the dangers of these insidious evils."[11] King's radio program was his primary means of communication. He received commendations from Governors

10   John Kersey, "Prince Frederick of Vilna and all of Byelorussia," https://san-luigi.org/royal-office/royal-house/prince-frederick-of-vilna-and-all-byelorussia/.
11   Ibid.

Ronald Reagan and George Wallace, Senator Strom Thurmond, and General Edwin Walker.[12]

The Bishop King Crusade was but one of many such organizations that proliferated in the 1960s – so much so a report on right-wing groups was prepared for President Kennedy in August 1963. It was estimated "that the radical right spent as much as $25 million annually, supported by about 70 foundations, 113 corporations, 25 utility companies, and 250 identifiable individuals."[13]

As for Ferrie, Raymond Broshears goes on to tell the DA's investigators that Ferrie was:

> Trying to tie Hale Boggs, a congressman here in Louisiana, trying to tie him in with Billy James Hargus [sic] and General Walker and H. Lemar [sic] hunt and this guy in New Jersey [Reverend Carl] McIntyre [sic]. He said it's part of the great, great white, Anglo-Saxon protestant plot to take over the country to keep their man in and I couldn't buy it. I really couldn't buy it then and I still have a hard – well, I'm not having as hard a time buying it, I'll be honest with you. I am not having as hard a time buying it now as I did then.

Broshears also included a personal detail, from Ferrie: "Ferrie told Broshears that he loved Lee Harvey Oswald and had some of his possessions including a hunter's hat with the initials 'L.H.' or the name 'Lee' on it."[14]

* * *

Archbishop Carl Stanley of Louisville was a 33-degree Freemason and was closely aligned with various Masonic orders.[15] Stanley also headed a pretend chivalric order, the Sovereign Order of St. John of Jerusalem, Knights Hospitallers, Priory of the Holy Savior, and gave the Orthodox Society of Jesus his blessing. Stanley formed his Kentucky Knights in 1960 as an offshoot of the Grand Priory of America of the Sovereign Order of St. John of Jerusalem, founded in New York in 1908. It annexed the Grand Priory of Russia in 1912. This order fancied itself as a genuine branch of the Orders of Malta, ostensibly the Russian line of the order; its membership largely consisted of displaced White Russians living in the United States, a membership that likely involved Archbishops Zhurawetzky and Ryzy-Ryzski, whose passion was assisting Ukrainians in diaspora. In 1936, its headquarters shifted from New York to Shickshinny, Pennsyl-

12   Ibid.
13   Russell, 11.
14   Ibid., 585.
15   Patrice Chairoff, *Faux Chevaliers, Vrais Gogos* (Paris: Jean Cyrille Godefroy 1985), 156.

vania. Its grand chancellor, chief executive officer and secretary-treasurer was "Colonel" Charles L. Thourot Pichel, a Catholic convert who lobbied in 1933 to become Adolf Hitler's U.S. representative.[16] Pichel and his cohort sympathized with National Socialism to best combat Bolshevism.

Pichel is a character who further brings us into this occultic and fascist milieu. Pichel was a convicted drug trafficker and invented origin stories about the Shickshinny Knights as a genuine offshoot of the Orders of St. John of Jersualem. Essentially, Pichel devoted his time to propagating secret societies of the Aryan race – white brotherhoods of anti-Semites and racists. This was particularly realized in Pichel's Ancient and Noble Order of the Blue Lamoo, which claimed its power and authority from "the Ancient and Immortal Atlantian Initiates of the Sun."[17]

As a Catholic convert, Pichel identified with the traditionalist aspects of the Roman religion. After Vatican II significantly changed many Catholic traditions – not the least being the actual structure of the Roman Mass as well as the liturgical calendar – the Catholic Traditional Movement, seeking a refuge from these modern changes, found solace within Pichel's Knights. We will return to this movement when discussing the wandering bishopric of Ngo Dinh Thuc.

The eugenic idea of Aryanism, of a white brotherhood, stretched beyond Nazism to its occult origins, indeed to Madame Helena Blavatsky, Theosophy, Rosicrucianism and Gnosticism: the inequality of the races and the purity of the white race. Such a notion was bolstered by Unitarian Charles Darwin's survival of the fittest theory as it related to white Europeans, which he outlined in *The Descent of Man* (1871). This basic tenet – what its believers would consider a fundamental right – gradually was challenged in the United States until reaching a watershed with the landmark *Brown v. Board of Education*.

There even existed an Armed Services Committee and Military Service Committee of the Shickshinny Knights, in which far-right military men like U.S. generals Charles Willoughby, Edwin Walker, Pedro del Valle and Lieutenant Colonel Phillip Corso were members.[18] Frank Capell, a far-right propagandist, was another member. "After the [President] Kennedy assassination, del Valle sent Capell a written account of his own concocted theory of the meaning of the assassination, which may have served

16   Russ Bellant, *Old Nazis, the New Right and the Republican Party* (Boston: South End Press, 1988), 45.

17   Pat McGrady, "'Aryan' Movement Outdoes Itself In 'Mystic Order of Blue Lamoo,'" *Jewish Daily Bulletin*, 2 August 1934.

18   Caufield, 193.

as a template for other similar far-right theories on the event."[19] Before he emerged as a master of disinformation in the aftermath of the President Kennedy assassination, Phillip Corso worked on the staff of C.D. Jackson's Operations Coordinating Board, an Eisenhower Administration effort providing oversight to covert operations. Moreover, Corso "liaised closely with Nelson Rockefeller, for some months Eisenhower's Special Assistant for Cold War Strategy."[20] Corso also was "connected with U.S. Army Intelligence for over twenty years, and for years furnished the FBI with information on alleged subversive activities."[21] This included involvement in Operation Paperclip, the disbursement of German scientists into the U.S. Ten years later, it was Corso who was the source of the rumor that Lee Oswald was a paid FBI informant.[22] And just before his death in 1998, Corso published the purported nonfiction memoir *The Day After Roswell*, with a foreword by Senator Strom Thurmond.

The generals decorated and honored by the Shickshinny Knights – Willoughby, del Valle and Walker – were all proteges of General Douglas MacArthur, a favorite of the far-right, particularly H.L. Hunt. General Willoughby was General MacArthur's chief of intelligence in the Pacific theater of World War II; MacArthur nicknamed him "my little fascist." Willoughby was a native of Heidelberg, Germany, born Adolf Tscheppe-Weidenbach in 1892. Another fervent anti-communist, Willoughby strongly backed the far-right American Friends of the Anti-Bolshevik Bloc of Nations (ABN), a bastion for anti-communist European exiles that was also pro-fascist and pro-Nazi. According to Christopher Simpson, author of *Blowback*, its executive board consisted of a half dozen "open Nazi collaborators."[23] Willoughby once said of Mussolini: "Historical judgment, freed from the emotional haze of the moment, will credit Mussolini with wiping out a memory of defeat by re-establishing the traditional military supremacy of the white race."[24]

In his retirement years, Willoughby was affiliated with a plethora of conservative groups: the International Committee for the Defense of Christian Culture, a board member of Young Americans for Freedom, and executive editor of *Foreign Intelligence Digest*. Like others on the radical right, Willoughby was frequently in touch with H.L. Hunt, who

19   Ibid., 194.
20   Burton Hersh, *The Old Boys* (New York: Scribners, 1992), 411.
21   Caufield, 194.
22   Ibid, 195.
23   Christopher Simpson, *Blowback* (New York: Open Road, 1988, 2014), digital version, 418.
24   Quoted in Phillip Nelson, *LBJ: The Mastermind of the JFK Assassination* (New York: Skyhorse, 2013), 180.

financially supported the Willoughby periodical. Both Willoughby and Hunt were sympathetic to, and great proponents of, the John Birch Society. On November 24, 1963, a Mexico City long-distance telephone operator heard a voice on an international call say, "The Castro plan is being carried out. Bobby is next." One of those telephone numbers traced to Emilio Nunez Portuondo, Latin American Affairs editor of *Foreign Intelligence Digest*.

One of Willoughby's proteges was fundraiser Reverend Billy James Hargis, a loyalist of Dr. Carl McIntire, ardent follower of the John Birch Society, and chaplain of the Constitution Party. Hargis visited Guy Banister's office in October 1963.[25] In September 1961, Hargis had "announced that a secret fraternity to coordinate right-wing activities would soon be formed."[26] It became known as the Anti-Communist Liaison, and met for the first time in March 1962. Army Lieutenant Colonel William P. Gale took the goals of the Anti-Communist Liaison to heart by organizing a paramilitary unit. He wrote a tactical guide, urging that "patriotic underground armies should be established, named the 'Rangers' who should train to assassinate, sabotage, and overthrow the 'People's Democracy.'"[27] Dick Russell reported the Anti-Communist Liaison attracted a "wide range of wanderers along an L.A.-to-Miami route."[28]

Of those in attendance at the March 1962 meeting were Willoughby, Gale, and John Rousselot, future congressman from California. Gale's home was in remote Mariposa, California, west of the Yosemite Valley. There he fomented white supremacist ideologies such as Christian Identity, even becoming ordained a minister by Wesley Swift in the Church of Jesus Christ Christian. Gale was deeply immersed in quasi-religious, crypto-fascist militia groups until the end of his life (he died in 1988). Of course, Gale would see himself as an advocate for white Christians, hence his formation of the Christian Defense League and named by Harry Dean as fundraiser for JFK's assassination.[29]

• • •

This flurry of activity during the centennial years of the Civil War shows just how deep-seated the antebellum way of life remained – and how much the presence of John Kennedy brought those sentiments, already boiling, to the surface. It was Mississippi native William Faulkner

---

25   Caufield, 376.
26   Russell, 111.
27   Ibid., 111-112.
28   Ibid.
29   Caufield, 590.

who remarked in 1956, "The South is armed for revolt. [White Southerners] will accept another Civil War knowing they are going to lose."[30]

If occultists of the 19th century found secret wisdom as an antidote to the forward sweep of the industrial age, then sympathizers of the Confederate States of America found in the "lost cause of the Confederacy" an idealized, mythological portrait of the antebellum South. Both the occultists of the pseudo-chivalric orders and the Confederacy sympathizers utilized the Maltese cross. In Atlanta in 1898, the United Daughters of the Confederacy honored Confederate veterans "as a local UDC chapter marked the graves of former Confederate soldiers with a small cross tombstone at cemeteries throughout the South. In doing so, the [United Daughters of the Confederacy] ... connect[ed] fallen Southern soldiers to an order of Christian knights involved in the Holy Wars of the Crusades against another type of infidel."[31]

Archbishop Carl Jerome Stanley, left, displays the Maltese cross on his vestment. Right, a commemorative marker from the United Daughters of the Confederacy

And just as medieval families supported the endeavors of local Templar commanderies and religious monasteries, the assassination plotters, hiding behind their fantasy world of religious and chivalric orders, were aided by sympathetic families of influence to achieve their objective.

30   "Faulkner Believes South Would Fight," *New York Times*, 15 March 1956.
31   Jon D. Bohland, "A Lost Cause Found: Vestiges of Old South Memory in the Shenandoah Valley of Virginia," Blacksburg, VA, 22 September 2006.

* * *

Time and again, H.L. Hunt and family emerged as the angel investors behind such clubs as John Rousselot's League of Right Wing Organizations and Billy James Hargis's Christian Crusade. Their worldview can be summarized thusly: "The pervasive attitude among the radical right in the 1950s was a disdain for President Roosevelt's New Deal, as well as for President Truman's Fair Deal, both of which were felt to be Socialistic. The far right felt that the civil rights position of the Fair Deal represented an assault on the sacred Southern institution of segregation."[32] Hargis and Major General Edwin Walker launched Operation Midnight Ride in February 1963, a national speaking tour referencing Paul Revere's famous midnight ride. Over the next few months, they galvanized audiences in close to twelve cities throughout the south and southwest with anti-Kennedy rhetoric.

As Walker, Willoughby, Hargis, and Gale whipped up the far right, retired Marine Corps Lieutenant General Pedro del Valle was writing incriminating letters about a coming World War III, a U.N. takeover of the United States, and the need for a military coup d'etat against not just the government, but against the foundations of the democratic process. Writing to the founder of the John Birch Society, Robert Welch, in September 1961: "The time has come for action, Treason sits enthroned in the seats of Power, and treason will soon land us in the Red One Worlder's Paradise unless we take steps to prevent it, and do it now and with decisiveness." del Valle went on to advocate armed resistance.[33] On another occasion, in a letter to the National States' Rights Party, del Valle wrote, "[W]hen a free people find their elected servants following a destructive course of action regarding the Constitution, the people must take effective action to restore same by taking the matter into their own hands and forcing the traitors out of power."[34]

To Gale, del Valle, Hargis and others, all this insurrectionist fringe business was ostensibly to prepare for a Communist takeover of the United States – whether by Soviet invasion, United Nations control, or a treasonous president, a closet Commie – and advocate for a return to limited government – nothing above county level – with unfettered use of firearms, and no prohibition on the Bible and public prayer in American society. This activity from retired high-ranking military officials was

---

32   Caufield, 138.
33   Ibid., 177.
34   Ibid., 341.

not lost on writer Fletcher Knebel, whose novel (co-written with Charles W. Bailey II) about an assassination attempt on the president by a general, *Seven Days in May*, was published in September 1962. John Frankenheimer, who previously helmed *The Manchurian Candidate*, directed the film version (with JFK allowing the production use of the White House). Knebel predated the novel with an article for *Look* magazine, "Rightist Revival: who's on the Far Right?" Knebel identified the failure at the Bay of Pigs, the stalemate of the Korean War, the Communist advancement in Southeast Asia, and the quashing of the Hungarian Uprising as factors in the rise of the radical right.

At the center of this faction was General Edwin Walker, who unsuccessfully ran for Texas governor in 1964, losing in the primary to John Connally. Two years earlier, President Kennedy pulled Walker from command in Germany for distributing John Birch Society propaganda to his troops. Walker was arrested on federal charges for inciting a major riot at the University of Mississippi protesting the use of federal troops enforcing the enrollment of black student James Meredith in September 1962; two people were killed in the riot. Walker called for 10,000 "patriots" to descend on Ole Miss in protest. A federal grand jury declined to indict Walker.

According to the Warren Commission, Lee Oswald supposedly fired his mail-order rifle into the Dallas mansion of General Walker on April 10, 1963. However, a teenage witness, Walter Coleman, identified three men outside the house at the time, with two escaping in a Ford, and the other pushing something down on the floorboard of a 1958 Chevy. That car was parked in an adjacent Mormon church parking lot before taking off.[35] Oswald did not have a driver's license, and some say didn't know how to drive. Brushing fragments of glass out of his hair when reporters arrived, Walker explained he was doing his taxes and moved a slight inch as the bullet struck the wall. He ran upstairs to get his own weapon, but the assassin was gone.[36] When asked who pulled the trigger, Walker replied, "There are plenty of people on the other side." Months later, only a week after JFK's assassination, a newspaper reported that Oswald was connected with the Walker shooting – the *Deutsch National-Zeitung und Soldaten-Zeitung*, a pro-Nazi paper out of Germany. But it was not until the first week of December 1963 when newspapers in the U.S. wrote of Marina Oswald's allegation that Oswald shot Walker. The Warren Commission accepted this, stating the attempt on Walker was a prelude to the later firing on the

---

35   Ibid., 197.

36   "Bullet Misses Gen. Walker By An Inch, Police Report," *San-Angelo Standard Times*, 11 April 1963.

Earl Anglin James relaxing at home, 1968

president. But how did the German paper get the scoop before Marina even went public with her allegation? As Jeffrey Caufield noted, "There is no way anyone else could have known about it – unless they had inside knowledge of the incident."[37] Most likely, it was General Walker himself who inserted Oswald into the suspicious narrative. After all, Walker at one point orchestrated his own kidnapping with accomplice Robert DePugh.

* * *

"They say I was involved, do they?" James told *Toronto Star* reporter Earl McRae. McRae's profile on James, "Garrison Probe touches Toronto," ran the week before Beckham's grand jury appearance in New Orleans in February 1968. "Well, I wasn't. I've never been to New Orleans in my life."[38]

Then why the gold key to the City of New Orleans on your watch chain, McRae asked.

---

37   Caufield, 402.

38   In 1970, James reported his wallet missing. Among the contents retrieved by Toronto police were business cards of dubious legitimacy: numerous ones from the state of Louisiana, such as one commissioning James as a "Colonel on the Staff of Earl K. Long" (then-governor of Louisiana); another naming the "Rt. Honorable Sir Earl A. James" as Honorary Attorney General in the State of Louisiana; another from the sheriff of Cook County, Illinois, Elmer Michael Walsh, who "requests you to extend every possible courtesy to Earl Anglin James." In Thomas Edward Beckham's deposition, he refers to the large amount of "cards" collected by Jack Martin.

"Oh, this,' he said fingering it gently, 'was sent to me by a Mr. Jack Martin of New Orleans in the mail. He had heard all about me and my fame and sent it to me. Very nice of him."

James made no mention of his true dealings with Martin. James denied knowing Ferrie. "I know nothing about this man Perry or whatever his name is. I received no phone calls from him. I don't know what it could be about." Yet the whole point of McRae seeking out James was because James's unlisted number appeared numerous times on Ferrie's phone records in 1962. Why would James deny knowing him?

Earlier, McRae asked him who he thought killed the president. "White Texans," James answered. "He went south to get the colored vote. They said, 'We'll stop this man.'"

CHAPTER EIGHT

DAVID'S FRIENDS

*I am distressed for thee, my brother Jonathan: very pleasant hast thou
been unto me: thy love to me was wonderful, passing the love of women.*
                                                          −2 Samuel 1:26

Throughout most of his 48 years of life, David Ferrie struggled to find his place.

Like Earl Anglin James, Ferrie constantly tried to integrate into the mainstream milieu – until he simply ignored the status quo and burrowed headlong into expressing his own identity, come what may. By the end of the 1950s and into the early 1960s there was no compartmentalization to his unusual life. Ferrie's homosexuality and sexual behavior with young men was a major aspect of his lifestyle, a pattern Ferrie shared with many Roman Catholic clerical abusers of mostly young adult males in the sexual abuse scandal that has decimated the Catholic Church in our time.[1]

Ferrie's unsuccessful attempts at becoming a Roman Catholic priest culminated in 1944 when he was dismissed for "emotional instability from St. Charles Seminary in Carthagena, Ohio," according to the FAA's background report on Ferrie (Ferrie clarified in a letter to George Augustine Hyde it was rather due to his "brashness and theological disagreements"). Fr. Francis Sullivan, seminary theology professor, went further than attributing it to emotional instability, calling Ferrie a "preconditioned psycho, [who] impresses people by pretending to be an expert on everything, [and who] definitely has a talent for character assassination."[2]

Ferrie, who was born in 1918, was allegedly molested by a priest at his boyhood parish, St. Pat's in Cleveland's West Park neighborhood, in the shadow of Hopkins Airport. The effects are incalculable. However, Ferrie graduated from St. Ignatius High a year ahead of his anticipated graduating class. This was discovered by inspecting the administration wing of St. Ignatius, the walls lined with senior class portraits. Indeed, there was

---

1   See "The Nature and Scope of Sexual Abuse of Minors by Catholic Priests and Deacons in the United States, 1950-2002: A Research Study Conducted by the John Jay College of Criminal Justice, The City University of New York," February 2004.
2   HSCA, X, n.19.

17-year-old Ferrie, the final portrait at the bottom, as if added at the last moment to the graduating class of 1935.

The all-male culture of St. Ignatius and John Carroll University (which became co-ed more than thirty years after Ferrie's time, in the fall of 1968), both under the tutelage of the Jesuits with their customary rigorous academic expectations and military-like discipline – earning them the nickname "God's Marines" – has historically too often been a culture of homophobia, and one that has led to tragic results.[3] Such has been the dichotomy of being a Catholic living with homosexual tendencies: an atmosphere that encourages individual self-expression within a stringent hierarchical structure. While homosexual activity is an active sin in Catholic teaching, one who is gay can still yet find creative outlets, particularly Jesuit, educational milieu that encourages self-expression and identity: the creative arts, such as musical theatre and the Glee Club, of which Ferrie participated; journalism and debating, in which Ferrie won student awards for his rhetorical skills; and music, where he played the organ at John Carroll's Spring Concert in 1938. Ferrie also showed a knack for fundraising, a vital trait for those discerning a priestly vocation, especially those groomed for high ranking positions of leadership like a university president or cathedral rector.

The expectation for young men being put through private school in pre-war America, particularly a Jesuit college preparatory high school as St. Ignatius, was that the young man was expected to be a success in his chosen profession, whether a family man or member of the clergy, but certainly a law abiding citizen – a patriot who loved God, country, and family. And yet, Ferrie could not follow the script written for him by either his parents or the expectations of his time and place, even if he loved the Catholic religion. That is not to suggest his inability to become an ordained priest was self-sabotage, but perhaps the respected role of parish priest (interestingly, Ferrie showed no interest in becoming a Jesuit, who are typically not assigned to parishes), a vocation not yet tarnished by the sexual abuse of minors that would rock the church at the turn of the 21st century, was not in the end what he really wanted. What perhaps attracted him was the concept of ritual, the "smells and bells" of the Roman Mass – namely, the Tridentine Rite, which would be largely abolished after Vatican II. In this way, perhaps he wanted to be part of an important secret society that valued ritual, but enabled him to do things that mattered in the here and now – not in the eternal afterlife that was to come.

And so David Ferrie channeled his passion and energy into the field of aeronautics. In 1945, he received his student pilot license after a three-

---

3   A student who identified gay in my own freshman class at St. Ignatius committed suicide over the Christmas holidays. He was 14.

year apprenticeship, the same year his brother Parmely returned home an Army Air Corps lieutenant who flew B-24s over Germany. David taught aeronautics at Cleveland's Benedictine High School, the all-boys Catholic school run by the Order of St. Benedict monks. His tenure on the faculty did not last long. He was fired in 1948 for reputedly taking students to a brothel, among other infractions. The HSCA report on Ferrie mentioned his firing from another Cleveland high school, Rocky River High, "for psychoanalyzing his students instead of teaching them."[4] Ferrie, however, disputed even being associated with that public high school.

A year earlier, Ferrie became an instructor in the local Civil Air Patrol unit (CAP), the official civilian auxiliary of the United States Air Force. According to HSCA testimony by one Jean Naatz, "[Ferrie] had done more for the Civil Air Patrol than anyone else and built up the squadron to one of the biggest squadrons in the State of Ohio."[5] Later, one of Ferrie's cadets in New Orleans was teenager Lee Oswald, who learned advanced aeronautics from Ferrie as part of CAP class studies.[6] Ferrie denied knowing Oswald in the wake of Oswald's own murder, but a squadron photograph showed Ferrie and Oswald at a CAP gathering in 1955. In an apparently random coincidence, the co-founder of CAP in Texas was multi-millionaire petroleum producer David Harold Byrd, owner of the Texas School Book Depository building where employee and former CAP cadet Lee Oswald worked for just over five weeks until November 22, 1963.[7]

4   HSCA, XII, 406.
5   HSCA, XII, 412.
6   Caufield, 32.
7   "Civil Air Patrol is Headed By D.H. Byrd," *Odessa American*, 24 December 1941.

Ferrie appears to have relocated to Florida in the late 1940s, where he taught in Turkey Creek, east of Tampa. In Tampa, Ferrie received his instrument rating at Sunnyside Flying School. This period is hazy, perhaps purposefully so. There are many questions: there never was a Sunnyside Flying School, for instance.[8] The HSCA document also reports, rather casually, that after taking lessons at Sky Tech Airway System in Cleveland, "[Ferrie] then worked as a pilot for an oil drilling firm which had jobs in South America," without mentioning Ferrie's role or the company's name.[9] Morris Brownlee, Ferrie's godson, believed Ferrie mentioned the name of the oil firm as Jade Oil.[10] This struck Daniel Hopsicker, author of *Barry & 'The Boys'* as a bit odd, noting this occurred when Ferrie was of "prime draft age in the middle of World War II, at a time when you needed more than a note from your local Congressman to evade military duty. And he's a *pilot* to boot!"[11] Alternating between Cleveland and Tampa – both towns with a powerful Mafia presence – Ferrie joined the U.S. Army Reserve back in Cleveland. In a letter to the commander of the U.S. First Air Force, Ferrie wrote in language reminiscent of Joseph Milteer's pamphlet blaming the JFK murder on the Jews. Ferrie then added, "Between my friends and I we can cook up a crew that can really blow them to hell … I want to train killers, however bad that sounds. It is what we need."[12] Here, Ferrie seems to have found himself: joining a booming business of ex-servicemen, pilots and soldiers of fortune in clandestine missions on behalf of U.S. intelligence and organized crime in the Caribbean and South America.

Hopsicker reported David Ferrie worked for another cover, Southern Air Transport (SAT), the proprietary commercial airline of the CIA with "hubs'" in the Congo, the Caribbean and Southeast Asia. "Both [Ferrie and Barry Seal] held – at different times – the same job, Southern Regional Manager, Aircraft Procurement and Deployment," Hopsicker wrote.[13] The Pentagon described SAT as "a civilian operation holding a $3.7 million contract to move mixed [unidentified] cargo and passenger loads on Far Eastern routes." SAT introduces us to Harvard alum and ice skating and square dancing fanatic Percival Brundage, President Eisenhower's director of the Bureau of the Budget (BOB). This seemingly innocuous CPA nev-

8   William Turner, "The Garrison Commission on the Assassination of President Kennedy," *Ramparts*, Jan. 1968.
9   HSCA, XII, 406.
10   Daniel Hopsicker, *Barry & 'The Boys': The CIA, the Mob, and America's Secret History* (Walterville, OR: TrineDay, 2006), 54.
11   Ibid., 53.
12   Edward Jay Epstein, "Garrison," *The New Yorker*, 13 July 1968, 38.
13   Hopsicker, 52.

ertheless gained a wealth of knowledge in back room politics; he became synonymous with rubber stamping black-budget operations. Brundage counted the Dulles brothers, Allen at CIA and John Foster at State, as close friends. He also sat on the Council of Foreign Relations.

And he was a Unitarian. CIA director Dulles found Unitarian members useful "to achieve the economic and political goals of U.S. Intelligence and the American Establishment."[14]

During the war and immediate postwar years, Percival Brundage was a director of the American Unitarian Association (AUA), investing most of his energies to helping refugees and displaced peoples. In 1949, Brundage became director of the Unitarian Service Committee (USC), which he held until joining BOB. In 1953, Brundage was employed at BOB and also president of the International Association for Religious Freedom (IARF), a charity organization which "promotes and nurtures inter-religious communication and understanding,"[15] and would become deeply involved with United Nations initiatives on religious tolerance.

That same year, Albert Schweitzer College was founded in Churwalden, Switzerland. Richard Boeke was the first president of the IARF's American chapter and glowed that Albert Schweitzer College was the "crown jewel" of the IARF.[16] In New York on April 17, 1953, the Friends of Albert Schweitzer College, the college's Board of Trustees, was incorporated. One of its directors was Percival Brundage.

A tiny, non-degree "school," Albert Schweitzer College evokes as much legitimacy as any of the diploma mills we have encountered. Its president, a Unitarian cleric named Hans Casparis, is a mysterious figure. Apparently Swiss, he was a student at the University of Chicago in 1946. Yet, only a year later, he is suddenly "a prominent Swiss educator"[17] who was sent by his government to study cutting edge American education strategies and write about it in the periodical *School and Society*. George Michael Evica extensively researched Casparis's background, and ultimately concluded Casparis never actually obtained a degree from anywhere.

The suspicious nature of Casparis as an educator evokes another administrator of ill repute, Earl Anglin James. Though Albert Schweitzer College offered no college credits, required no entrance exam or any kind of previous academic work or transcripts,[18] it was the school Lee Oswald, still

---

14   See "Essay Four: Allen Dulles & the Destabilization of Eastern Europe" in George Michael Evica, *A Certain Arrogance*, 105-167, (Walterville, OR: TrineDay, 2006, 2011).

15   "International Association for Religious Freedom," us@iarf.net.

16   See "Essay Three: Schweitzer College New Evidence and Analysis" in Evica, 83-102.

17   *Chattanooga Daily Times*, 26 May 1947.

18   "Schweitzer College Head Here, Describes Goals," *Atlanta Constitution*, 30 August 1958.

**ALBERT SCHWEITZER COLLEGE,
CHURWALDEN (4,000ft.), SWITZERLAND**
For adolescents and adults. A balanced edu-
cation, courses in modern social, ethical, etc.,
problems, language instruction, mental and
physical recreation, worthwhile holidays.
SKI AND STUDY COURSE, Feb. 20th-
March 3rd. Fr. 13 per day inclusive.
SKI COURSE, at Easter. Fr. 9.50 per day
inclusive.
SUMMER COURSES of 14 days' duration in
July and August. Fr. 10 per day inclusive.
YEAR COURSES: Three 11-week terms,
Oct. to June. Fr. 950 per term inclusive.
Inquiries to Professor H. Casparis,
Albert Schweitzer College,
Churwalden/Gr. Switzerland.

1956 advertisement for Albert Schweitzer College in the London Observer

in the Marine Corps, applied to and was accepted in 1959. But rather than attend, Oswald decided to renounce his country and defect to the USSR.

* * *

When Lee Oswald and his young family moved from Texas to New Orleans in the spring of 1963, Ruth Paine, who had befriended Lee's wife Marina when the young Russian lived in Irving, wanted to see how she was faring in New Orleans. Paine used Unitarian connections to find someone to check on Marina. She started with the secretary of the Dallas Unitarian Church and finally ended up connecting with a Mrs. Kloepfer, a member of Revered Albert D'Orlando's First Unitarian Church in New Orleans. Kloepfer dutifully stopped by the Oswald residence on Magazine St. in New Orleans, making two visits. On her second visit in September 1963, Lee was there – as was Ruth Paine, ready to escort Marina back to Texas. The Oswalds' time in New Orleans was over. Lee had other plans, telling the guests he was planning on going to Philadelphia "or somewhere in the East." This struck Kloepfer – who had never met Lee Oswald before or since – as somewhat vague. Lee only said it was for "business."[19] By now, Oswald's "business" seemed to be tracking the president: JFK was in Philadelphia at the end of October 1963. Indeed, Oswald was reportedly in Chicago ahead of JFK's planned visit on November 2. According to

---

19   CE 1929.

the FBI, Oswald visited the University of Illinois inquiring about Cuban student groups, a mission that evoked Guy Banister's tactic of investigating college students and their affiliations.[20] Secret Service agent Abraham Bolden risked his own career and freedom to publicly state the Chicago Secret Service office was on alert that "an attempt to assassinate the President would be made on November 2, 1963, by a four-man team using high-powered rifles."[21] The president canceled the trip at the last moment, ostensibly because of the November 1 coup in South Vietnam.

Although it is not mentioned in the FBI reports included in the Warren Commission exhibits, Mrs. Kloepfer was a member of the New Orleans Committee for Peaceful Alternatives (NOCPA), one of three "so-called Communist fronts" Lee Oswald infiltrated along with the Fair Play for Cuba Committee (FPCC), and the Congress of Racial Equality (CORE). CORE was a civil rights group that ran a voter registration line in Clinton, Louisiana where Ferrie and Clay Shaw allegedly drove Oswald to register to vote, the lone white in line, and thus easily recognizable.[22] According to Jeffrey Caufield, the New Orleans Committee for Peaceful Alternatives was a "liberal, 'ban the bomb' group at Tulane University, which was dedicated to nuclear proliferation."[23] In the case of Ruth Paine, one of the central characters in the Oswald tragedy, the role of religion became a convenient tool for a handler to remain in contact with her charge. Paine was a Quaker, a religion compatible in many ways with Unitarian Universalists. For example, both are rooted in pre-Council of Nicea Christianity, but neither would consider themselves theists. Perhaps Joseph Campbell's quote, "All the gods, all the heavens, all the worlds are within us,"[24] accurately reflects Quaker and Unitarian Universalist worldviews.

Less than a year after JFK's assassination, Quaker author Jessamyn West interviewed Ruth Paine for *Redbook*. The sympathetic piece, framing Paine and her husband, Bell Helicopter engineer Michael Paine, as Good Samaritans to the inscrutable monster that was Lee Harvey Oswald, tells us Ruth's mother was a Unitarian minister in Columbus, Ohio. Her parents were both Methodists before becoming Unitarians, but while still a teenager Ruth gravitated to Quakerism. She attended Antioch College in Yellow Springs, Ohio.

---

20   Cf. Lamar Waldron, *The Hidden History of the JFK Assassination* (Berkeley: Counterpoint, 2013), 287. See also Patsy Sims, *The Klan* (Lexington: Kentucky, 1996, second ed.), 257 wherein Klan Imperial Wizard James Venable confirmed to author Sims an individual fitting Oswald's description visited Venable's Atlanta law office asking for names of Chicago-based right-wing leaders.

21   NARA 180-10070-10273, HSCA interview with Abraham Bolden.

22   Caufield, 202; 620-621.

23   Ibid., 616.

24   See Joseph Campbell, *The Power of Myth* (New York: Anchor, 1988), 46.

ALBERT SCHWEITZER COLLEGE
CHURWALDEN (GR)
SWITZERLAND

March 22nd, 1960

Mr. Leo H. Oswald
MCAF, MACS-9
Santa Barbara, Calif.
U.S.A.

Dear Mr. Oswald,

Due to a number of circumstances we found ourselves
forced to make a slight change in the arrival and departure
dates of the third term. The first lecture will be held
on Tuesday afternoon, 16.00 o'clock, April 19th, instead
of taking place on the 21st, with arrival day on the 20th.
It will mean that the students arrive either on the evening
of Monday, the 18th, or before noon on April 19th. This
change, however, makes it possible to end the term on the
weekend of July 2nd, instead of the 6th as originallyplanned.

We hope that you will still be able to fit this change
of dates into your travel plan. Should it not be possible
for you to arrive on the earlier date we of course understand the difficulty. In the latter case, please drop us a
line so that we know.

Looking forward to your coming, we are,

Sincerely yours,

ALBERT SCHWEITZER
COLLEGE

Prof. Hans Casparis
President

COMMISSION EXHIBIT 229

A year after graduating, she taught folk dancing at a Quaker-affiliated school in Philadelphia, where she met Michael Paine. The couple moved to Irving Texas, had two children, and separated. Ruth told West she met the Oswalds at a party in February 1963, when a friend with whom she "sang English madrigals together," invited her to attend, for the specific purpose of meeting

Marina Oswald.[25] This was chemist Everett Glover, who worked for Socony Mobil Oil Co. (now ExxonMobil). Glover was of the mind Ruth Paine, who apparently had interest in the Russian language, might hit it off with Marina. In assassination research, this is known as the Magnolia party. Oswald was going to speak at the gathering on his experiences in the USSR. Glover's idea to connect Ruth Paine with Marina Oswald hatched after Glover met Marina Oswald at a dinner at the home of George de Mohrenschildt and his wife. It is interesting to note Glover was an ice skater, and met Mrs. de Mohrenschildt at a rink sometime in the late-1950s, according to his Warren Commission testimony.

It also should be noted here that days after Oswald's own assassination, the associate pastor of First Unitarian Church in Dallas, Rev. Byrd Helligas, was asked to describe Oswald's personality. Helligas described Oswald as "erudite." Helligas said, "In the dictionary definition of the word 'intellectual' he was an intellectual."[26] The Unitarian minister and Oswald met at the October 25 meeting of the American Civil Liberties Union Dallas chapter.

* * *

How did Lee Oswald even come to hear about such a placeas Albert Schweitzer College? Its total enrollment in 1958 amounted to only 24 students. One possibility is Kerry Thornley, whose Warren Commission testimony makes for fascinating reading. Thornley was a fascinating individual himself: a prolific writer, with instincts on human nature and behavior, eccentric though they may be, coming through in his statement to the Warren Commission. Indeed, might Kerry Thornley – who later parodied the religious storefront church business by "founding" Discordianism, which worships Eris, Greek goddess of discord and strife – have helped in Oswald's application? A native of southern California, Thornley was a Marine Corps reservist attending USC when he was summoned to active duty. He met Oswald at the Marine Corps Air Station in early 1959, just when Oswald applied to Albert Schweitzer College. Thornley was intrigued by Oswald from the outset. Later that year, he was stationed in Japan when he read of Oswald's defection to the Soviet Union. Thornley even wrote a book based on Oswald in 1962, *The Idle Warriors*. In his Commission testimony, Thornley shared this insight:

> [Oswald] looked upon the eyes of future people as some kind of tribunal, and he wanted to be on the winning side so that 10,000 years from now people would look in the history books and say,

25   Jessamyn West, "Prelude to Tragedy: The woman who sheltered Lee Oswald's family tells her story," *Redbook*, July 1964. See Commission Exhibit No. 1439.
26   *Washington Post*, 2 December 1963.

"Well, this man was ahead of his time. This man was – " he wanted to be looked upon with honor by future generations. It was, I think, a substitute, in his case, for traditional religion.[27]

Lee Oswald

A nexus of sorts emerges between Oswald, Percival Brundage, and Kerry Thornley in the person of David Ferrie. Oswald joined the Marine Corps on his 17th birthday, October 18, 1956. It may have been Ferrie, dressed in a military-style uniform, who visited Marguerite Oswald at her home to encourage Lee to join the Marine Corps.[28] And it was aeronautics, Ferrie's great passion, where Oswald worked in the marines.[29] It is possible Ferrie himself, or Ferrie via Thornley, introduced Albert Schweitzer College to Oswald as a cover to get into Russia. As we will see later, Kerry Thornley was in New Orleans in the summer of 1963.

Percival Brundage

Albert Schweitzer College was an offshoot of Percival Brundage's Unitarian Service Committee, specifically the American Unitarian Youth program. In all likelihood it was a recruiting effort, disguised as a cultural relations/ education program of the State Department. Young people from Unitarian families were recruited to attend Albert Schweitzer College in a kind of study abroad program and return to their hometown to share their experiences.

Kerry Thornley

This might have been Oswald's initial plan post-Marines, until something more daring presented itself: defection to the Soviet Union.

There is one other possibility we must consider regarding Oswald's introduction to Albert Schweitzer College: none other than Earl Anglin James. Albert Schweitzer College was the product of the Unitarian-Universalist Association, its headquarters formerly on Boston's Beacon Hill, near Calvin Coolidge College, "alma mater" of James associate Pericles Voultsos.

---

27   Warren Commission Hearings, Volume XI, 97.
28   Ibid.,, 32.
29   Ibid., 33.

James was "Dean" of an India degree factory, the World Jnana Sadhak Society, "a silent world fellowship of culture, faith and unity." It sought "to attain the goal of the basic unity of all Faiths and Cultures and to eliminate cankers of Colourphobia, apartheidness and untouchability."[30] Apparently founded in 1956, it appeared to promote the publications of its founder and president, Bhabes Chandra Chaudhuri. The titles and honors amassed by Chaudhuri suggest the entire persona is an alias of Earl Anglin James. One such work, *Rural Ghost*, "a masterpiece of national satire – a glorious production that adds a worthy tribute to the memoirs of The Gandhian Centenary," is a nonsensical rambling that reads as if it were written by James himself. More to the point, the World Jnana Sadhak Society considered Albert Schweitzer as an honorary advisor. Furthermore, one of its publications was titled *The Evolution of Science: Darwinisim in Vedantic View*, a look at the work of another Unitarian, Charles Darwin.[31] Darwin was named on Oswald's application to Albert Schweitzer College as a person of influence. An author highlighted in the World Jnana Society's publications is Gustaf Stromberg, the Swiss-American astronomer. Stromberg worked at Mount Wilson Observatory in California, and moved deeper into psychic phenomena "and God's place in modern science."[32] Stromberg wrote *The Searchers* in 1948, wherein he advocated a life-generating force as a basic component of the universe.[33] A character in the novel is a Russian Marxist refugee (Boris Charkov) who infiltrates a group called the Searchers, a group seeking enlightenment about the meaning of life.

30   Bhabes Chandra Chaudhuri, *Rural Ghost* (Calcutta: Alpha-Beta Publications, 1966), 50-51.
31   Ibid.
32   Ibid., 52.
33   René Fueloep-Miller, "Reviewed Works: What is Life by Erwin Schroedinger; Sound of the Universe by Gustaf Stroemberg; The Searchers by Gustaf Stroemberg; Life on Other Worlds by H. Spencer Jones," *The American Scholar*, Vol. 19, No. 3, summer 1950, 378.

Chapter Nine

Truth and Consequences

And my wrath shall wax hot, and I will kill you with the sword;
and your wives shall be widows, and your children fatherless.

— Exodus 22:24

When not in the shadows of black ops and flying missions for New Orleans godfather Carlos Marcello, David Ferrie was a commercial airline pilot for Eastern Air Lines, whose Chairman of the Board was World War I flying ace Capt. Eddie Rickenbacker. Rickenbacker made a note for Ferrie's file: "This man's efforts bear watching and his qualifications justify his being used and helped whenever possible in line of duty-and even beyond."[1] An Eastern Air pilot would have been an ideal career for someone of Ferrie's disposition, except he falsified his application in 1951, overlooked at the time as many pilots were engaged in the Korean War. When he was arrested on a morals charge in August 1961 (sexual behavior with a 15-year-old boy, indecent behavior with three others; an extortion charge was also added), he at last lost that job. The company conducted a two-year investigation on Ferrie's charges, and though Ferrie went down fighting on appeal, the company issued its final decision against him in 1963.

The HSCA noted Ferrie "found an outlet for his political fanaticism in the anti-Castro movement."[2] Following Castro's takeover in 1959, Ferrie is moving like a maniac: he's purchasing rifles at the Cadet Rifle Club in New Orleans; he's the executive officer for the Civil Air Patrol; he's flying firebombing raids for his friend and Tampa crime boss Santos Trafficante underling, former Cuban congressman and exile leader Eladio del Valle – the same Eladio del Valle who would be murdered the day before Ferrie's death in 1967, shot in the heart and his skullcap sliced open by a machete. In 1960, Ferrie formed a CAP-like cadet training squad called the Falcons. By March 1961, he's close friends with Sergio Arcacha Smith, the New Orleans delegate to the Cuban Revolutionary Council (CRC). The Cuban Revolu-

1   HSCA, Vol. X, n.66.
2   Ibid., 410.

tionary Council "had direct access to President Kennedy and top White House aides."[3] Its existence was to prepare for the Bay of Pigs landing.[4]

CRC's chairman was CIA's E. Howard Hunt, the future organizer and recruiter of the Watergate break-in. CRC's intent, once Castro's 26th of July government was toppled, was to install Cuban investment banker Mario Garcia Kohly as Cuba's new president. A principal backer of the CRC was H.L. Hunt, whom Kohly visited in Texas in December 1962.[5] The post-Castro era was to be the task of Operation 40, established under the Eisenhower Administration; Kohly met with Vice President Dick Nixon in October 1960 for this express purpose.

Kohly, of course, never succeeded Castro; his guerilla army of 300 men were routed in the Escambray Mountains in March 1961. There's something medieval about the CIA's relentless strategy of regime change, invasions, and coups in Latin America and elsewhere. These power grabs were not unlike the sixty year period of Latin kingdoms occupying the Greek empire of Constantinople in the thirteenth century, with a steady stream of mediocre Frankish nobles hoisted onto the Byzantine throne, with no business being there in the first place, wandering from kingdom to kingdom raising money by selling relics to wage their wars. To be anybody in the Middle Ages was to be of the nobility; there is no room in medieval history for peasants. It was who you knew, where you came from, who your family was. Kinship and politics have never gone out of style: monarchies, dukedoms, lordships, the ability to command armies and to usurp the infidel – that was what mattered. It was also the case in the Caribbean of the twentieth century: big business oligarchies influencing covert operations. We see one small example in the family of Mario Garcia Kohly. His second cousin was Marcos A. Kohly, the same Marcos Kohly affiliated with the Eloy Alfaro Foundation.

Ed Haslam reported Ferrie first went to Washington to meet with CIA Deputy Director Gen. Charles Pearre Cabell with the directive to fly from Florida's west coast, Ferrie piloting, and record radio signals in Cuba's Sierra del Chorrillo Mountains. The mission was accomplished, but not before the plane was strafed by Cuban troops. Within twenty four hours, however, the Bay of Pigs was an unmitigated disaster, with over 1,000 exiles captured. The air support the CIA expected never came.

Ferrie was livid. Three months after the Bay of Pigs, Ferrie was at a dais before the New Orleans chapter of the Military Order of World Wars. The topic: the Kennedy Administration and the Bay of Pigs. When Ferrie veered

3   HSCA, Appendix 4: "Cuban Revolutionary Council: A Concise History."
4   "Castro Foe Sees An Early Invasion," *The Town Talk*, 11 April 1961.
5   Russell, 378.

into excessive criticism of the president, he was escorted offstage.[6] It is tempting to dismiss Ferrie as a ranting madman, partly from his unusual physical
appearance, partly perhaps from Joe Pesci's portrayal of the Ferrie character
in Oliver Stone's *JFK*. But Ferrie was at home in public speaking, which he
continued to do long after his Jesuit debate club days, such as in December
1954 when he spoke to 75 businesswomen at a Birmingham, Alabama Episcopal church on the rise of mental illness in the U.S. and ways to curb it.[7]

Also in 1961, Ferrie drew the attention of the FBI with the launch of
Omnipotent, Ferrie's training of young men to help train others in the event
of an all-out attack on the U.S. A steward for Eastern Air, John Harris, alerted the FBI that coworker Ferrie had access to a cache of arms somewhere
around New Orleans, Houma, and the Mississippi Gulf Coast, and was attempting to purchase a C47 in the range of $30,000-$45,000.[8] Moreover,
Harris mentioned a kind of cult-like knit that Ferrie had with young adult
males, which Harris found disturbing. Ferrie's morals arrest that August put
him on extended leave from Eastern with no pay. The report goes on to say:

> Harris stated that it has been his observation that Capt. Ferrie has
> been holding something over the heads of the boys in this group and
> suspects that he is keeping them doped up with narcotics, liquor and
> with hypnotism. He stated that he believes that Capt. FERRIE has
> taken pornographic pictures of the various boys in this group which
> he is holding over their heads to make them cooperate with him.[9]

Harris also reported Ferrie procured passports for the boys in the
group, and seemed to be making preparations for a flight out of New Orleans in early October 1961. When Jefferson Parish Deputy Sheriff Joseph
Battaglia searched Ferrie's home – finding loads of ammo and guns, even
two mini-submarines – Ferrie admitted he worked for the Cuban Democratic Revolutionary Front, brought under the ownership of the Cuban
Revolutionary Council the same month as John Harris made his report.
The CRC's new address was the Newman Building in New Orleans, a corner structure that shared two street addresses – 544 Camp St. and 531 Lafayette St. Guy Banister's private investigation office was at 531 Lafayette;
the Cuban Revolutionary Council at 544 Camp St. Intriguingly, before
moving to the Newman Building, both Banister and the CRC were located in the Balter Building on Camp St.[10] Clearly, Banister was provid-

6   HSCA, X, 404.
7   "Worry over trivia scored by speaker," *Birmingham News*, 02 December 1954.
8   FBI Report on David William Ferrie, October 30, 1961.
9   Ibid.
10   HSCA, X, 431.

ing support via his private detective agency through background checks, building leases, and other operations management for the anti-Castro Cubans.[11] The CRC also reveals the link between Banister in New Orleans and H.L. Hunt in Dallas, whose "oil operations in Louisiana were plagued by continuous thefts of drilling equipment, and Hunt retained Banister and [Banister associate Joseph] Oster to investigate the problem," Jeffrey Caufield noted.[12] Banister successfully bolstered the security of Hunt's equipment. After Banister's death, Oster picked up the Hunt contract, and told Caufield, "Banister also did security work for Sun Oil and Texas oilmen Clint Murchison and Sid Richardson."[13]

* * *

In late 1961, Ferrie, Arcacha Smith, Banister and Omnipotent members participated in seizing munitions from Schlumberger Well Service in Houma, Louisiana. According to Eric Tagg, Attorney General Robert F. Kennedy himself not only knew of the raid, but authorized it. The munitions purportedly came from the French right-wing terrorist group OAS, anti-de Gaulle militants angry over Algerian independence from France, which JFK supported. RFK wanted those munitions seized to prevent further OAS attacks, or for use by Castro forces or further south in Guatemala. Tagg writes, "[Jack] Martin and [Dave] Lewis noted in their affidavit that Robert Kennedy had established his own secret channel of communication to communicate with Banister, bypassing J. Edgar Hoover and the local FBI special-agent-in-charge."[14]

Moreover, as described earlier the confluence of these groups in the same building – whose owner, Bluford Balter, was a Nazi financier – was its sympathies to Nazi ideology, characterized by the inherent racism and anti-Semitism of Banister and his associates. Jeffrey Caufield noted, "David Ferrie was, perhaps, the first Nazi in Lee Harvey Oswald's life."[15] Jim Garrison also obtained a transcript of a letter from Ferrie wherein he "shared his dream of the re-unification of Germany and living in a world where all the currency was in Deutschmarks." Furthermore, it "spoke of the need to kill all the Kennedys and Martin Luther King, Jr. Ferrie wrote that he was being 'suffocated by the n******s and Jews."[16] The letter was

---

11   Ibid., 484-487.
12   Caufield, 306.
13   Ibid.
14   Eric Tagg, *Brush with History* (Garland, TX: Shot in the Light Publishing, 1998), 64. On the Schlumberger Raid and RFK knowledge, see 61ff.
15   Caufield, 85.
16   Ibid., 86.

sent to Garrison by Glenn Pinchback, who worked in the mailroom of the Operations Command at Fort Sill outside Lawton, Oklahoma. Pinchback described the letter as a "Neo-Nazi plot to enslave America in the name of anti-Communism," and "a neo-Nazi plot gargantuan in scope."[17]

* * *

It is interesting to note how the First Vatican Council (1869-1870) and the Second Vatican Council (1962-1965) both factor in our investigation. We have seen how the dogma of papal infallibility galvanized the Old Catholic Church. In a January 1970 letter, Patriarch Zhurawetzky wrote, "One hundred years ago the Almighty restored his true (Old) Catholic Church and has raised up modern prophets and Apostles to direct the work. Under the guidance of heaven, powers of priesthood have been brought back to earth by the ministry of angels. They did not come from any political unit."[18] As for the ramifications of Vatican II, the most impact was the change from the centuries-old Latin liturgy to a newly-designed Mass in the vernacular. This was a great betrayal to many Catholics, so much so that schismatics sects rejected the "modernist" changes wrought by Vatican II and chose to continue celebrating the traditional Latin Mass. Some of these "traditionalists" found solace in the Old Catholic Church, despite being cut off from Rome.

Pope John XXIII (1958-1963) and Paul VI (1963-1978) were the two popes of Vatican II; Pope John died of cancer in June 1963 after overseeing only the first session of the Council. JFK and Pope John were like-minded: John XXIII by opening the windows of the Church to the modern world, JFK looking to a post-Cold War political landscape. Moreover, John XXIII's policies, such as his outreach efforts to Nikita Khruschev, who welcomed them, were met with resistance within the Catholic faction of *sedevacantists* (Latin for "vacant seat"), the general name for those who rejected Vatican II as valid and even doubted the legitimacy of Pope John as the true pope – and thus every pope elected after him.

Conservative Democrat (and Catholic) Senator Thomas Dodd put it succinctly, "I'll say of John Kennedy what I said of Pope John [XXIII] the day he died: it will take us fifty years to undo the damage he did to us…"[19]

As Dodd insinuates, not all U.S. Catholics supported the first Catholic president. An example of the faction of Catholics against JFK and his policies is Delphine Roberts, secretary and mistress to Guy Banister, who was

---

17   Ibid.
18   Kersey, "Patriarchate."
19   James Boyd, *Above the Law* (New York: New American Library, 1968), 106.

adamantly opposed to integration because she thought it was a Communist ploy. Roberts was a member of the Daughters of the American Revolution and president of the National Confederation for Conservative Government. When the Fifth Circuit Court of Appeals conducted its hearing on student James Meredith's attempt to register for classes at the University of Mississippi in 1962, Roberts picketed outside the New Orleans courthouse. Banister was instrumental in arranging members of the pro-segregation White Citizens Council to continue picketing for the entire week of the Meredith hearing, September 25 to October 2, 1962; Roberts, too, became a member of the New Orleans chapter. On the 28th, Roberts' sign read: "Gov. Barnett, do not agree to any face saving compromise with Kennedy Bros., Have that showdown. Interposition will work."[20] Interposition, first broached by James Madison, meant that a state could declare itself exempt from a federal mandate. Like the rest of the Deep South, the Louisiana Legislature cited interposition in 1960 when the state refused to recognize the decision of *Brown v. Board of Education*.[21] A week ahead of JFK's May 1962 trip to New Orleans, Roberts picketed outside City Hall: "Is President Kennedy planning to use New Orleans as the place from which to issue the second emancipation proclamation…?" her placard read.[22] Roberts is referring to Martin Luther King, Jr.'s visit to the Kennedy White House in the fall of 1961. While giving a tour of the White House, JFK pointed out the table Lincoln used to sign the Emancipation Proclamation in September 1862. "I would like you to sign a Second Emancipation Proclamation on this very table," King told the president, seizing the moment.[23]

Perhaps the most vocal diatribe from Delphine Roberts came in a July 27, 1963 letter to the editor published in the *Shreveport Journal*:

> Has action to start the needed situation for the take-over of the United States begun?
>
> The NAACP stands guilty of insurrection on a nation-wide scale by way of its sit-ins and protest marches.
>
> If the White South and other true American conservatives sit idly by and watch, the Negores – led and guided by Socialists-Communists directed by the Kremlin and backed by the Kennedy Brothers – will succeed in overthrowing our Republican form of government by default. The Negroes are being used purposely in this "plan" for they are the means by which the take-over of our country can be accomplished.

---

20   Caufield, 351.
21   *Bush v. Orleans Parish School Board.*
22   "Pickets Protest Kennedy Speech," *The Town Talk*, 27 April 1962.
23   Quoted in Steven Livingston, *Kennedy and King* (New York: Hachette Books, 2017), 205.

In the Supreme Court is a brief filed by Robert Kennedy deny-ing Article IV, Section 4 of the Constitution "limiting the powers of the Executive" is still in effect. If the Supreme Court rules in Ken-nedy's favor, a military dictatorship will be created and the Consti-tution and the United States completely destroyed.

Immediately the numerous Executive Orders issued by JFK now on file in the Federal Register, will go into effect wiping out ownership of all private property and the denial and suppression of all liberties and freedoms.

It is of utmost importance that we demand Congress to remove the Kennedy Brothers and impeachment procedures against both be begun immediately while we are still under the Constitution and can still act under it, or it will be too late! Because of the immi-nence of the situation, it is extremely urgent to contact your gover-nor and state representatives and senators immediately to instruct your Congressional Representatives in Washington, D.C. that their impeachment is the action people back home want and demand!!

We can save our country! But if we do NOT save it – we must live forever in the cruel bloody chains of slavery!!!

MRS. DELPHINE ROBERTS

National Confederation for Conservative Government,

P.O. Box 4193

New Orleans, 18, La.

Roberts even aimed her zealotry towards her own church. She spoke at the Catholic White Layman's League and picketed outside St. Patrick's Catholic Church during Sunday Mass protesting desegregation. Roberts held a sign: "Jesus was born of the house of David. – Of pure white stock in Judea – A white country – it is our sacred duty to preserve the white race of Jesus." This was flanked by other signage: "Will excommunication of Roman Catholics be used to govern the United States via religious inter-ference with government?" "Have Socialist agents infiltrated the Catholic religion? Integration is part of an international communist conspiracy?"[24] While "the white race of Jesus" claim echoes of both Christian Identity a similar Rosicrucian thought that we will examine later, it also simply sug-gests support of white supremacy. Racism was a unifying theme for those who populated the Banister orbit – Banister and Roberts included.[25]

Roberts also was a picketer in front of Archbishop Rummel's residence, this time with a sign: "Caroline Kennedy is segregated – excommunicate

---

24   "Appeal to Pope Sent By Segregationist," *Lake Charles American Press*, 16 April 1962. See also Edgardo Goyret, *La Revolución Incruenta* (Montevideo: Omega, 1962), 125.

25   Cf. Caufield, 53.

111

her father." Roberts herself was eventually excommunicated. She was joined in this ignominious distinction by Judge Leander Perez, "a devout Catholic, the leader of the integration resistance movement and was close to Guy Banister, as well as Joseph Milteer."[26] As early as 1955, Perez also backed the pro-segregation alliance of Southern states, the Federation for Constitutional Government.[27] According to informant Willie Somersett, "Leander Perez was a financial backer of the Kennedy assassination."[28] A third excommunicant, Jackson Ricau, former investigator for Banister and higher up in the Louisiana Citizens' Council, published the racist newsletter *Citizens' Report*. Like Roberts, both Ricau and Jackson connected back to Guy Banister. In his interview with Miami Police the Tuesday after the assassination, Willie Somersett quoted Joseph Milteer: "Kennedy appointed all the Jews he could get," adding, "A lot of Catholics are just as much against Kennedy as anybody else. There was probably a lot of Catholic money that helped to get him killed," because "Catholics were against [JFK] for appointing all the Jews up there to office. A lot of Patriots had been too slow in realizing these things."[29]

At this point, the non-profit Information on the Council of the Americas (INCA) emerges within this milieu, the great passion of Tulane's surgery department chair, Dr. Alton Ochsner. Founded in May 1961 its mission was simple: to battle Communism creeping into the Western Hemisphere. INCA was the organization that later produced a record album of Lee Oswald debating Carlos Bringuier – whom Oswald tussled with while passing out Fair Play for Cuba Committee leaflets, leading to both of their arrests –

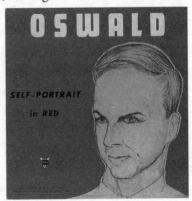

with interventions by Ed Butler, INCA's executive director, pushing Oswald's purported Marxism. Butler was essentially the front, the face of INCA, while its mission and identity was shaped by Ochsner. The whole "debate" was a farce, part of an overall coordinated effort that appears to be masterminded by Guy Banister and Ed Butler to prop Lee Oswald up as a Communist – not, initially,

OSWALD

SELF-PORTRAIT
in RED

---

26   Ibid., 95.

27   James L. Dickerson, *Dixie's Dirty Secret: how the government, the media, and the mob reshaped the modern Republican Party into the image of the Old Confederacy* (Jackson, MS: Sartoris Literary Group, 2016), 1.

28   Ibid., 279.

29   Document 0062e, "Miami Police Informant Information on Milteer," 26 November 1963, Cuban Information Archives.

to set him up as a patsy in the eventual murder of the president, but to pose as a communist, infiltrate so-called communist organizations, not unlike Boris Charkov in Gustaf Stromberg's *The Searchers* – namely those aligned with the integration movement – ingratiate the members, and ultimately have them arrested under the Communist Control Act for associating with a known Communist. Eventually, if the convoluted plan worked, integration would be discredited as nothing more than a Communist effort. This may have been the playbook Oswald was following by infiltrating things like the Congress on Racial Equality.

INCA's strongest financial supporter was Patrick J. Frawley, a California-based keen businessman who built his fortune with the Frawley Pen Company, maker of Paper Mate, which was later acquired by Gillette. He also oversaw the color processing company Technicolor, Inc. and Eversharp, producers of Shick razor blades, which had a plant in Cuba before Castro closed it down. Ochsner was an Eversharp board member. Frawley also supported Nixon in the 1960 campaign and Barry Goldwater in 1964.

Ed Butler caught Frawley's attention and gave Butler a job in California after the Kennedy assassination.[30] Frawley sponsored a Butler-produced and narrated "documentary," *Hitler in Havana*, that aired on WOR-TV in New York in 1966. *New York Times* critic Jack Gould called it "a tasteless affront to minimum journalistic standards....With inflammatory words and pictures but no pretense to hard documentation, the program invited the conclusion that Premier Fidel Castro, through use of propaganda, aroused Lee Harvey Oswald to violence and therefore was responsible for the assassination of President Kennedy."[31]

This seeming attempt at misinformation belies informant Willie Somersett's allegation that the shooters in Dealey Plaza were Theodore "Ted" Jackman, R.E. Davis, and Dallas police officer Jefferson Davis "J.D." Tippit.

Tippit was killed shortly after the president was shot in the Oak Cliff neighborhood, where Oswald rented a room. Oswald was first charged with the Tippit killing before he was charged with assassinating the president. Tippit, 39, father of three children, was shot four times, once in the head at close range. Tippit died instantaneously. One witness reported seeing a shooting suspect flee inside the nearby Abundant Life Temple.

It is tantalizing to consider the Abundant Life Temple as a pre-planned safe house. At the time, the church was managed by the Rev. Dr. O. B. Graham of the United Missions of America. Graham, a healing preacher in the

---

30   Caufield, 192.

31   Jack Gould, "TV: Right-Wing Propaganda and Razor Blades," *New York Times,* 28 October 1966.

Full Gospel Assembly tradition (Pentecostal), bought the former Oak Cliff Christian Church at the intersection of Tenth and Crawford in April 1962. Graham sold the property only months after the assassination. In the summer of 1964, Graham visited Moscow.[32] He died in Dallas in 1974. The purported encounter between Tippit and his murderer echoes an incident involving Rev. Wesley Swift thirty years earlier when a group of kidnappers were stalking Swift and his young wife. When Swift's mother was threatened by the gang outside the Angelus Temple, Swift's mother escaped her assailants by rushing inside the church, shaking off her potential kidnappers.[33]

O.B. Graham

Tippit, who worked off-duty as a bouncer, was on the cusp of a divorce. An outpouring of support for his widow amounted to over $650,000 dollars. Among the many who donated was Abraham Zapruder, who sold his 8mm recording of the assassination to *Time-Life*, and gave the proceeds to Mrs. Tippit.

It is not out of the realm of possibility, if R.E. Davis – a notorious Texas fraudster, forger, and Imperial Wizard of the Original Knights of the KKK – was involved in the shooting, that he sought refuge in the Abundant Life Temple after the murder of Tippit. After all, both Davis and O.B. Graham were associated with the Pentecostal movement. For years Davis ran the First Pentecostal Baptist Church of God. He baptized William Branham, a leading healing revivalist who also, incidentally, championed Wesley Swift's Christian Identity theology. As Davis took Branham under his wing, Branham later did the same for Jim Jones of Jonestown infamy. Meanwhile, O.B. Graham was building his career starting similar churches in the Carolinas, Michigan, Oklahoma, and Texas. His pattern appeared to launch a church, get it up and running, and within a short

Abundant Life Temple

amount of time turn around and sell it, though Graham seemed to always be connected to the buyers. An incorporator with Graham in United Mis-

32   "Address by Tulsa Pastor Postponed," *Northwest Arkansas Times*, 04 December 1964.
33   "Husband Routs Kidnaping Band," *Los Angeles Times*, 14 December 1932.

sions of America, Inc., George Sherrell, thought "Graham was something of a crook where money was concerned."[34]

* * *

The Rev. Dr. Theodore "Ted" Jackman was a "retired minister" from Glendale, California who liked to stoke the flames of the radical right in conspiracy-laden speeches.[35] He was a friend and "violent associate" of Joseph Milteer, who Willie Somersett called "one of the toughest killers."[36] And he was considered in the "high command" who pushed for "violence and armed resistance," particularly incensed over the Kennedy administration's disarmament policy.[37] Earlier in life Jackman was a Christian minister in the Pacific Northwest before moving his family to Israel, where he "collected" antiquities he said dated back to the time of King David.[38] In the 1940s he was the Near East representative of the World Christian Fundamentals Association.

* * *

As for Ferrie's internal wrestling over the events of the assassination in the final three years of his life, Raymond Broshears said Ferrie "told the truth about the assassination to four other people": Broshears, Jim Garrison, a woman, and a minister in the Orthodox Old Catholic Church of North America."[39] This could mean any number of individuals – Jack Martin, Archbishop Stanley, Bishop Frederick King, Thomas Beckham, Peter Zhurawetzky, Uladyslau Ryzy-Ryski, even Walter Propheta or Earl Anglin James.

---

34   Tagg, 158.
35   "So-Called Patriots Terrify Thousands," *Greenville News*, 3 May 1963.
36   Cf. Caufield, 609, 181, 142.
37   Ibid, 181.
38   "Rare Valley Collection of Biblical Antiquities," *Valley Times*, 1 September 1952.
39   Ibid., 588.

John Fitzgerald Kennedy and Allen Dulles

CHAPTER TEN

WAR AND RUMORS

*I will stir up Egyptian against Egyptian – brother will fight against broth-
er, neighbor against neighbor, city against city, kingdom against kingdom.*
— Isaiah 19:2

O ur circle of wandering bishops becomes complete in the most
unlikeliest of places: Vietnam. To begin, let us revisit the par-
titioning of Vietnam, where we encounter familiar figures from
our narrative. After the French withdrew following the decisive Battle of
Dien Bien Phu in 1954, the Geneva Accords split Vietnam at the 17th Parallel: Ho Chi Minh ruled in Communist North Vietnam; Emperor Bao
Dai in the South. Free elections in the South were set for 1955. However, a meeting had been convened at New York's Metropolitan Club while
Dien Bien Phu was still being waged. The host was C.D. Jackson. Twelve
U.S. government officials were in attendance, three from State and three
from CIA: Allen Dulles, Richard Bissell, and Frank Wisner. There, Walt
Whitman Rostow "unveiled his plan for cutting Vietnam into two irreconcilable pieces, neatly flanked by independent Laos and Cambodia."[1]

With the French loss at Dien Bien Phu, their Indochina war was over.
"Catholic militia streamed north to Hanoi and Haiphong, their hearts
filled with anger at French abandonment," CIA station chief in Saigon
Edward Lansdale's team report noted.

When JFK came into office, Walt Rostow moved into the White
House as a chief Kennedy advisor. Rostow was obsessed with finding a
way to swarm troops into the Mekong Delta without really calling them
"boots on the ground." One idea had infantry men (between ten and
fifteen thousand) arriving under the cover of "agricultural technicians."[2]
Hence, the growing number of American "advisers" present in Vietnam.
In the end, Rostow got the boots on the ground: "In September of 1961
President Kennedy, stung by failure at the Bay of Pigs and by his Vienna

<hr>

1   William J. Gill, *The Ordeal of Otto Otepka* (New Rochelle: Arlington Press, 1969), 100-101.
[The meeting is also referenced in Document 15, "Lansdale Team's Report on Covert Saigon Mission
in '54 and '55" in The Pentagon Papers.]
2   Ibid., 103.

meeting with Khrushchev, increased the American commitment in South Vietnam from the small core of military advisers authorized by Eisenhower to an American army of some 30,000 men. The die was cast. The United States had embarked on a policy that was to produce incalculable agony in coming years."[3]

The free elections occurred as the Geneva Accords required, although they were rigged to benefit Jean-Baptiste Ngo Dinh Diem, who was hoisted up first as prime minister under Bao Dai, and then became president of the Republic of Vietnam, deposing Bao Dai. A solemn man, Diem was a pious Catholic, having considered the priesthood early in life; he eventually became a third order Benedictine and remained celibate throughout his life. Indeed, his older brother, Pierre-Martin Ngo Dinh Thuc, rose to become a bishop in the Catholic Church. His nephew, Francis-Xavier Nguyễn Văn Thuận, was ordained a priest, rose to the rank of cardinal (by Pope John Paul II in 2001), and declared by Pope Francis a Venerable – the first step towards sainthood – in 2017.

Through his Church connections, Bishop Thuc was largely responsible for introducing Diem to western leaders. During the nine years of the Diem regime, Diem's right-hand man was his other brother, Ngo Dinh Nhu. Nhu, once a bookish archivist interested in a particular Catholic philosophy (personalism), became head of the Diem regime's secret police, the Cần Lao Party. His wife was the fiery Madame Nhu, a convert to Catholicism who was on a speaking tour in the U.S. at the time of the coup and subsequent execution of her husband and brother-in-law.

The French brought Catholicism by way of Jesuit missionary Alexandre de Rhodes in the 17th century. The Ngo family converted soon after the arrival of the missionaries. As young men, the Ngo brothers had the luxury of studying and living abroad. Diem even spent time at Maryknoll seminaries in New York and Jersey, where he met a freshman congressman from Massachusetts, John Kennedy. However, it is important to note that the Ngo understanding of Catholicism was imbued with a certain Confucianism; Diem "was the product of a Vietnamese culture unknown to the American foreign service."[4] In other words, according to Bernard Fall, Diem was "a spiritual son of a fiercely aggressive and militant faith rather than of the easygoing and tolerant approach of Gallican Catholicism."[5]

---

3   Drew Pearson and Jack Anderson, *The Case Against Congress: A Compelling Indictment of Corruption on Capitol Hill* (New York: Simon and Schuster Press, 1968), 359.
4   Ellen Hammer, *A Death in November: America in Vietnam, 1963* (Oxford: Oxford UP, 1987), 48.
5   Bernard Fall, *The Two Viet-Nams* (New York: Praeger, 1967), 236.

The intensely Catholic Ngo family ruled over a predominantly Buddhist population; only ten percent of Vietnam's population was Catholic. Thanks to the influence of Bishop Thuc, Catholic refugees from the north were brought into South Vietnam. There they were awarded generous land grants and other favors – a direct affront to the native Buddhists. This mass migration – 750,000 Catholics, according to author Douglas Valentine – was the responsibility of Edward Lansdale. These Catholics, Valentine wrote, "became the vanguard of the US-designed war against the Viet Minh nationalists."[6]

The Ngo Family Dynasty months before the U.S.-backed assassinations of President Diem (second from right) and his political advisor brother, Ngo Dinh Nhu (third from right). The third brother is the Catholic archbishop Ngo Dinh Thuc. Madame Nhu, wife of Ngo Dinh Nhu, stands next to her priest brother-in-law.

However, the Diem regime "ran roughshod over their own ostensible Catholic ideals, indulging in extortion, racketeering, fraud, currency manipulation, and murder."[7] As Diem's paranoia grew, more extreme measures saw Ngo Dinh Nhu's Can Lao Party infiltrate all aspects of life, and retort with vicious brutality against detractors when necessary. Madame Nhu, on her end, "banned divorce, dancing, and large portions of press

---

6 Douglas Valentine, *Pisces Moon*, (Walterville, OR: TrineDay, 2023, 237.)

7 Ed Jarvis, *Sede Vacante: The Life and Legacy of Archbishop Thuc* (Berkeley: Apocryphile Press, 2018), digital version, 12.

activity. It did not take long for someone to label her 'the Vietnamese Lady MacBeth.'[8] Furthermore, resentment from the Buddhist majority over Diem's mistreatment and favoritism towards Catholics was boiling over: "the religious conflict in Vietnam was much more significant than the political conflict."[9]

The Geneva Accords prescribed a national referendum for 1956 that would have reunited the country – "which Ho Chi Minh," Valentine wrote, "would have won in a landslide."[10] Diem ignored the stipulation, effectively creating an unofficial dictatorship. Meanwhile, Senator John Kennedy remarked in 1956: "Vietnam represents a test of American responsibility and determination in Asia. If we are not the parents of little Vietnam, then surely we are its godparents. We presided at its birth, we gave assistance to its life, we have helped shape its future…. This is our offspring – we cannot abandon it, we cannot ignore its needs."[11] Here historian Brian Crozier argues that while Kennedy was less interested in Diem's shared Catholicism, he nevertheless was an advocate for the "Vietnam Lobby" in Washington.

* * *

Malachi Martin, a kind of wandering cleric in his own right, former Jesuit and purported one-time Vatican adviser, told author John Cooney that "the Pope wanted the United States to back Diem because the Pope had been influenced by Diem's brother, Archbishop Thuc." While Peter Dale Scott contends this point, Cooney claimed "Spellman and [Joe] Kennedy helped form a pro-Diem lobby in Washington."[12] Moreover, Spellman "enlisted the support of Vice President Nixon for a substantial amount of U.S. aid for South Vietnam as well as military advisers."[13] As such, Diem's Catholicism convinced some circles South Vietnam was a quasi-theocracy, and that Diem himself "possessed the Confucian Mandate of Heaven, a moral and political authority that was widely recognized by the South Vietnamese, Buddhist and Catholic alike. This devout Roman Catholic leader never lost his mandate to rule in the eyes of his people," Geoffrey Shaw wrote in his sympathetic biography on Diem, *The Lost Mandate of Heaven*.[14]

8   Ibid., 44.
9   Brad O'Leary and L.E. Seymour, *Triangle of Death* (New York: Thomas Nelson, 2003), 10.
10   Valentine, 237.
11   "Remarks of Senator John F. Kennedy at the Conference on Vietnam Luncheon in the Hotel Willard, Washington, D.C., 1 June 1956."
12   John Cooney, *The American Pope: The Life and Times of Francis Cardinal Spellman* (New York: The New York Times Book Company, 1984), 242.
13   Pearson and Anderson, 357.
14   Geoffrey Shaw, *The Lost Mandate of Heaven* (San Francisco: Ignatius Press, 2015), 17.

This feeling of invulnerability – if not megalomania – ultimately con-tributed to the family's downfall. For the time being, "they staffed the gov-ernment and military with loyal members of their Can Lao (Personalist Labor) Party, which promoted the idea that people owed allegiance to a charismatic leader rather than a party or ideology. To enforce loyalty to President Diem, SEPES [Office of Political and Social Research] chief [Dr. Trần Kim] Tuyến created a vast intelligence network of Catholic emigres and beholden Can Lao cadres to control and influence all levels of the administration. Tuyen likewise used the Military Security Service (An-Ninh Quân-Đội) to monitor the many unhappy military officers who were plotting coups."[15]

By the time of Kennedy's presidency, Diem and his brothers still clung to power, but things in Saigon had taken a turn for the surreal:

> Elder brother Ngo Dinh Thuc, archbishop of Hue, used his polit-ical clout to augment church property. One critic charged that his requests for contributions "read like tax notices." He bought farms, businesses, urban real estate, rental property, and rubber planta-tions, and he employed ARV [Army of the Republic of Vietnam] troops on timber and construction concessions. Ngo Dinh Can, the dictator of Hue, accumulated a fortune as head of a smuggling syn-dicate that shipped huge loads of rice to Hanoi and large volumes of opium throughout Asia. Ngo Dinh Luyen, the South Vietnam-ese ambassador in London, became a multimillionaire speculating in piasters and pounds using insider information gleaned from his brothers in Saigon. More bizarre still were the antics of Ngo Dinh Nhu. By 1963 Nhu was smoking opium every day. His ambition long since turned into a megalomania symbolized the Personal-ist Labor Revolutionary Party, or Can Lao – secret police known for torture and assassination. Can Lao troops, complete with Na-zi-like goose-step marches and stiff-armed salutes, enforced Nhu's will. Madame Nhu had her own stormtroopers, a group known as the Women's Solidarity Movement and Paramilitary Girls, which worked at stamping out evil, or at least what Madame Nhu consid-ered evil – dancing, card playing, prostitution, divorce, and gam-bling. The Nhus amassed a fortune running numbers and lottery rackets, manipulating currency, and extorting money from Saigon businesses, promising "protection" in exchange for contributions. After reading a CIA report on the shenanigans, President Kenne-

---

15   "The Life and Times of a South Vietnamese Special Police Officer:, Douglas Valentine interviews Nhuan Le," *rat haus reality press*, April 10-20, 2017.

dy slammed the document down on his desk and shouted, 'Those damned sons of bitches.'[16]

The network of Ngo brothers also controlled the flow of opium: "While Can sold opium in Hue that his brother's police confiscated in Saigon, brother Luyen's preserve was in Europe."[17] By the end of the Diem regime, while President Diem was relying more and more on the Nhus, brother Ngo Dinh Nhu, according to the Pentagon Papers, had become addicted to opium:

> Nhu came more and more to dominate Diem in the last year of the Diem rule. But as his power increased, Nhu's grip on reality seems to have slipped and he was reported in that last year to have been smoking opium and to have been mentally ill[18]

The more dissatisfied Washington seemed with Diem, the more draconian Diem became. Olson and Roberts stated frankly that by now "South Vietnam was a dictatorship: dissidents were imprisoned, tortured, or killed; elections were manipulated; the press, radio, and television were controlled; and universities were treated as vehicles for government propaganda."[19]

It was clear something had to be done about the Ngo Family. Finally, in 1963, drastic action was taken after images of a Buddhist monk, Quang Duc, showed setting himself ablaze in a Saigon street. Duc was protesting the oppression of the Diem regime. The pictures of the burning monk were printed in U.S. newspapers. "If the Buddhists wish to have another barbecue," scoffed Ngo Dinh Nhu, "I will be glad to supply the gasoline and the match."[20] Yet for every crackdown against the Buddhists by the Ngo regime, the more monks set themselves ablaze – calm, prayerful, their mind elsewhere.

This self-immolation crisis was preceded by the hypocrisy exercised by the regime when Archbishop Thuc celebrated his silver jubilee as a bishop, which featured billowing flags of the Holy See. However, when the birth of Buddha was celebrated on May 7, 1963, troops tore down the Buddhist flags. At a subsequent demonstration, tear gas grenades were

16   James S. Olson and Randy Roberts, *Where the Domino Fell: America and Vietnam, 1945 to 1990* (New York: St. Martin's Press, 1991), 99-100.
17   Hilaire du Berrier, *Background to Betrayal: The Tragedy of Vietnam* (Belmont, MA: Western Islands, 1965), 156.
18   Department of Defense, "United States-Vietnam Relations, 1945-1967: The Overthrow of Ngo Dinh Diem," Book 3 of 12, 1.
19   Ibid.
20   Neil Sheehan, *The Pentagon Papers: The Secret History of the Vietnam War: As Published by the New York Times* (New York: Racehorse Publishing 2017), 138..

fired into the crowd of thousands; eight died as a result.[21] Diem put martial law in effect.

Only when news of the Buddhist crisis spread throughout the world
did Washington finally move on Diem. There would be a coup from Vietnamese generals – the public was not to know that it had the backing of
the U.S. government. CIA operative Lucien Conein was the go-between
between the plotting generals and the office of ambassador Henry Cabot
Lodge, Jr. Kennedy was not told when the coup would take place, only
that it would be sometime in the autumn of 1963. Evidently, the president
was also not aware that his counterpart would be murdered in the uprising. However, during the coup on November 1, Conein was "in steady
contact with McGeorge Bundy at the White House Situation Room."[22]

Attorney General Robert F. Kennedy broached the topic of disengage-
ment from Vietnam completely. According to "The Pentagon Papers,"
Kennedy reasoned "if the war was unwinnable by any foreseeable South
Vietnamese regime, it was time to get out of Vietnam. But, if the Diem
regime was the obstacle, he contended, then Ambassador Lodge should
be given the power to bring about the necessary change."[23]

When the coup finally occurred, the brothers fled the palace, finding
refuge at St. Francis Xavier Church in the Chinese business district of
Cholon. When the diary of the driver, Lieutenant Tho, was found years
later, Diem's last words to him were recorded as: "I don't know whether
I will live or die and I don't care, but tell [General] Nguyễn Khánh that I
have great affection for him and he should avenge me."[24] On the morning
of November 2, the brothers were found in the church – after Diem alerted the mutinous generals of their location, under the auspices they would
be given safe passage out of Vietnam. They had received Communion,
and in the photos taken after their execution, Diem can be seen wearing a
priest's cassock. They were taken from the church, thrown into the back of
an APC (armored personal carrier), and quickly thereafter shot a number
of times at close range and then stabbed, leaving behind unrecognizable,
bloodied corpses.

"I was shocked by the death of Diem and Nhu," President Kennedy
said into his dictation microphone on November 5. "I'd met Diem with
Justice Douglas many years ago. He was an extraordinary character. While

21   See Charles A. Joiner, "South Vietnam's Buddhist Crisis: Organization for Charity, Dissi-
dence, and Unity," *Asian Survey*, Vol. 4, No. 7 (Jul., 1964), 915-928.
22   O'Leary and Seymour, 29.
23   Sheehan, 181.
24   Hammer, 294.

he became increasingly difficult in the last months, nevertheless over a ten-year period he'd held his country together, maintained its independence under very adverse conditions. The way he was killed made it particularly abhorrent."[25] In the very same recording, Kennedy admits, "I feel that we must bear a good deal of responsibility for it." Frederick Nolting, former ambassador to South Vietnam (1961-1963), wrote years later: "[T]he Kennedy administration set the stage for the tragedy that followed."[26]

Only a day after the coup, before her husband and brother-in-law were assassinated, Madame Nhu commented to the American press, "No coup can develop without American backing and American involvement."[27] Three days later, Madame Nhu gave a press conference in the United States on the murders of her husband and brother-in-law: "Whoever has the Americans as allies does not need any enemies…I can predict to you all that the story in Vietnam is only at its beginning."[28] When asked if she would seek asylum in the U.S. Madame Nhu responded, "I cannot stay in the country that stabbed me in the back."[29]

The Diem question was lingering for months before November 1, occupying its Washington plotters while leaning on its media cronies to push for regime change: journalists David Halberstam and Neil Sheehan wrote that "the war in South Vietnam was being lost mostly because of Diem's corrupt and self-serving government," and Clare Boothe Luce attacked Madame Nhu in a full-page ad in the New York Times paid for by the National Review – "The Lady Is for Burning: The Seven Deadly Sins of Madame Nhu" – from an article of the same name Luce wrote earlier in the year, and was reprinted in National Review the week after the Diem coup.[30]

Anticipating the immediate chaos the coup would ignite, the Kennedy administration knew it had to get Diem's extended family out of the way beforehand, namely, Madame Nhu and Archbishop Thuc.

* * *

It will be recalled that one of the decisive outcomes of Vatican II was the change in Catholic liturgy from the traditional Latin Mass to a new rite in the vernacular. It was a change not entirely welcomed. J.R.R. Tolkien, for instance, was so crestfallen he shouted out the Latin responses to

25   "JFK's Memoir Dictation on the Assassination of Diem."
26   Frederick Nolting, From Trust to Tragedy: The Political Memoirs of Frederick Nolting (New York: Praeger, 1988), 3.
27   "Mme. Nhu Says U.S. Incited Revolt," New York Daily News, 2 November 1963.
28   Monique Brinson Demery, Finding the Dragon Lady (New York: PublicAffairs, 2013), 214.
29   "Mme. Nhu Says U.S. Incited Revolt," New York Daily News, 2 November 1963.
30   Shaw, 163n30. See also Clare Boothe Luce Papers, Manuscript Division, Library of Congress, Box 304 and Box 777.

the English rejoinders, to the embarrassment of his son Christopher. To some, there were accusations the Council was a communist or masonic plot to shake the Church's foundations, the work of what excommunicated Jesuit-turned-sedevacantist Joaquín Sáenz Arriaga called *las falsas derechas* – "the fake Right."[31]

The most famous participant in Vatican II to break from the Church was French archbishop Marcel Lefebrve, who founded the Society of St. Pius X (SSPX) in 1970. SSPX priests and worshipers only celebrated the traditional Latin Mass, a direct affront to the changes incurred by Vatican II. When Lefebrve consecrated four bishops, ignoring Pope John Paul II, Lefebrve and his associates were excommunicated. Lefebrve died in 1991. Today, there are six SSPX seminaries and hundreds of active churches around the world, and it remains separated from the Church of Rome.

But there was one other bishop from Vatican II who became a sedevacantist, who also consecrated men to the episcopacy – many with dubious credentials – and was duly excommunicated because of it, a "wandering bishop" in the truest sense of the word: he was banned from returning to his homeland after the overthrow of his brothers, and left to roam rural Italian and French parishes for twenty years. His name was Ngo Dinh Thuc, the brother of the overthrown and executed President Ngo Dinh Diem and Ngo Dinh Nhu.

---

31   Luis Herran Avila, "Las Falsas Derechas: Conflict and Convergence in Mexico's Post-Cristero Right after the Second Vatican Council," *The Americas*, 79:2, April 2022, 322.

TIME

THE WEEKLY NEWSMAGAZINE

SOUTH VIET NAM'S DIEM
The hour is late, the odds are long.

CHAPTER ELEVEN

MARY, MARY QUITE CONTRARY

But we will certainly do whatsoever thing goeth forth out of our own mouth, to burn incense unto the queen of heaven, and to pour out drink offerings unto her, as we have done, we, and our fathers, our kings, and our princes, in the cities of Judah, and in the streets of Jerusalem: for then had we plenty of victuals, and were well, and saw no evil.

– Jeremiah 44:17

The Ngos thought they could do no wrong. This mentality was largely forged by the oldest surviving brother, Pierre-Martin Ngo Dinh Thuc, born in Hue in 1897. The eldest brother, Khoi, was executed by the Vietminh at the end of World War II. Imprisoned with Khoi was Diem. *Time*, in a 1955 cover story on Diem, chronicled an exchange between Diem and Ho Chi Minh:

"Come and live with me at the palace," Ho put it to him.

Diem: You killed my brother. You are a criminal.

Ho: I know nothing about your brother.... You are upset and angry. Stay with me. We must all work together against the French.

Diem: I don't believe you understand the kind of man I am. Look me in the face. Am I a man who fears?

Ho: No.

Diem: Good. Then I will go now.

Ho let him free.[1]

Thuc was ordained a priest in the diocese of Hue in 1925. He then studied at the Gregorian University in Rome, earning three doctorates, including one in canon law. Thuc taught for a short time at the Sorbonne before returning to Hue. In 1938, Pope Pius XI appointed Thuc as titular bishop of Sesina and apostolic vicar in Vietnam. In 1960, John XXIII named Thuc archbishop of Hue and assistant to the pontifical throne.

---

1   "The Beleaguered Man," *Time*, 4 April 1955.

During this rise, Thuc cultivated extensive relationships with both Church hierarchy, such as Cardinal Spellman, and Catholics in government. It was Dean Rusk, then head of the Asian division for the State Department, who sought to meet Bishop Thuc; Thuc and Diem met Rusk and other officials at the Mayflower Hotel in October 1950.[2] The brothers also were received by Cardinal Spellman at the archbishop's residence. To those at State, who "wanted a nationalist in high office in South Vietnam to blunt some of Ho Chi Minh's appeal,"[3] Diem emerged as the ideal choice to become prime minister. This was made possible by the clerical connections fostered by Thuc.

With Diem claiming the presidency in 1955, the future seemed bright not only for the entire Ngo family, but also Bishop Thuc. "In Thuc's naivete Diem was the 'father of the Republic'; exalted, revered, a mandarin, a good Catholic – as long as Thuc was alive, the Ngo family delusion would live on."[4] In 1962, Archbishop Thuc participated with other Catholic bishops in the first session of Vatican II. "[I]n many ways," Ed Jarvis argued, Archbishop Thuc was "profoundly theologically progressive, in harmony with his anticolonial third-world theology roots. His Asian Catholicism verged on syncretism,"[5] that is, an amalgamation of different religions. Indeed, Thuc's intervention during the first session of the Council echoed this leaning: "I salute the non-Catholic Christian Observers but where are the observers from the other non-Christian religions?"[6] This perspective is – theologically – very much in line with the direction hoped for by the liberal faction of the modern Catholic Church.

And so, when Thuc veered into traditional Catholicism in the 1970s, it was a remarkable – and perplexing – shift.

But before discussing Thuc's foray into independent Catholicism, we cannot ignore the State Department's role in forever altering the destiny of Ngo Dinh Thuc. The May-June 1963 Buddhist protests against the regime certainly caught the world's attention. But it was the regime's brutal reaction that "stunned Washington" when special forces in white helmets "carried out midnight raids against Buddhist pagodas," leading to 1,400 arrests, mostly monks, with many beaten.[7] "Two days later, the army generals conspiring against President Diem first sought official American

---

2   Cooney, 240-241.
3   Ibid., 241.
4   Jarvis, 55.
5   Ibid., 12.
6   Yves Congar, My Journal of the Council (Collegeville, MN: Liturgical Press, 2012), 324.
7   Sheehan, 172.

support."[8] The Pentagon's analysis unequivocally states, "For better or worse, the Aug. 21 pagoda raids decided the issue for us."[9] Still further, Ambassador Lodge cabled on Aug. 25: "We are launched on a course from which there is no respectable turning back: the overthrow of the Diem Government. There is no turning back in part because U.S. prestige is already publicly committed to this end in large measure and will become more so as facts leak out. In a more fundamental sense, there is no turning back because there is no possibility, in my view, that the war can be won under a Diem administration."[10] But the big news in the press that week was the civil rights march in Washington. The *Washington Post* devoted significant coverage to the march, while running two small articles, the headlines reading: "Nhu Called Real Viet-Nam Ruler" and "Vietnamese Regime Headed for Showdown with U.S."[11]

"We will do all that we can to help you conclude this operation successfully," Kennedy cabled Ambassador Lodge on August 30.[12] Officials including Ambassador Lodge later denied American involvement in the deadly coup, but there was no way around it: the administration with the CIA colluded with the conspirators, all while placating Diem. At the same time, the Diem question created a feud in both Washington and those in Saigon, like Diem supporter John Richardson, Lansdale's successor as CIA station chief in Saigon: "For if the Diem regime was a house divided against itself, so was the Kennedy Administration," Hedrick Smith wrote.[13]

Members of the National Security Council met on Aug. 31, a "where do we go from here?" meeting – "the sense of an administration adrift."[14] That same day, Dean Rusk sent a telegram to Ambassador Lodge. While Rusk advised Lodge to stress "common interest in defeating Viet Cong," he was cognizant that the president would be pressed on the repressive actions of the regime at a coming press conference. JFK was mere months from formally launching his re-election campaign; how could he possibly explain away pictures of monks setting themselves aflame? Rather than take drastic measures against the generals, Rusk pushed Madame Nhu "leave country on extended holiday." Rusk had another suggestion: "[W]ould you think it useful if we tried to get Vatican to summon Archbishop Thuc to Rome for lengthy consultations?"[15]

8   Ibid.
9   Ibid.
10   Ibid., 178.
11   Fredrik Logevall, *Choosing War: The Lost Chance for Peace and the Escalation of War in Vietnam* (Berkeley: University of California Press, 1999), 3.
12   Sheehan, 168.
13   Ibid., 169.
14   Ibid., 180.
15   "Instructions for Ambassador Lodge on Dealing With Diem Regime Repression," 31 Aug. 1963.

And so it came to pass that not only was Madame Nhu and her oldest child ushered out of Vietnam – to the United States on September 9, for an extended speaking tour where she openly criticized the administration – but Archbishop Thuc was duly summoned to Rome for the second session of Vatican II, convened from September 29-December 4. Another brother, Ngo Dinh Luyen, was in London at the time of the coup, as ambassador to the U.K. With this diaspora, the State Department was taking measures to protect certain Ngo family members in anticipation of the pending coup – purportedly commenced at a time chosen by the insurgent generals.

The official records of the Holy See state Pope Paul announced the date of September 29 a few days after his June election.[16] Edward Miller, author of *Misalliance: Ngo Dinh Diem, the United States, and the Fate of South Vietnam*, reports Thuc left for Rome on September 7, a week after Rusk's cable. Miller also notes that it was Nhu who ushered these family members, including his wife and children, out of the country.[17] But once in Rome, Thuc wasted no time speaking his mind. *Giornale D'Italia* quoted Thuc upon his arrival saying "the United States spent $20 million in an effort to replace [Diem]."[18] A papal audience between Thuc and Paul VI was inexplicably canceled days later; a day later, Thuc was on a plane for New York. There, he told reporters the Vatican ordered him to stop talking about the political situation in South Vietnam.

Things were reaching fever pitch. Thuc issued a lengthy statement for Catholic readers addressing the Buddhist situation: "International adventurers, furious that President Diem refused to obey them blindly, found the occasion favorable for provoking a coup d'etat under the pretext of protecting Buddhism, but in reality as an attempt to set up a Vietnamese Government subservient to their ambitions."[19] Thuc never explained who the "international adventurers" were.

On November 5, Madame Nhu's three youngest children – ages 15, 11, and 4 – arrived in Rome. Archbishop Thuc skipped that day's Council sessions to settle them in at the hotel suite where he was staying. Madame Nhu and her oldest child, Le Thuy, were in California at the time of the coup and subsequent assassinations. A week later, Paul VI met the three children and their archbishop uncle in a private audience. Madame Nhu

---

16   *Acta Apostolicae Sedis: Commentarium officiale,* 55 (1963), 581; cf. John W. O'Malley, *What Happened at Vatican II* (Cambridge: Harvard UP, 2008), 167.

17   Edward Miller, *Misalliance* (Cambridge: Harvard UP, 2013), 298.

18   "Diem's Kin a Prelate," *Lancaster New Era,* 7 September 1963.

19   Peter Kihss, "Archbishop of Hue Defends His Brother's Regime, *New York Times,* 13 September 1963.

reunited with her other children on November 15, secluding themselves in a convent hideaway arranged by Archbishop Thuc. The family later lived in exile in France.

When Thuc had left Vietnam for the second session of the Council in September 1963, he was a wealthy prince of the church, the spiritual figurehead of the reigning, if embattled, Ngo Family dynasty. He was chancellor of Dalat University, founder of the Personalism Training Center, owner of vast real estate holdings, and overseeing the building of a new cathedral. By the session's close, the dynasty, his brothers Diem and Nhu – everything Thuc knew beforehand – were dead. Within a year, this proud Viet was forbidden by the Vietnamese, the Americans, and evidently even the Holy See from returning to his diocese, or from entering Vietnam at all. Thuc appealed to the pope: "I do not know what the Holy Father Paul VI did, but he took advantage of the impossibility of my return to the Archepiscopal See of Hue to ask for my resignation and to name in my place his favorite, Mgr. Diem."[20]

For the next twenty years, Thuc was a true wandering bishop, assisting at remote Italian parishes, becoming increasingly problematic to the Holy See. Edward Jarvis observed, "Thuc was in abysmal standing; he was seen as an intriguer, a miser, a politicker, the archetypal eminence grise. The occasionally-heard conjecture that his episcopate was exemplary (or even just normal) is a willful denial of the evidence."[21]

Within ten years of the close of Vatican II, the theologically progressive Thuc had become a hardline traditionalist, a sedevacantist. How this shift came to be is difficult to explain. One cannot ignore the mental and physical strain Thuc endured in exile from his homeland – a homeland torn asunder by war, his brothers brutally murdered; another, Ngo Can, was kidnapped and executed. But Thuc – and the Ngo Family in general – were largely forgotten.

And for as ostensibly tolerant as Thuc appeared to other religions, which he made continually known at Vatican II, Thuc was adamant that the nearby town of La Vang, which was the site of a reported Marian apparition in 1798, become the site of a great Marian shrine – much to the consternation of the local Buddhists. This pious gesture, however, revealed a larger conflict at play in Vietnam: in Hue, especially, between Thuc's Catholic minority population (his pastoral region ministered to

20   Ngo Dinh Thuc, *Autobiographie de Mgr. Pierre-Martin Ngo-dinh-Thuc*, French ed., 1982, 79.
21   Jarvis, 86.

about 35,000 Catholics), and the majority Buddhist population under the leadership of Buddhist monk Trich Tri Quang.

In the Catholic Church, the controversy regarding schismastic traditionalists was about the suspended Archbishop Marcel Lefebrve and his Society of St. Pius X seminary. In 1974, Thuc visited the SSPX seminary to give a lecture. A year later, echoing the wandering bishop mills of Henry Carmel Carfora and Carl Jerome Stanley – let alone Earl Anglin James – Archbishop Thuc made a significant number of dubious consecrations. Somehow, Thuc agreed to journey with total strangers when he was visited by a group of Spanish lay men wanting Thuc to ordain them to the priesthood – instantly. Thuc spent the next three days on a road trip with the men he apparently never knew. They told Thuc the Virgin Mary required his service. Among them was Clemente Dominguez y Gomez, subsequently jailed in Madrid for heresy by impersonating a bishop, who later announced himself the true successor of Pope Paul VI, calling himself Gregory XVII.

Upon arriving in a town outside Seville, Dominguez y Gomez told the 78-year-old Thuc that Paul VI bilocated to Spain and personally told him that he must be ordained by a Catholic bishop. The ceremony took place on New Year's Eve, 1975. The participants wore hastily strewn satin miters.

Less than two weeks later, Thuc raised two of these young men to the episcopacy. They were part of the Palmar de Troya group, formed out of a purported appearance of the Virgin Mary to four girls in 1968. When Dominguez y Gomez visited the site shortly after the first apparitions, he supposedly had a number of mystical experiences. The Catholic archbishop of Seville dismissed the apparitions as hysterical – "collective superstition" and "harmful to the faith" – but that did not stop people like Dominguez y Gomez and his close friend, Manuel Alonso Corral, an insurance broker, from trying to build a major Marian pilgrim center.[22] Dominguez y Gomez also founded a religious order, the Carmelites of the Holy Face, completely unrelated to official orders of the Roman Catholic Church. He also believed the real Paul VI was imprisoned in the Vatican, replaced by an imposter. A car accident rendered Dominguez y Gomez blind, his eyes enucleated. He mutilated parts of his body to claim he was a stigmatist. In 1978, when he proclaimed himself Gregory XVII, the true successor of Paul VI, Dominguez y Gomez announced the creation of the Palmarian Christian Church. Followers were restricted from interacting with any-

---

22   Magnus Lundberg, *A Pope of Their Own: El Palmar de Troya* (Uppsala: Uppsala University, 2017), 19.

one outside the church. Arms and legs must be covered. Women must wear veils. Before Dominguez y Gomez died in 2005, he confessed to acolytes he was sexually incontinent, and harrassed both nuns and bishops in his church; he was known in the gay community of Seville. Today, the Cathedral-Basilica of Our Crowned Mother of Palmar, walled off the country road by slabs of concrete, is considered by its followers to be the Palmarian version of the Vatican.

Needless to say, Paul VI excommunicated Thuc and those he ordained "in accordance with a 1951 canonical law banning consecrations without Vatican approval."[23] On the other hand, "Thucites" – those consecrated by Thuc and who could thus claim apostolic succession from the "Thuc line" – were off and running, now free to consecrate whomever they wanted to the episcopacy, and Dominguez y Gomez was no exception. As the 1980s dawned, the lust for apostolic succession was alive and well: an "episcopal carnival," as the Vatican called it.[24]

But how did Clemente Dominguez y Gomez manage to emerge from Andalusian anonymity to lead Archbishop Thuc into schism? Earlier in 1975, months before he encountered Thuc, Dominguez took his message on tour. He was invited to speak in Orwell, Vermont, population 851, by the pastor of St. Paul's Roman Catholic Church, Fr. Anthony H. Brackett. Dominguez spoke no English, but Brackett oversaw the regional distribution of his messages (visions). Dominguez warned of a coming world war and foresaw the Catholic Church falling into schism after Paul VI's death. One wonders, however, how Fr. Brackett got to know this purported seer in the first place, and what compelled him to devote so much effort to promoting the Spainard's message.

Anthony H. Brackett, a priest in the Diocese of Burlington since 1959, was a U.S. Army Air Corps veteran of World War II. From 1960-1964, Brackett was chaplain of the Civil Air Patrol in Bennington, Vermont. In late 1973, Brackett made local headlines for his fire and brimstone sermons about the approaching comet Kohoutek in 1973. Brackett said he obtained his information about Clemente Dominguez y Gomez from various Marian Centers in Canada and the U.S.[25] As Ngo Dinh Thuc envisioned a Marian shrine in La Vang, so too did Clemente Dominguez Gomez envision Palmar de Troya to become a major Marian shrine. But

23   Jacques Leslie, "Order Rebels Against Catholic Church," *Los Angeles Times*, 18 February 1976.
24   "Pope: Reached Evening of Earthly Day," Associated Press, 27 September 1976.
25   Aldo Merusi, "Orwell Priest Praying to Avert Comet's Wrath," *Rutland Daily Herald*, 28 December 1973.

Thuc was not the first bishop of choice – that, of course, was Marcel Le-febrve, whose blessing was nothing short of a prerequisite for schismatic traditionalists. When Lefebrve begged off, the Palmar group looked to Lefebrve's understudy in such matters: Archbishop Thuc.

The accounts of Thuc's wandering through independent Catholicism usually depicts Thuc as aimless, ambivalent to the abuses of his faculties as a successor of the apostles, that ultimately he did not know what he was doing. If Lefebrve thought the group too radical, clearly Thuc must not have known what he was doing when he performed the ordinations and consecrations. What other rational explanation was there?

One possibility: that Thuc was already familiar with the fringe and mi-cro-churches of those who sought him out. And not only familiar, but ap-proved of them enough to go forward with the consecrations. For instance, in September 1982 Thuc consecrated one Christian Marie Datessen, who was already consecrated a year earlier by Andre Enos. However, once Da-tessen received the Thuc consecration, he turned around and consecrat-ed Enos, putting Enos in the Thuc line of succession. Andre Enos was a former Roman Catholic priest. After apostatizing he was made bishop in the Old Holy Catholic Church – the church founded by British Israelism supporter Archbishop Charles Brearley. Recall Brearley was a member of the Sovereign Order of Cyprus, the de facto chivalric order of Bishop Wal-ter Propheta's American Old Catholic Church. It will be remembered, too, that the lay representative of the Old Holy Catholic Church was Count Dr. Pericles Voultsos-Vourtzis, honorary attorney general of Louisiana and ambassador of King Ntare V of Burundi, among other fraudulent titles: namely, grand master of the Sovereign Order of St. Dennis of Zante. Voult-sos was also a member of the Sons of the American Revolution and a 32nd degree Mason in the Parthenon Lodge No. 1101 of New York.

According to Peter Levenda, a mysterious character named Father Fox, a Fordham-educated "priest" affiliated with the Sovereign Order of St. Dennis of Zante, traveled frequently to South Vietnam for reasons not entirely spiritual.[26] It is not out of the realm of possibility Fox interfaced directly with Archbishop Thuc, prior to the fall of the Ngo Family.

In the world of the wandering bishop, one could never have too many lines of apostolic succession. In the case of Andre Enos and Christian Marie Da-tessen, the source of their initial consecrations was a character who fancied himself the Roman emperor, Grimaldi-Lascaris. Grimaldi-Lascaris owed his consecration to Johann Frederik Van Assendelft-Altland, the bishop who con-

26   Email correspondence with Peter Levenda, 31 May 2023.

secrated Archbishop Stanley of Louisville, founder of the Église Catholique Apostolique Primitive d'Antioche Orthodoxe et de Tradition – the same church in which David Ferrie and Guy Banister's cabal were ordained in 1961. Grimaldi-Lascaris also conferred upon Bishop Frederick King, of the Bishop King Crusade and John Birch Society, the title of Marquis de St. Laurent.

There is another possibility: Archbishop Thuc met Archbishop Stanley during the third session of the Vatican Council in 1964. Indeed, Carl Jerome Stanley of Kentucky, one of Earl James's consecrations, a man with a criminal record and key to exposing the New Orleans cabal of fake bishops, was invited to the session as an ecumenical witness, a perplexing invitation indeed.[27]

Mere propinquity? Perhaps. It's possible that there was an intense desire to be consecrated by an actual prince of the Catholic Church, the church whose first pope was St. Peter, built by Christ himself (cf. Mt. 16:18), and Thuc was the one who could do it, a poor man's Marcel Lefebrve. Thuc, at age 84, formally declared the seat of Peter vacant in 1982:

> How does the Catholic Church appear today as we look at it? In Rome, John Paul II reigns as "Pope," surrounded by the body of Cardinals and of many bishops and prelates. Outside of Rome, the Catholic Church seems to be flourishing, along with its bishops and priests. The number of Catholics is great. Daily the Mass is celebrated in so many churches, and on Sundays the churches are full of many faithful who come to hear the Mass and receive Holy Communion.
>
> But in the sight of God, how does today's Church appear? Are the Masses – both the daily ones and those at which people assist on Sundays – pleasing to God? By no means, because that Mass is the same for Catholics as it is for Protestants – therefore it is displeasing to God and invalid. The only Mass that pleases God is the Mass of St. Pius V, which is offered by few priests and bishops, among whom I count myself.
>
> Therefore, to the extent that I can, I will open seminaries for educating candidates for that priesthood which is pleasing to God.
>
> Besides this "Mass," which does not please God, there are many other things that God rejects: for example, changes in the ordination of priests, the consecration of bishops, and in the sacraments of Confirmation and of Extreme Unction.
>
> Moreover, the "priests" now hold to:
> 1) modernism;

27   "Louisville Orthodox Prelate On Way To Vatican Council," *The Courier-Journal*, 23 Sept. 1964.

135

2) false ecumenism

3) the adoration [or cult] of man;

4) the freedom to embrace any religion whatsoever;

5) the unwillingness to condemn heresies and to expel the heretics.

Therefore, in so far as I am a bishop of the Roman Catholic Church, I judge that the Chair of the Roman Catholic Church is vacant; and it behooves me, as bishop, to do all that is needed so that the Roman Catholic Church will endure in its mission for the salvation of souls.

February 25, 1982

Munich

+Peter Martin Ngo-dinh-Thuc

Archbishop

Thuc was again excommunicated in 1983, seven years after his first excommunication. Following Thuc's death in 1984, the Vatican stated Thuc once again reconciled with the Catholic Church, recanted his claims, and affirmed John Paul II was truly the Successor of St. Peter. From what we have shown, however, the world of independent Catholicism and wandering bishops is a small one, and the shadow of Earl Anglin James looms even over the fate of Ngo Dinh Thuc. Thuc, in many ways a pivotal figure in America's deepening involvement in Vietnam was, in the end, affiliated with clerical charlatans. Harmless, one one hand, with their love of liturgical vestments and solemn knighting ceremonies. Dangerous on the other: frauds so convinced of their delusions that the world of the occult became their reality. Consider Archbishop Brearley's title as Paladin of the Athenian Order, which in the 1960s was composed of an "élite of Literati and Illuminati with a Rosicrucian ethos."[28]

As we move further into the occult, particularly the role of hypnosis and religion in assassinations, we will first examine one more relationship linking the "Thuc bishops" of the Palmarian Church with Earl Anglin James – the story of James's protege.

* * *

By the mid-1960s, James's chief associate was Guy F. Claude Hamel (1935-2008), convicted felon, Rosicrucian, and author of such books as *The Egocentric Masterpiece, Humanity at a Glance,* and *Broken Wings: A*

---

28   John Kersey, "Ministry of Abbess Mary Francis at Cusworth, and of the Old Holy Roman Catholic Church," https://san-luigi.org/churches/catholicate-of-the-west/mission/ancient-catholic-church/ministry-of-abbess-mary-francis-at-cusworth-and-of-the-old-holy-roman-catholic-church/.

Collection of Poems. On February 19, 1965, with assistance by Peter A. Zhurawetzky, James consecrated Hamel as a bishop in the Old Catholic Church (Orthodox Orders). However, Hamel claimed he was first consecrated in 1962 by a French "cardinal" of a fake pope, Clement XV. This cardinal will later align himself with the Palmarian church.

At first, James was enticed by Bishop Hamel, more than thirty years James's junior and the heir apparent to James's vast bishopric: James named Hamel coadjutor and bestowed upon Hamel the right of apostolic succession. James dreamed of an enormous cathedral that Hamel would build – the Earl Anglin James Cathedral, of course – which would also function as the bishop's "palace," housing the archbishop primate (James) and also housing the rector of the cathedral (Hamel, who had a boon of children). The cost for this great undertaking? James figured somewhere in the ballpark of $500 million.[29]

Hamel maintained a publishing house for release of his own material, CSP (Congregation of St. Paul, not to be confused with the Roman Catholic congregation, Society of St. Paul, SSP). One of the regular writers for *CSP World News* was the John Bircher we met earlier, Bishop Frederick King, who had formed an alliance with Hamel in the 1960s.[30]

"We are now serving under Archbishop-Primate, Sir Anglin 'Laurentius I' James; from him we are learning the Art of TRUE PATIENCE under the Load of PERSECUTION," Hamel wrote in one newsletter.[31] Hamel was ordained only a year before, by William Pavlik of the Ontario Old Roman Catholic Church. Only two months later, Pavlik deposed and excommunicated Hamel. Perhaps the archbishop got wind of Hamel's sordid past: in Montreal, Hamel rented a room in a woman's house while her husband was in prison. Hamel and the women left the children, and moved to Winnipeg where Hamel was a short-order cook, and eventually stripped the furnished apartment bare on their way out of town. Hamel's newsletter told of harrowing tales of the woman's alleged foray into prosti-

29   CV, 31.
30   John Kersey, "Prince Frederick of Vilna and all of Byelorussia,
31   CV, 34.

by Emily Medaugh.

It was a truly inspiring experience for me when I went to the Altar built by the Most Reverend Father Guy F. Claude Hamel, at Cordova Lake, where he is going to build, with the help of God, and many kind hearted friends (who love to help children.)

I felt as though I were standing on Hallowed Ground and the great Peace in the silence was like the Presence of God, pronouncing a benediction.

tution, all while Hamel was married to another woman, Marguerite, with whom Hamel had six boys.

After Pavlik, Hamel aligned himself with "the true pope," a heavyset 61-year-old named Michael Collin. Ensconced in a cinder block building within a cinder block wall on the French-German border lived Collin, alias Clement XV. The grounds were called Le Petit Vatican de Clemery. Collin was a defrocked and excommunicated Roman Catholic priest who claimed John XXIII personally made him pope. He was associated with a Quebec hostel run by the "Apostles of Infinite Love." He also distributed literature for Hamel throughout the Lorraine area of France urging donations for Hamel's signature ministry, "the Metropolitan's Children's Home," and to send cash or checks to a Toronto P.O. box.[32]

But this orphanage proved to be Hamel's undoing, exposing a pattern of fraud and abusive behavior. It would lead to Hamel's 1970 con-

---

32   "Head of Sect Declines to Talk of Quebec Hostel," *Calgary Herald*, 28 January 1967.

viction for fraud, and act as the catalyst for James's attempted comeback as Universal Patriarch, only to be resisted by his former underling. Long before this conviction, Hamel's reputation preceded himself. In a 1967 letter from the Anglican archbishop of Toronto to a Concordia Seminary professor, Arthur Piepkorn, the Venerable G.H. Johnson did not mince words about the reputation of both Hamel and James:

> He is associated at times with a man called Earl Anglin James who is also an individual to beware of. My advice to you with respect to both of these persons is to use extreme caution. They are both on our list of "Clergy Warnings" for the Diocese of Toronto.[33]

After the inevitable fallout with Clement XV, Hamel moved under James, who in turn quickly consecrated him a bishop. James wrote in his CV, "[He] is doing a noble and honorable Duty in bringing about 'the Metropolitan Children's Home' – Needs Larger Shelter!" Hamel ventured on fundraising tours into other places like Philadelphia, where he hoped to establish a beachhead in the form of "St. George's Mission" led by "Cardinal" Leo Christopher Skelton of "The Congregation of St. Jude Thaddeus." The *Philadelphia Inquirer* checked with various police departments in Ottawa: Hamel and friends had a list of felonies and convictions. Philadelphia's DA was put on notice.[34]

Just as quickly as he ascended to the heights of becoming the successor of Earl Anglin James, Hamel broke from his affiliation with James, and formed his own sect, crowning himself His Holiness Claudius I. One of the individuals he reputedly made a cardinal was Anton LaVey, the San Francisco-based founder of the Church of Satan.[35] In turn, LaVey counted Hamel his "filial wizard" of Canada. Hamel longed for instruction in satanic rituals while Hamel's partner in crime, "Sr. Mary," continued to solicit funds for the non-existent children's home.

Hamel's fall out with James appeared to be around the strange case of John and Mary Wilson – the very same "Sr. Mary." John, alias Bishop Frederick, BD, LL.D, Ph.D, owed his letters courtesy of James. Only John Wilson was illiterate. In 1968, the Wilsons were put on trial for defraud-

---

33   Johnson letter to Piepkorn, April 4, 1967.
34   '1-Man Church Seeks Funds; D.A. Watching," *Philadelphia Inquirer*, 05 February 1968, 1, 6.
35   Burns to Piepkorn, 22 June 1970.

ing the public over non-existent religious and charitable institutions.[36] A psychologist testified both husband and wife had the mental equivalent of a six-year-old. Earl Anglin James was arrested for failing to respond to a subpoena related to the case. When asked about his qualifications to distribute diplomas, especially to people with mental disabilities as the Wilson, Anglin James testified, "I'm permitted to give degrees just like the Salvation Army makes captains and sergeants," he said under oath.[37] Both John and Mary Wilson were convicted of defrauding the public.

Hamel was accused of forcing himself on Mary Wilson, among other women. It then became evident there was no children's home, and Hamel pocketed all those donations for himself – about $60,000 over nine years. He was convicted in 1970, sentenced to nine months in jail and three years' probation.[38]

"Shakespeare couldn't have written anything funnier than the story of this church!" James laughed in an interview. "Write a movie about it. I am willing to play myself in any drama. The public would love it, now that the church is about as extinct as the dodo bird."[39]

---

36   "Psychologist Says Wilson Mental Equal of 6-Year-Old," *Ottawa Journal*, 27 February 1968, 6.
37   Ibid.
38   "'Church' Leader Was a Con Man," *Calgary Herald*, 2 July 1970.
39   "A Satanic benediction for the wildest sect in Ontario," *Weekend Telegram*, 23 May 1970.

CHAPTER TWELVE

THE BUSINESS OF THE LORD

The wicked shall see it, and be grieved; he shall gnash with his teeth, and melt away: the desire of the wicked shall perish.

– Psalm 112:10

On the night of the president's murder, David Ferrie collected two young male companions and set out for Texas. It was about 9PM. Ferrie drove 350 miles in his 1961 Mercury Comet blue station wagon through a blinding thunderstorm before reaching Houston about 4:30AM. The trio checked into Room 19 of the Alamotel, owned by Carlos Marcello. When the president was shot, Marcello was in court. Ferrie joined him, assisting defense attorney G. Wray Gill. Marcello was acquitted.[1] As Ferrie made his mad dash west, fellow bishop Jack Martin was telling the New Orleans district attorney's office and FBI that Ferrie taught Oswald how to shoot with a telescopic sight, and that Ferrie was to be a getaway pilot for the assassin. Very quickly, David Ferrie was being sought as a person of interest by New Orleans authorities. Martin soon recanted his story.

Ferrie later said he and his young buddies went goose hunting and ice skating with the intent of possibly buying a rink. Indeed, the trio did visit Houston area rinks, but Ferrie spent his time on the telephone. At 11PM on Saturday, the three arrived at the Driftwood Motel in Galveston. They arrived back in New Orleans on Sunday night. Ferrie voluntarily turned himself in on Monday, but was released quickly thereafter. It wasn't until three years later when Ferrie emerged as a key witness in Jim Garrison's investigation. But Ferrie died only days after that news became public. When Garrison indicted Clay Shaw on charges of conspiracy to kill the president, Ferrie was posthumously named co-conspirator.

All of this is both highly suspicious and yet does not implicate Ferrie or friends in anything nefarious. After all, he was the kind of guy who might just undertake a journey with two men over twenty years his junior – ideal alibis in any case.

---

1 Marcello was facing charges for conspiracy and defrauding the U.S. government. It was later revealed Marcello bribed a juror.

While at the Alamotel that Saturday, November 23, Ferrie (or his boy pals) made two long distance calls that are strange for someone supposedly just wanting to get away and relax: the New Orleans radio-television studio WDSU and radio station WSHO. Why would such innocuous calls be of any consequence?

* * *

In New Orleans, beginning on March 23, 1962, the cancer research Drs. Alton Ochsner and Mary Sherman at Tulane University were conducting became something else entirely: to create a cancer that would kill Fidel Castro.[2] The incredible story is told in Edward T. Haslam's *Dr. Mary's Monkey*, a story which took a tragic turn when Dr. Mary Sherman was found murdered in 1964, a crime that remains unsolved.

The "debate" with Oswald was part of a WDSU-TV and WDSU-AM program called "Conversation Carte Blanche" hosted by Ed Slatter. It was recorded in August 1963 and was practically shown on loop during NBC's nonstop coverage the weekend of the assassination. CIA/FBI informant William Gaudet "felt Bringuier's altercation with Oswald was on purpose and that Ed Butler put on the whole thing."[3]

In one of INCA's first public events, in July 1961, Dr. Boris Klosson, Soviet expert from the State Department, presented a talk on tactics the Communist Party readily employed to infiltrate a country. Butler followed Klosson with his own lecture centered on psychological warfare: "Are You a Brainwar Casualty?"[4] Butler is using CIA verbiage here, as in a "brainwar" with the Communists, an intelligence takeaway culled out from the carnage of the Korean War. CIA director Allen Dulles expanded on this concept in a letter to President Eisenhower: "[The Russians] take selected human beings whom they wish to destroy and turn them into humble confessors of crimes they never committed or make them the mouthpiece for Soviet propaganda. New techniques wash the brain clean of the thoughts ... and, possibly, through the use of some 'lie serum,' create new brain processes and new thoughts, which the victim, parrot-like, repeats."[5]

Latin America was INCA's battleground against the ubiquitous communist and his subversive tactics. In the fall of 1961, INCA boasted it was setting up regional councils. An op-ed calling for support of INCA con-

2   See Ed Haslam, *Dr. Mary's Monkey* (Walterville, OR: TrineDay, 2014).
3   Caufield, 37.
4   "Butler To Be Speaker at Civil League Meet," *St. Bernard Voice*, 28 Jul. 1961.
5   Allen Dulles, "Brain Warfare," National Alumni Conference of the Graduate Council of Princeton University, 10 April 1953.

cluded, "The INCA program is just beginning, but its people-to-people approach is one that the Reds have no ready-made means of combatting."[6]

In his influential journal article on INCA, Arthur E. Carpenter cut through the anti-communist propaganda that coated INCA's PR campaigns: "By identifying social radicalism with an alien totalitarianism, it tried to shield a wealthy, conservative elite from fundamental change."[7] This was the heart of the matter, ultimately, in Cold War ideology, couched as it was in frantic paranoia about godless communism because, in truth, *something* needed to be the scapegoat for the postwar existential crisis permeating America that exploded in the antiwar movements. Carpenter goes on to state INCA served not the laborer, the blue-collar worker, but the New Orleans elite with certain interests who had a lot to lose if the dominoes of Latin America fell to the Red Menace.

INCA skewed to the radical right, where Ochsner preferred to be. His interests in Latin America dated back decades earlier, when he formed the Ochsner Clinic and the Ochsner Family Foundation. He built a reputation throughout Latin America, treating leaders and their families: Juan Peron of Argentina, the Somozas of Nicaragua, Fuentes of Guatemala.

Carpenter points out how integral Latin America was to the success of businesses and politics (and their leaders) in New Orleans. Strong relations with Latin America was an absolute necessity, for instance, for the existence of the International House and International Trade Mart of New Orleans. "Trade was New Orleans' biggest business, and seventy-five percent of it was with Latin America."[8]

New Orleans was intended to be the "premier gateway to the Americas."[9] On July 30, 1941, the Office of the Coordinator of Inter-American Affairs was established by Executive Order. Its objective was to "provide for the development of commercial and cultural relations between the American Republics" and strengthen "the spirit of cooperation between the Americas in the interest of Hemisphere defense."[10] Its coordinator was Nelson A. Rockefeller, and in 1946 the Office of Inter-American Affairs came under the umbrella of the State Department. The Office of Inter-American Affairs was its own tightly run – but unofficial – intelligence

---

6   "Fighting Latin Communists," *Shreveport Times*, 11 October 1961.

7   Arthur E. Carpenter, "Social Origins of Anti-Communism: The Information Council on the Americas," *Louisiana History*, Vol. 30, no. 2, Spring 1989, 118.

8   Ibid., 119.

9   Joshua L. Goodman, *Gateways to Latin America: Pan Americanism as a Business Strategy in Gulf South Port Cities, 1940-1970* (Tulane University, 2017), 76.

10   H. Steven Helton, "Preliminary Inventory of the Records of the Office of Inter-American Affairs" (Washington, D.C.: National Archives), 1952, 1.

bureau. Rockefeller had agents canvassing Latin and South America. Rockefeller contracted with Yale's Cross-Cultural Survey "to produce a Strategic Index of Latin America, which divided the cultures and subcultures of the area into roughly one hundred regional units."[11] Through the recon done by this office, the State Department had a thorough understanding of the region, like "meteorological conditions, food and water supplies, and the vectors of disease – all information useful to an occupying force."[12]

One of the domestic interests of the Office of Inter-American Affairs was the Pan-American Center in New Orleans, an initiative of longtime New Orleans Congressman F. Edward Hebert, with the notion it would advance "commercial and cultural relations between the American Republics."[13] For our purposes, the Pan-American Center symbolizes how central these "American Republics" of Latin America were to New Orleans business and trade. If the relationship dried up, so did New Orleans. It was a relationship with great latitude and little oversight. Like the Trade Mart, founded in 1946, and International House, founded in 1945, the Pan-Am Center was self-supported and not-for-profit; politics was to keep out.[14] Nelson Rockefeller referred to the International House as "our Good Neighbor Policy in action." Its slogan was "World Peace, Trade and Understanding."[15]

Of course, there were more clandestine objectives. Inter-American Affairs was in reality a "U.S. intelligence agency that intercepted Nazi activity in South America.[16] Rockefeller was informally connected with the spy agency BACC (British-American-Canadian Corporation), which merged into the World Commerce Corporation in 1947. Additionally, the State Department's other purpose for these NGOs was as bulwarks against Soviet propaganda in Latin America. "As long as Latin American countries remained anti-communist and stable, the theory goes, Washington was content to take minimal action, especially regarding funding for economic development."[17] The Private Enterprise Corporation, a bureau of the State Department, envisioned the creation of cultural and educational

11 Farish, 65.
12 Ibid.
13 Ibid.
14 Gary A. Bolding, "New Orleans Commerce: The Establishment of the Permanent World Trade Mart," *Louisiana History: The Journal of the Louisiana Historical Association*, Vol. 8, No. 4, Autumn 1967, 356.
15 Alonzo G. Ensenat, "The Story of International House and International Trade Mart," 1974, 3.
16 Ralph Ganis, *The Skorzeny Papers* (New York: Hot Press, 2018), 26.
17 Goodman, 23.

exchange programs for working professionals and young people, a PR campaign to ease perceptions from both the U.S. and Latin America. It again echoes both FDR's Good Neighbor Policy and later President Truman's Point Four program. It also echoes the clear-cut goal of Operation Mockingbird. The official platform of the Republican Party in 1956 stated proudly:

> The American Republics have taken effective steps against the cancer of Communism. At the Caracas Conference of March, 1954, they agreed that if International Communism gained control of the political institutions of any American republic, this would endanger them all, and would call for collective measures to remove the danger. This new Doctrine, first proposed by the United States, extends into modern times the principles of the Monroe Doctrine.
> A first fruit of the Caracas Doctrine was the expulsion of the Communist regime ruling Guatemala. Today, Guatemala is liberated from Kremlin control. The Organization of American States has grown in vigor. It has acted promptly and effectively to settle hemispheric disputes. In Costa Rica, for the first time in history, international aerial inspection was employed to maintain peace. The Panama Conference was probably the most successful in the long history of the Organization of American States in its promotion of good will, understanding and friendship.[18]

Weirdly, Ed Butler orchestrated a press conference the day after the murder of RFK in 1968 where two conspiracy theorists, Anthony Hilder and John Steinbacher, spoke of RFK's assassination as a plot carried out by the Illuminati. The claims, authors William Turner and Jonn Christian argued, obscured the role the radical right likely played in the slaying.[19] In this way, Butler reprised his role as media manager of disinformation as he did regarding Lee Oswald in New Orleans.

All of this brings us back to the night of the assassination, when Oswald's "debate" was endlessly replayed. There was another guest brought in to interview on WDSU only hours after the president's death – Kerry Thornley.

Kerry Thornley wound up in New Orleans at the same time as Oswald – the summer of 1963. Thornley seemed to "accidentally" run into a number of persons of interest: "Thornley stated he 'accidentally' met Guy Banister in 1961 and discussed the book he was writing based on Oswald,

18   Republican Party Platform of 1956, 20 August 1956.
19   See William Turner and Jonn Christian, *The Assassination of Robert F. Kennedy* (New York: Carroll & Graf Publishers, 1978), 55-57.

who was in the Soviet Union at the time. Thornley met David Ferrie in 1962 and claimed his contact with him was also 'accidental' and that no significant conversation transpired. In September 1963, Thornley visited Mexico City – the same month as Oswald – allegedly as a tourist. Interestingly, Thomas Beckham, a regular at Banister's office, told the HSCA that Kerry Thornley was part of Banister's cell, along with Lee Harvey Oswald."[20]

Thornley was interviewed at WDSU TV about Lee Harvey Oswald, and followed up that appearance in the New Orleans *States Item*, in which Thornley called Oswald a "real loser" and "a little psychotic."[21] It was as if Thornley's job was to smear Oswald and spread disinformation, because Thornley's media appearances contradict what he told WSHO Radio program director Cliff Hall. According to Jim DiEugenio, after the WDSU interview "Thornley and Hall went out for a drink. Thornley now admitted that he *had seen* Oswald since the service. It was in New Orleans. Hall asked him if he knew Oswald well and he said yes he did."[22]

Was Ferrie calling both WSHO and WDSU to ensure Thornley got his time on the air to sully Lee Oswald?

Lee Oswald never lived to have his day in court. There is precious little information that exists to understand what was going on behind closed doors in the 12-hour interrogation of Oswald from November 22-November 23. What we do have available is the seemingly endless parading of Oswald up and down police station hallways from one room to another. Each time he is swarmed by newsmen, like a young Dan Rather, shouting at him. Watching the clips, Oswald's demeanor is striking. He seems more bothered by the bruise under his eye – "A policeman hit me!" he exclaims, outraged, when a reporter asks about it, as well as the injustice over not securing a lawyer – than the kind of defiant, seething, or enraged behavior one might expect from a ruthless, Communist assassin who just murdered the leader of the Free World in broad daylight. Instead, the way Oswald was being treated at the police station suggests Ruby, the de facto avenging angel of a mourning Kennedy family, might dart in at any moment, armed and loaded; he was there, posing as a newsman, waiting for the moment.

Simply, the treatment of Oswald suggests he was already deemed guilty before even being charged. The footage we have shows how archaic things

20   Caufield, 228.
21   Quoted in Jim DiEugenio, "Kerry Thornley: A New Look (Part One)," 13 June 2020, https://www.kennedysandking.com/john-f-kennedy-articles/kerry-thornley-a-new-look-part-1/.
22   Ibid.

were done in Dallas in 1963, how wild west it still was, with the police station's creaking doors and stoic men in Stetsons dragging Lee Oswald around for the cameras like a fifth rate dog and pony show. Most telling is the Kafkaesque midnight "press conference," with Oswald paraded into the identification room...

> *Oswald, handcuffed, is brought before a loud and crowded assembly of the press. It's ten minutes after midnight on November 23, 1963.*
>
> **OSWALD:** ...I know nothing about this situation here. I would like to have leg--uh, legal representation.
>
> *A long pause. Inaudible. Oswald continues.*
>
> **OSWALD:** Well, I was, uh, questioned by a judge, however I, uh, protested at that time that I was not allowed legal representation during that, uh, uh, very short and sweet hearing. Uh, I really don't know what this situation is about. Nobody has told me anything, except that I'm accused of, uh, of, uh, murdering a policeman. I know nothing more than that. I do request, um, someone to come forward to give me, uh, a legal assistance.
>
> **REPORTER:** Did you kill the president?
>
> **OSWALD:** No. I've not been charged with that. In fact, nobody has said that to me yet. The first thing I heard about it was when the newspaper reporters in the hall, uh, asked me that question.
>
> **REPORTER:.** You have been charged with that.
>
> **OSWALD:** (leans in) Sir?
>
> **REPORTER:.** You have been--
>
> **VOICE IN BACK:.** Nobody said what? Nobody said what?
>
> *Oswald looks to the back where the voice comes from. He scans the crowd. He frowns.*
> *The press conference ends. Oswald is led away.*
>
> **REPORTER:.** How'd you hurt your eye, Oswald?
>
> **OSWALD:** *(leans towards reporter, deeply offended)* A policeman hit me!

It seems to dawn on Oswald at that moment that he's all alone. He'd had his share of arrests and some jail time in the past. He was accustomed to the bullying, he could take the haranguing from authorities. But this was entirely different: not only charged with the killing of one of Dallas's finest, but the president of the United States! What, then, was Lee Oswald's motive? How much did he obsess over how he was going to do it? What was his getaway plan? A deadly Communist assassin relying on public transportation to flee the scene of the crime of the century? He didn't even have a driver's license.

He said *repeatedly* – whenever he could – *that he didn't do it*. We know from his Dallas interrogators he never budged on that position under questioning – interrogations that transpired without a lawyer, it should be noted, with no transcriptions or recordings of said questioning. There was little to no respect shown for the rule of law during Oswald's time in police custody.

Perhaps the most infamous phrase to come out of Oswald's brief imprisonment was "I'm just a patsy!" Actually, the whole of it, as he again is transferred down a hall, is: "They're taking me in for the fact that I lived in the Soviet Union. I'm just a patsy!" Rarely are the two sentences put together. But understood as a whole, Oswald seems to be saying he's the patsy for the Dallas police, that the reason he was singled out and arrested was because of his 1959-1962 defection to the USSR. More often than not, "I'm just a patsy" is taken to mean Oswald was asserting his patsy role in the assassination by those conspiring to kill the president. In this context, one wonders if Oswald was truly ignorant of what was to come to pass at Dealey Plaza that Friday. Was he really telling the truth or lying? Either way, Oswald was innocent until proven guilty – and he never was proven guilty by a court of law.

Looking back on Oswald's movements following his return from Russia fills in the picture a bit.

Upon arriving in the United States in 1962, his contact on arrival in New York was one Spas T. Raikin, who worked in the foreign department of the Traveler's Aid Society. A native of Bulgaria, Raikin was tremendously committed to helping Bulgarian refugees escape Communist clutches. A decade earlier, Raikin fled Bulgaria to Greece, where he completed his education with the support of the World Council of Churches.[23] At the time, Raikin was also the secretary-general of the Anti-Bolshevik Bloc of Nations, which received strong support from General Willoughby.

* * *

On June 11, 1963, President Kennedy appeared live on television from the White House. He was introducing to the American people legislation

---

23   *Pocono Record* (Stroudsburg, PA), 2 December 1969.

that would ultimately become the Civil Rights Act of 1964. He called it "a moral issue." "One hundred years of delay have passed since President Lincoln freed the slaves, yet their heirs, their grandsons, are not fully free..."

Meanwhile, six weeks after the televised presidential address of June 11, Lee Oswald gave a speech of his own, to Jesuit scholastics at Spring Hill College in Mobile, Alabama. The 23-year-old was invited by his cousin, Eugene Murret, who was then studying to become a Jesuit priest (Murret eventually left the Society of Jesus and became a lawyer), to speak on his experiences in Russia. Though Lee was baptized Lutheran, his cousin's family were soundly Catholic, largely influenced by the Jesuit schools in New Orleans. Oswald's notes for the thirty-minute address are preserved, and open with quite a hook: "Americans are apt to scoff at the idea, that a military coup in the U.S., as so often happens in Latin american countries, could ever replace our government. but that is an idea that has grounds for consideration."[24]

Oswald's next point: segregation. "It, is, I think the action of the active segregationist minority and the great body of indifferent people in the South who do the United States more harm in the eyes of the worlds people, than the whole world communist movement."[25] And on USSR-U.S. relations, the purported killer of JFK says this: "our two contries have too much too offer too each other to be tearing at each others troughs in an endless cold war."

It is also worth noting Oswald rather admired the president and the First Family. In her book *Accessories After the Fact*, Sylvia Meagher documents all the witnesses who commented on Lee Oswald's positive attitude towards JFK: among them, George de Mohrenschildt, Michael Paine, Lee's aunt Lillian Murret, and Lee's cousin Mary Murret.[26]

As we have seen, JFK's commitment to de-segregation and opposition to that policy has largely been obscured by focusing on the CIA and the military-industrial complex in relation to motives for assassination. "I am, therefore, asking the Congress to enact legislation giving all Americans the right to be served in facilities which are open to the public – hotels, restaurants, theaters, retail stores, and similar establishments. This seems to me to be an elementary right. Its denial is an arbitrary indignity that no American in 1963 should have to endure, but many do."[27]

24   "Lee Oswald: Speech to a Jesuit College in Alabama," 22november1963.org.uk. Oswald's dyslexia learning disability is evident in his spelling errors.
25   Ibid.
26   Sylvia Meagher, *Accessories After the Fact* (New York: Skyhorse Publishing, originally published in 1967 by Hood College), 504.
27   "Televised Address to the Nation on Civil Rights," 11 June 1963.

It was another salvo from JFK that the old ways would not do. But the president only had five months left to live. "[A] substantial minority of citizens believed that Kennedy's pro-civil rights stance meant that he 'had it coming for him.'"[28]

* * *

Meanwhile, Dallas at this time of social change was really run by a hidden governing body of influential WASP men, one which yielded tremendous control over policy and public image of Dallas. This was the Dallas Citizens Council, launched in 1937 and composed of about 250 high-ranking businessmen and industrialists with the singular purpose to "improve Dallas."

A 1964 *New York Times* story aptly titled, "Group of Businessmen Rules Dallas Without a Mandate From the Voters," tells us education became a major point of interest to the Dallas Citizens Council, namely the issue of integration. On April 6, 1961, a federal court ruled that Dallas' public school system must desegregate. "When the Dallas school board reported in the late 1950's that all legal steps to keep the system segregated had failed, the Citizens Council set to work," *The Times* wrote.[29]

Their solution was to produce a short film about non-violent desegregation, *Dallas at the Crossroads*, hosted by CBS news anchor Walter Cronkite. The film was widely exhibited and viewed throughout the South over the summer of 1961. What's striking about the film is the notable absence of any blacks: the film's target audience obviously were whites. While the film's theme is to promote desegregation, *Dallas at the Crossroads* appears to have no interest in the black community at all, and integration is a "problem" to be overcome – with a very intentional message to its white audience: avoid violence when integration begins in schools that fall. However, the resultant peaceful integration process in Dallas received nationwide recognition and praise from the White House.

"The political hooliganism that preceded the assassination of President Kennedy is foreign to the Dallas Citizens Council. Before the assassination, business leaders resented the fact that the action of a few persons, with no standing in the city, should be taken as representative of Dallas. To offset this, the Citizens Council had agreed to cosponsor the luncheon for President Kennedy on Nov. 22," the *Times* reported.

---

28   Matthew Dallek, *Birchers: How the John Birch Society Radicalized the American Right* (New York: Basic Books, 2022), 107.

29   "Group of Businessmen Rules Dallas Without a Mandate From the Voters," *New York Times*, 19 January 1964.

Another aspect of Dallas in the early 1960s was its reputation as a safe haven. For instance, the former prime minister of Hungary, Ferenc Nagy, cultivated a public image in the U.S. as a lecturer, speaking about the situation in Hungary, the refugees and displaced peoples flung out of that country, and the overall theme of repelling a Soviet communism intent on routing Judeo-Christian religion from the earth. Once settled in Dallas after a stint on a farm in Falls Church, Virginia, Nagy almost certainly would have interacted, or at the very least had been aware of, the Hungarian Cistercian monks at the University of Dallas in nearby Irving. The conservative Catholic university – the only one of its kind in Texas – was the pet project of Dallas bishop Thomas Gorman. From 1960-1962, its second president was a layman from New Jersey, Dr. Robert Morris, at one time General Walker's attorney. Morris proved to be a fish out of water during his time in Texas – later unsuccessfully opening his own school, the short-lived University of Plano, which succumbed to the status of an unaccredited diploma mill[30] – and made the Diocese of Dallas and the trustees of the University of Dallas nervous with his outspoken views. Morris made a name for himself as chief counsel of the Senate Judiciary Committee in the 1950s, a subcommittee that hunted Communists. In Dallas, Morris joined Gen. Edwin Walker and H.L. Hunt in the John Birch Society. The concentration of the infamous "Wanted for Treason" flyers attacking JFK on his arrival into Dallas was to students at the University of Dallas. "In his testimony before the Warren Commission, [Jack] Ruby directly alluded to the largely anti-Semitic John Birch Society and its most militant member, General Walker, as the powerful force that had used him because he was a Jew."[31] This is strong language and suggests certain Dallas forces that may have hung over Ruby the weekend he killed Lee Oswald. For now, whatever was going through Jack Ruby's mind when he shot Oswald in the basement of Dallas Police headquarters – fear of an antisemitic conspiracy, of more murders ahead – perhaps he moved to silence Oswald in order to *protect* Oswald from whatever these forces were that controlled him.

As stated earlier, Ruby did not materialize out of thin air. His past life would have made him known to the Banister/Ferrie anti-Communist-arms dealers in New Orleans. Indeed, Ruby himself was a gun smuggler. His path in this regard echoed the black op and paramilitary missions once undertaken by Ferrie. Based on testimony by FBI informant

30   "Plano accused of mail degrees," *The Paris News*, 28 June 1976.
31   Caufield, 523..

Blaney Mack Johnson, in the early 1950s Ruby and close collaborator Eddie Browder arranged illegal arms exports out of Miami to Castro forces. Both Browder and Ruby utilized the Florida Keys, where Ruby owned a cottage in Islamorada. Ruby and Browder contracted smuggler Joe Marrs's Marrs Aircraft to transport arms to Carlos Prio Soccaras, the deposed Cuban president.[32] This connection ties Ruby to a group with links to soldier of fortune and adventurer Frank Fiorini, alias Frank Sturgis, one of the future Watergate "plumbers."[33]

* * *

JFK was thus everything those who ran Dallas were not: progressive, liberal, Ivy League, Boston, Irish, Catholic. A carpetbagger. He didn't win any of them over when he let it be known in his only inaugural address that "the torch has been passed to a new generation of Americans – born in this century, tempered by war, disciplined by a hard and bitter peace, proud of our ancient heritage – and unwilling to witness or permit the slow undoing of those human rights to which this nation has always been committed." As his successful campaign showed, Kennedy made concerted efforts to connect with the black voter of 1960: "promises of federal action on education and housing, pocketbook issues, and most strikingly, Africa."[34] To those in the South, the old ways – the way things have always been done – were gone. Integration was inevitable, and the youngest elected president in the nation's history, an Irish Catholic no less, would see to it.

This was the lurking atmosphere when President and Mrs. Kennedy landed at Love Field on November 22, 1963.

32   See Lisa Pease, "Gunrunner Ruby and the CIA," *Probe*, July-August 1995 (Vol 2., No. 5).
33   Interestingly, Sturgis started his own church out of his Miami home, the Independent Church of God, Inc., in 1970, and a fictional non-profit, the Help the Homeless Fund, which received tax exempt status three days befo.re Sturgis was arrested at the Watergate Hotel. The total contributions to the church for FY 1972 was $201.00, according to a 1974 letter from Janet Sturgis to the IRS. See HSCA, "Sturgis Deposition," 183-185; NARA Record Number: 180-10088-10086.
34   James H. Meriwether, "Worth a Lot of Negro Votes': Black Voters, Africa, and the 1960 Presidential Campaign," *Journal of American History*, December 2008, 737.

CHAPTER THIRTEEN

THE DEVIL MADE THEM DO IT?

And in his place shall arise a vile person,
to whom they will not give the honor of royalty;
but he shall come in peaceably,
and seize the kingdom by intrigue
— Daniel 11:21

The postwar period saw an influx of Americans settle in Mexico, particularly its capital city and the southern tropical resort town of Cuernavaca. These people of wealth and influence were the opposite of expatriates – mostly from Southern states, namely Texas, they were committed to their vision of the United States and were dedicated to helping that vision however they could. Samuel Montague, a career public relations advance man from New Orleans, was one of those who resided in an American neighborhood in Mexico. To counter apparent anti-Americanism in Mexico – "Cuba si, Yanqui no" and other variations of the "imperial Yankee" theme – Montague formed the Comite Norteamericano Pro Mexico in 1954. Nicknamed Operation Amigos, Montague asserted it was geared as an organization of only civilians – no government agencies. In fact, Operation Amigos was a propaganda initiative called for by the Private Enterprise Corporation.

The treasurer of Operation Amigos was sometime emcee for the Eloy Alfaro Award, Marcos A. Kohly. Among the contributing companies to Operation Amigos in 1956 was Eastern Air, Gillette, *Time Life*, Coca Cola Export, Sydney Ross Co., and DuPont.[1] On two occasions Operation Amigos presented parchment scrolls honoring two of Dallas's favorite sons: in 1957 to Stanley Marcus, of Neiman-Marcus, "for his outstanding work in recent years to promote better relations between the people of Mexico and the people of Texas;" two years earlier, to Ted Dealey, *Dallas Morning News* publisher. In 1961, Leo M. Roy became president of Operations Amigos, whose day job was running the Mexico department of Pan-American Life Insurance, the New Or-

---

1   *In Mexico it's the custom, Senor!*, 1964, 70.

leans insurance company which was the mortgage holder for the International Trade Mart.

This exercise in public relations and propaganda were framed by the ever-present specter of Communist advance. An Operation Amigos letter inserted into the Congressional Record in August 1961 supports this:

> [W]e ask you not to let the Communists hoodwink you. The next time you see a headline shrieking 'Anti-American Riot in Mexico,' read the full story. It will probably say that only a few individuals were involved, and that they were led by known agitators, that no Americans were molested, that the government stepped in and broke it up. Such a "riot" definitely does not represent "anti-American" feeling on the part of the people themselves. We who live here may not even hear about it until we read about it in our hometown papers from the States. Visit Mexico. See for yourselves what the wonderful country has to offer. Let's all help keep Mexico where it belongs, one of the free and democratic nations of the world.[2]

The same letter was printed in dozens of American newspapers at the same time.

"Dr." Bruce Vickers, yet another acolyte of Earl Anglin James, was one of these "American businessmen," supporting promotional campaigns of his compatriots to attract American tourism and work to Mexico.[3] A longtime resident of Mexico during the Good Neighbor Policy era, Vickers was an adviser to the mayor of Cuernavaca, executive president of its Citizens' Committee, and in 1968 assumed the enviable role of president of the National Association of Committees of Sister Cities. This portrait of a responsible American, dedicating himself to fostering peace and understanding among diverse peoples, however, is another instance of Earl James's network of fraudsters and phonies.

The FBI noted Vickers's duplicitous character: "VICKERS, although ostensibly a leading member of the American community in Cuernavaca, is a highly questionable character, having passed himself as a medical doctor, Ambassador of Togoland and as 'Sir' Bruce Vickers."[4] Little wonder Earl Anglin James, who supplied Vickers with these fake titles and degrees, called Vickers his "aide-de-camp."

2   "Anti-American Feelings and Trend Toward Communism in Mexico," Senate Congressional Record, 18 August 1961, 16349.
3   Congressional Record, U.S. Senate, 1 September 1961, p. 1961.
4   NARA Record Number: 124-10208-10137; FBI file #92-3171-2080. 25 August 1967.

Vickers was born Boris Viktorov in Riga, Latvia on May 19, 1908. In 1931 he married Boston resident Lillian Sussmann and petitioned for naturalization in October 1932, thereby renouncing the USSR. When the couple became engaged, Lillian was a secretary to Clark University president Wallace W. Atwood. His son, Dr. Rollin S. Atwood, worked in the State Department's Bureau of Inter-American Affairs and later chief of special operations at the In-

Boris Victorov, aka Bruce Vickers, aide-de-camp to Earl Anglin James and "highly questionable character" according to the FBI

ter-American Development Bank. Before this, he was the first director of the Institute of Inter-American Affairs at the University of Florida, preceding A. Curtis Wilgus. Victorov's later connection with inter-American affairs likely stemmed from the Atwoods.

Victorov became a second lieutenant in the Reserve Corps, living in Queens. At about this time Boris Victorov of Russia becomes Bruce Vickers of the USA. During World War II, Vickers was a lobbyist, a foreign agent for Mexico during the Lend-Lease program, representing Gen. J. Salvador S. Sanchez, chief of staff to Mexico's then-president, Gen. Manuel Alvaro Camacho. Vickers was a member of the U.S.-Mexico Defense Commission.

Vickers developed a reputation of being "an American high up in Communist circles,"[5] a probable confidant to the avowed Marxist Vicente Lombardo Toledano,[6] and having a "questionable character."[7] Vickers was the Mexico representative for a newly created private firm out of the conservative American Federation of Labor, the Inter-American Construction Corporation (IACC). Ostensibly formed to assist Juan Peron's dictatorship in Argentina with its five-year plan, Peron paid the envoy $1.1 million for "engineering services."[8] IACC was not above using paramili-

---

5   NARA Record Number: 124-10208-10126.

6   Ibid.

7   NARA Record Number: 124-10208-10137.

8   "Argentine Job Nets Profit for U.S. Firm," *Birmingham Post Herald*, 5 September 1950.

tary brigades to shut up Argentine unions and labor organizers, such as shooting workers in the head for arguing about wages.

Dubbed the City of Eternal Spring, the history of Cuernavaca, this odd, fascinating place under the volcano of Popocatepetl is rife with subversive and suspicious activity. Bruce Vickers was a resident – one of its chief residents, according to the FBI – of Cuernavaca's elite, palatial subdivision Rancho Tetela, an enclave of antebellum mansions owned almost exclusively by Americans – particularly Texans. The sprawling property was originally the estate of Harry E. Stewart of Dallas, owner of a highly successful farm machinery import/export business, patriarch to a respected, influential Dallas family, and member of the oldest masonic lodge in Texas, Holland Lodge No. 1. At one time, Stewart owned the Dallas Stoneleigh Hotel, until he sold it to Leo F. Corrigan in 1943; Stewart married his future ex-wife there in 1935. She was Edith Little Lewis, whom the FBI later characterized as "very astute and distrustful, and much feared by her servants."[9] In 1956, now on her fourth marriage, to Col. Louis Bunde, Edith pulled a gun on ex-husband Stewart demanding a $200,000 promissory note, then shot at him. He signed.[10] Stewart died in 1961, and Edith then assumed management of the Rancho Tetela property, where she lived with Bunde until his death in 1962. Even Bunde, from a well-to-do family of Wisconsin jewelers, could not escape the Bureau: the FBI regularly looked into Louis Bunde's activities after he visited the Soviet Embassy in Mexico City in 1956.[11]

Edith's registration at the U.S. embassy cited Dallas banker Fred Florence as a reference. A prominent member of the Dallas community, president of Temple Emanu-El, and one of the first members of the Dallas Citizens' Council, Florence headed the parent company of the Republic National Bank of Dallas, exposed in 1967 by the *Washington Post*'s Richard Harwood as a conduit for CIA funds since the late 1950s, mainly The Howard Corp, a shell company created by Florence.

Medford Evans compared the influence in Dallas of H.L. Hunt to Fred Florence in his 1968 book on the LBJ administration, *The Usurpers*:

> You're always hearing about H.L. Hunt. Mr. Hunt is a real loner. And he puts on his own kind of show. He is a subject of diverting conversation. He is incredibly rich. So is the Sheik of Kuwait. Mr. Hunt produces oil. He's got to sell it. He sells lots of it to Jersey

---

9   NARA Record Number: 124-10208-10110
10   Ibid.
11   Ibid.

Standard. Mr. Hunt is a remarkable man, but he is not Dallas, and he is not influential in Dallas, compared to, say, Fred Florence of the Republic National Bank. The Republic National and the First National of Dallas are the only two banks in the South with deposits over a billion dollars (as of June 30, 1965).[12]

According to author Russ Baker, Florence was a member of the Texas Crusade for Freedom, joining Dallas mayor Earle Cabell, D.H. Byrd, Ted Dealey, H.L. Hunt, Clint Murchison, and Bernard Gold, "owner of Nardis Sportswear, which employed both Abraham Zapruder and Mrs. George de Mohrenschildt."[13]

In 1956, Florence was appointed chairman of the "People to People" program banking committee by President Eisenhower in 1956. Similarly, Edith represented Texas Governor Beauford Jester's Good Neighbor Commission as envoy to Mexico in 1948.[14] Later that year, the commission orchestrated a ten-day visit throughout Texas of "Mexican debutants," which included the daughters of the British and Chinese ambassadors to Mexico. Edith oversaw the "get acquainted" tour, which included tea with University of Texas with Austin sorority girls and a weekend in Dallas. There they were "entertained" by Mr. and Mrs. D.H. Byrd. In Fort Worth, their hosts were Mr. and Mrs. Neville Penrose. Travel accommodations were "private planes owned by Byrd, Bentsen Brothers of McAllen, Renoir Oil Company, Clint Murchison of Dallas and Pete Coffield of Rockdale."[15]

The Good Neighbor Commission of Texas was established by Governor Coke Stevenson in 1943 with its principal aim to tackle discrimination and improve labor relations for Mexicans living and working in Texas. Its origins come from Nelson Rockefeller's Inter-American Affairs. And it followed a formulaic script, justifying its existence with typical, over-the-top imagery: "The world's woods are on fire, the fires spread, they may reach our shore, we would prepare by uniting all Americas to fight the flames."[16] It was an ambitious mandate for one state to foster relations with an entire country. Ostensibly to support the working class, it

---

12   Medford Evans, *The Usurpers* (Boston: Western Islands, 1968), 249.

13   Russ Baker, *Family of Secrets* (New York: Bloomsbury Press, 2008), n18, Ch. 5.

14   "Good Neighbor Group Appoints Mexico Envoy," *Corpus Christi Caller-Times*, 26 June 1948.

15   "Mexican Girl Emissaries Reach Austin," *Fort Worth Star Telegram*, 4 November 1948.

16   Hubert C. Herring, *Good Neighbors; Argentina, Brazil, Chile and Seventeen Other Countries* (New Haven: Yale University Press, 1942), 327; cited in Nellie Ward Kingrea, *History of the First Ten Years of the Texas Good Neighbor Commission*, and discussion of its major problems (Fort Worth: TCU Press, 1954), 6.

relied on PR pieces like the goodwill tour of the nubile socialites to en-
hance its image. Clearly the "who's who" of Texas elite were tapped to
lend their resources, revealing the two faces of the Good Neighbor Commission: the public face, to help the Mexicans – and Latin Americans in
general – in Texas; and the hidden, private citizens with personal interests
in Mexico. Consider the names:

- Oil magnate Neville Penrose, future chairman of the Good
Neighbor commission and father-in-law of CBS correspondent
Bob Schieffer. Also owned property in Cuernavaca;

- H.H. (Pete) Coffield, wealthy oil magnate with ties to Lyndon
Johnson and deeply involved in the Texas prison system;

- Lloyd Bentsen, Sr., then a senior colonel in the Texas State Guard
Reserve Corps, and father of future senator Lloyd Bentsen, Jr.;

- D.H. Byrd, owner of the building later known as the Texas
School Book Depository in addition to his petroleum interests and
other investments.

- Clint W. Murchison, whose oil interests stretched from Franco's
Spain to Haiti and whose wealth extended to owning a private island off the Gulf of Mexico in Veracruz.[17] He also employed George
de Mohrenschildt at Three States Oil and Gas company.

These same influential and powerful individuals also comprised the
infamous Suite 8F Group, in reference to a suite in Houston's Lamar Hotel where those who defined Texas politics and business hammered out
deals and other ventures. In sum, the Good Neighbor Commission, with
the blessing of the governor and the help of the Office of Inter-American
Affairs, operated as a de facto government-within-a-government, another example of the duplicitous nature of local government in Texas: there
were those duly elected to serve the people, and there were those who
really ran things behind the scenes.

Many of these fellows were also directors on the board of Nafco Oil
and Gas and close to its president, John Alston Crichton. Crichton is
at the nexus of Texas oil interests home and abroad, particularly Cuba,
Spain, and the Middle East. In his quest to extract oil from Cuba during
Fulgencio Batista's dictatorship, Crichton became friendly with George
de Mohrenschildt. Born in Louisiana in 1916, Crichton worked in the
OSS during the war, and in 1956 became commander of a Dallas-based

---

17   Ernestine Orrick Van Buren, *Clint: Clinton Williams Murchison: A Biography* (Fort Worth:
Eakin Press, 1986), 184.

Army Reserve unit, the 488th Military Intelligence Detachment. Many Dallas PD officers were in this unit, a kind of homegrown stay-behind army. Dorchester Gas Producing was another Crichton company; D.H. Byrd was a director there. Fabian Escalante has indicated Dick Nixon, when overseeing Operation 40, asked two Texas oilmen to fund the squad of saboteurs-assassins: "Jack" Crichton and George H.W. Bush. When the Secret Service wanted to question Marina Oswald about her husband, it was Crichton who arranged for a Russian interpreter. Lastly, Crichton was recognized as an Elder at Preston Hollow Presbyterian Church.

D.H. Byrd was another immensely wealthy oil figure teasingly nick-named "Dry Hole" Byrd for his early follies in the business, namely, drilling fifty-six dry holes in the 1920s. Still, the money flowed from Byrd Oil Corp. Of course, Byrd factors in every JFK assassination narrative: he was

the owner of the actual red brick building at 411 Elm St. where the Texas School Book Depository leased space. It should be clarified that the Texas School Book Depository company did not own the building proper – Byrd did – although it became commonplace

A glimpse into the sloppy workings of the Texas School Book Depository

to refer to the building as "the Texas School Book Depository." And, this is where 24-year-old Lee Oswald, allegedly armed with a 1940s-era bolt action rifle and with uncanny poise and precision, fired off three shots from a six floor window in just a few seconds, killing the president and wounding Governor John Conally. Byrd, however, missed all of this: he was hunting in South Africa on a rare trip outside North America. Byrd owned the building since 1936. The Texas School Book Depository company only moved into that building months before the assassination – from the first floor of the Dal-Tex Building just across the street at 501 Elm.

An additional element that concerned the Texas Good Neighbor Commission was education. What exactly did the Texas School Book Depository company do? Until his death in 1927, the proprietor of the Texas School Book Depository was Hugh Perry. By the time he relocated his retail book business, the Hugh Perry Book Depository, from Sherman in northern Texas to Dallas in 1903, the company was becoming the premier seller and distributor of school textbooks, with 800 depositories scattered around the state.[18] Indeed, "The books which [Perry] handles have been officially adopted by the state of Texas for use in the public schools."[19] In the 1940s, the Good Neighbor Commission, in tandem with the State Department of Education and a grant from Rockefeller's office weighed in on recommendations to change text books in order "to be used in teaching Latin American children and in influencing Anglo-American children to have a greater appreciation of Mexican culture."[20] The commission tentatively approached the topic of segregation as something to amend then, but ultimately kicked the issue down the road.

Once the Warren Report's conclusion that Lee Oswald killed the president from the southeast window on the sixth floor of the Texas School Book Depository, D.H. Byrd had the window removed from "that window," and had it installed at his home, like some kind of trophy. It stayed there until his death in 1986, when his son returned it. The fifth and sixth floors of the building are now a museum commemorating the assassination. Another "trophy" was Byrd's friend H.L. Hunt procuring a first edition copy of Abraham Zapruder's 8mm searing, snuff-like home movie that captured the fatal shot to JFK's head within 72 hours of the killing. Byrd and Hunt – two major Texas oilmen, both with prized, if morbid, relics of the assassination.

* * *

Let us return to Edith Stewart. It would seem natural that after the death of her husband Louis Bunde in 1962 widow Edith might connect with someone like Bruce Vickers, who shared a similar background in Mexican-American affairs, community outreach, hospitality, and tourism. And that is exactly what happened, according to the FBI legat in Mexico City. With "more money than she can count from profits in oil and real estate," Edith married Vickers sometime in the mid-1960s.[21] Vickers died in Houston in 1973 and is buried in Flushing, NY.[22] Edith finally died in Mexico in 1977.[23]

The problem is that both of their death certificates make no mention of the other: Edith's spouse is listed as the late Louis Rudolph Bunde; for

---

18   *Austin American-Statesman*, 18 December 1908.
19   L.B. Hill, ed., *A History of Greater Dallas and Vicinity, Vol. II* (Chicago: Lewis Publishing Co., 1909), 324.
20   Kingrea, 45.
21   *Racine Journal-Times*, 15 November 1954. See obituary for Edith's father, W.F. Little (d. 1968). *Charlotte Observer*, 27 April 1968.
22   Bruce Vickers death certificate.
23   Edith Bunde death certificate.

Vickers, his longtime wife, Lillian Sussmann. Did the FBI get their reputed marriage wrong? Or was Vickers living a double life in Mexico? An example of Vickers's squirrely nature is the case of Norma van Etten. Van Etten, an American who lived in Mexico City, died in June 1962. Norma's nephew, Richard E. Allen of Miami, was notified of her death in a letter from Vikers three weeks after she died. Allen later learned that his aunt was buried the same day she died. Allen was especially suspicious about Vickers when he discovered Norma changed her will a week before her death, naming Dr. Bruce Vickers the beneficiary. Allen wrote a letter to the State Department asking for more information on the nature of his aunt's death and the reason for her hasty burial.[24] It is not known if he ever received an answer.

According to the Bureau's files, Edith and Bruce Vickers were the proprietors of Cuernavaca's Rancho Tetela by 1967. There, in a plush, walled residence nicknamed "San Cristobal," Chicago mobster Sam Giancana lived out a good portion of his Mexican seclusion period. In 1966, to avoid testifying before a grand jury, Giancana fled Chicago. It was an open secret among Rancho Tetela residents that Giancana, alias Richard Sczaletti, alias Sam De Palma, made his home there, although Edith and Bruce denied knowing the identity of the occupant. Giancana's stay in Rancho Tetela kept the FBI at bay for nearly a decade. It also enabled Giancana to do business beyond his Chicago interests. Like Trafficante, Giancana was interested in mining the lucrative black market possibilities of Central America. Whether Bruce Vickers and Edith Stewart Bunde deliberately obfuscated federal investigations on Giancana is unconfirmed.

During Lee Oswald's trip to Mexico two months before the assassination, he visited Cuernavaca. He met Honduran Luis Fernandez Gonzalez, a member of the Movimento de Liberacion Nacional (the National Liberation Movement) in front of the Hotel Reforma on September 28. He introduced himself to Gonzalez as "John White."[25] The next day, Fernandez joined "John White" and Saul Lopez, press chief of the National Liberation Movement in Mexico, on a trip to Cuernavaca, spending the day at the Casino de la Selva, a resort from a bygone era that used to entertain the likes of Al Capone and Bugsy Siegel before the hotel's casino was shut down. In the 1960s, however, it was mainly known as the leading

---

24   Department of State, Memorandum of Conversation, "Death of Mrs. Norma Van Etten," 11 July 1962. In 1964 the US Court of Appeals for the Third Circuit heard *United States of America v. Bankers National Life Insurance Company, Norma F. Van Etten, Lillian Vickers and Bruce Vickers, Also Known As Boris Victorov, bankers National Life Insurance Company, Appellant, 333 F.2d* 145.
25   CE 2121.

nightclub in Cuernavaca. The FBI noted that Sam Giancana frequented it when he lived at nearby Rancho Tetela.

The sheer number of elite and successful Texan businessmen and socialite women shuttling back and forth to Dallas from Cuernavaca has gone totally unexplored. While Sam Giancana is a favorite suspect in the Mafia conspiracy theory in the JFK assassination, his presence in Rancho Tetela speaks volumes about the veil of secrecy that surrounded that enclave, its compounds de facto safe houses for those who could afford them.[26]

A resident of both the U.S. and Cuernavaca, according to the Warren Report, was the mysterious Alexander Albert Osborne, an elderly man who sat next to Lee Oswald on the Flecha Roja Bus into Mexico at the end of September 1963.[27] There was a great amount of speculation in the Warren Commission exhibits over Osborne's identity. The name on the tourist card Osborne used to board the bus was not "Albert Osborne" but "John Howard Bowen," born in England in the 1880s. Osborne, under the alias Bowen, reportedly made his living as an itinerant missionary, primarily in remote parts of Oaxaca with the indigenous Mixteca people. In 1929, he founded a group for boys in Knoxville, Tennessee called Campfire Council, to curb juvenile delinquency. He stepped down from running Campfire Council in 1943.[28] Only later was it made known he resigned over allegations of sexual advances he made on Campfire Council boys.[29]

Bowen/Osborne then moved to Dallas to reportedly work for the United Service Organizations.[30] The work took him abroad, primarily to the Caribbean.[31] Yet, within three years, Bowen was now the highly respected "Brother Bowen" of the National Baptist Church, having sold all his possessions – a 1941 Buick among them – and preaching the Gospel of Jesus in remote Mexican villages.[32] In short, trying to sort out the truth on Albert Osborne/John H. Bowen leaves us with a tangled mess. [33]A Baptist minister familiar with this character, Rev. James Timmons, told the FBI that "to his knowledge [Osborne] had not attended any ministerial school."[34] Another Baptist pastor, Fred Allen Jr., remarked when

---

26   See Virginia Snow, "The Mexican Parade," *Austin American,* 30 January 1955.

27   CE 2195.

28   "Campfire Council Loses J.H. Bowen," *Knoxville Journal,* 14 April 1943. The article quotes Bowen as 62 years old.

29   Jim Balloch, "JFK: Oswald trail led to ex-Knox man," *Knoxville News-Sentinel,* 28 November 1993.

30   "J.H. Bowen in USO Post in Dallas, Tex," *Knoxville News-Sentinel,* 23 April 1943.

31   *Knoxville News-Sentinel,* 29 August 1943.

32   L.P. Ramsey, "Baptist Work in Mexico," *Baptist and Reflector,* 16 May 1946.

33   For a thorough look see John Kowalski, "The Dual Life of Albert Osborne, 21 July 2017, https://www.kennedysandking.com/john-f-kennedy-articles/the-dual-life-of-albert-osborne.

34   CE 2195

Osborne spoke at his church in September 1962, "[Osborne] felt it was a very dangerous thing for the United States to have a Catholic as president."[35] During and after the assassination, Osborne happened to be on a speaking tour in Europe.[36]

Mr. Bowen

Again and again a religious persona appears to maneuver the mechanics of the plot. Given what we have encountered in our exploration of wandering bishops and ministers, we can be fairly certain Alexander Albert Osborne's humble vocation as a missionary in the vineyard of the Lord – with a curious amount of press coverage to boot – was mere cover for more clandestine duties. When Osborne died in 1966 he was staying at a small mission in San Antonio run by a Baptist pastor, Lyman Erickson. In 1993, Erickson told *Knoxville News Sentinel* journalist Jim Balloch, "[Osborne's] words to me were, 'I traveled to Mexico with Lee Harvey Oswald,

Alexander Albert Osborne, twenty years before he sat next to Lee Oswald, or someone impersonating him, on the overnight bus ride into Mexico.

and I was called in and questioned about it.' Not, 'I just happened to sit next to Oswald,' but 'I traveled *with* Oswald.'"[37]

---

35   Balloch, "JFK: Oswald trail led to ex-Knox man," *Knoxville News-Sentinel*, 28 November 1993.

36   "Bowen Leaves for Overseas," *Knoxville Journal*, 14 November 14 1963.

37   Rachel Ohm, "Was mystery caller in JFK files 'missionary' from Knoxville area?" *Knoxville News-Sentinel*, 29 October 2017. Emphasis mine.

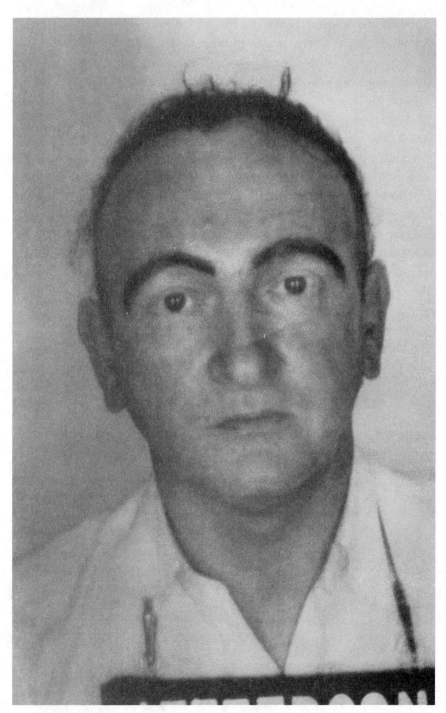

David Ferrie Mugshot

CHAPTER FOURTEEN

FALLING INTO A TRANCE

Now as he was speaking with me,
I was in a deep sleep on my face toward the ground:
but he touched me, and set me upright.

– Daniel 8:18

In a Dec. 1963 FBI report, David Ferrie mentioned how prominent the phony diploma mill business was within his circle. But he also went even further, suggesting the nation's foremost expert on hypnosis, Dr. Harold Rosen from Johns Hopkins University, might be able to determine if someone like a Lee Harvey Oswald was under hypnosis when the president was killed – a kind of "Manchurian Candidate" scenario played out in real time.[1] Ferrie's remark cannot be dismissed out of hand as the rantings of a madman. And, it should be noted, Jack Martin "told the FBI three days after the assassination 'that he believed Ferrie was an 'amateur hypnotist' who may have been capable of hypnotizing Oswald.'"[2]

In Earl Anglin James's acceptance speech of the Eloy Alfaro Grand Cross of Panama, this archbishop of the Old Catholic Church references not the Triune God of Christianity – Father, Son, Holy Spirit – but, rather, "the Great Spirit." This is a clue into James's lingering connection with Spiritualism, twenty years after he was preaching at the Metaphysical Spiritualist Church with Harry Gaunt. In fact, in none of the extant documentation this author could find does James mention anything about the theology or practices or dogmas of the Old Catholics – including their somewhat improbable hybrid of Eastern Orthodoxy and Roman Catholicism. Indeed, he admitted in the 60s, "I really haven't done anything for my church since 1945."[3] Spiritualism, however, hinges on the very things that have occupied James and his bishop brethren. And it is more Spiritualism than Christian Orthodoxy or Catholicism with which James identified. Matthew Wills, writing on famed Russian mystic H.P. "Madame"

1   See "Re Dallas tel to New Orleans, 12/9/63, 3:17 PM, CST (18-02.pdf (hood.edu)).
2   Russell, 672.
3   McRae, "Garrison Probe."

Blavatsky, summarizes her contribution to Spiritualism this way, echoing James's own interest: "Blavatsky gave occultism an Eastward orientation and helped turn Europeans and Americans towards Eastern religion."[4]

The National Spiritualist Association of Spiritualism defines Spiritualism as: "The science, philosophy, and religion of continuous life, based upon the demonstrated fact of communication, by means of mediumship, with those who live in the Spirit World."[5] This concept in Spiritualism stands on the work of Franz Mesmer (1734-1815), whose work on animal magnetism led to the term "mesmerism." In *Modern American Spiritualism*, Emma Hardinge writes, "In nearly every city, town, or hamlet, the itinerant mesmerizer made his rounds, operating upon chance subjects as opportunity offered, and alternately exciting In superstitious terror or wrathful antagonism by the exercise of his seem-

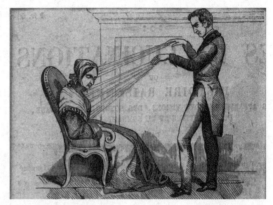

ingly magical powers."[6] In New Hampshire in 1860, for example, a spiritualist and mesmerizer, Henry Farmer of New York, came to visit his sick second cousin. He said the spirit of his mother sent him to help the woman, Betsey Farmer, write up a will. Farmer then proceeded to induce Betsey into a trance and produce the will; Betsey died a few days later. She left $5,000 to the Baptist Church, although she hadn't been to church in fifteen years.[7]

In 1951, a 32-year-old former Danish Nazi named Palle Hardrup held up a Copenhagen bank and shot and killed two tellers. On arrest, Hardrup claimed no knowledge of what he had done. After three years, the truth emerged from the work by Dr. Paul J. Reiter, when Reiter administered Hardrup a truth serum under hypnosis. Reiter later detailed the account in his book, *Antisocial or Criminal Acts and Hypnosis, A Case Study*. Hardrup then wrote a confession implicating Bjorn Nielsen, 40, who was able to put Hardrup in a hypnotic state by having the letter X act as the trigger

---

4   Matthew Wills, "Spiritualism, Science, and the Mysterious Madame Blavatsky," *Jstor Daily*, 25 October 2016.

5   Rev. Ronald Koch, *Introduction to Modern Spiritualism*, Church of Spiritual Illumination, 2006, 4.

6   Emma Hardinge, *Modern American Spiritualism*, 1870, 22.

7   "A Funny Old Maid," *Buffalo Courier*, 9 February 1860.

point. From here, he could then command Hardrup to do anything Niel-sen wished – including murder and armed robbery. Reiter diagnosed Har-drup's condition at the time of the killings as the personality of a paranoid schizophrenic. Bjorn Nielsen was sentenced to life in prison.[8]

Spiritualism, mesmerism, occultish rituals – these were woven into the early fabric of Puritan America as far back as the seventeenth century. The very foundation of what became the United States was built as a refuge for religious outcasts; the wandering bishops are just a few of the eclectic pilgrims in this North American Canterbury tale.

In the beginning, before MK-ULTRA or its two predecessors, Arti-choke and Bluebird, there was Allen Dulles. The son of a Presbyterian minister, Phi Betta Kappa honor society member at Princeton, senior law partner at Sullivan & Cromwell, and director of the Council on Foreign Relations, he was the younger brother of John Foster Dulles, Secretary of State in the Eisenhower Administration. As CIA deputy director of plans, Allen Dulles wasted no time in diving into the Agency's mind control projects. In his book *Poisoner in Chief: Sidney Gottlieb and the CIA Search for Mind Control*, Stephen Kinzer writes, "[Dulles] saw [mind control projects] as an indispensable part of the secret war against Communism that he was charged with waging."[9] Dulles had a very basic question for Operation Bluebird's senior officers, Frank Wisner and Richard Helms: "Can a person under hypnosis be forced to commit murder?"[10] Dulles was certainly aware of the unethical, or at least illegal, nature of testing subjects on U.S. soil, so places like West Germany and Japan became two popular locations for the CIA to unlawfully detain, interrogate, and im-prison people. In Japan, for instance, "Bluebird interrogation teams inject-ed captured North Korean soldiers with drugs including sodium amytal, a depressant that can have hypnotic effects."[11]

Bluebird expanded into Artichoke once Dulles hired Dr. Sidney Got-tlieb, the 32-year-old, square dance-loving biochemist. Gottlieb hop-scotched from one agency to another before landing at CIA: the Depart-ment of Agriculture, the FDA, and the National Research Council. Ira L. Baldwin, Gottlieb's mentor in bacteriology and its department chair at the University of Wisconsin, recommended Gottlieb to Dulles. During World War II, Baldwin ran the secret germ warfare operations at Camp (now Fort) Detrick in Maryland.

---

8   "Hypnotist Gets Life Term in Murders," *The Province*, 17 July 1954. See also "Conspiracy Proof Ignored, Book Says," *Atlanta Constitution*, 30 Oct. 1970.
9   Stephen Kinzer, *Poisoner in Chief* (New York: Henry Holt and Co., 2019), 39.
10   Ibid., 40.
11   Ibid., 44.

Operations Bluebird and Artichoke fed off the rampant paranoia that a Communist invasion on American soil was imminent. And if not a physical invasion akin to the opening scene of *Red Dawn*, then a psychological, or psychic invasion – brainwashing. Richard Helms later said, "We felt that it was our responsibility not to lag behind the Russians or the Chinese in this field, and the only way to find out what the risks were was to test things such as LSD and other drugs that could be used to control human behavior."[12] A case frequently cited as an example is the 1949 imprisonment of Catholic archbishop Jozef Cardinal Mindszentsky of Hungary, then a Soviet satellite state. According to *The Tablet*, the cardinal was arrested on no actual charges, but purportedly confessed to the crime of "high treason" once secret police administered the priest with a "will-destroying drug." When he was put in the dock at a show trial, "Mindszenty appeared as if he were drugged and was reciting rehearsed lines."[13] What most concerned CIA was what kind of drug was used (alcheton, the generic brand of Benzedrine).

MK-ULTRA took drug experimentation on witting and unwitting pa-tients to new extremes; LSD the drug of choice for Sidney Gottlieb and his interrogators. The story of Frank Olson is one of the most compel-ling to come out of these tests. Olson, who had a PhD in bacteriology from the University of Wisconsin (whose thesis advisor was Army-hired biological warfare expert Ira Baldwin[14]), was a captain in the U.S. Army Chemical Corps during World War II, a biological warfare scientist, and a committee member on Project Artichoke. Olson rubbed elbows with fellow biological warfare scientists and ex-Nazis brought to the U.S. via Operation Paperclip. By 1953, Olson led the Special Operations Division at Fort Detrick when he went on a retreat with others from the division to a remote, forested CIA retreat center, Deep Creek Lake. It was the week before Thanksgiving, 1953.

The LSD trip irrevocably changed Olson. "I've made a terrible mis-take," he cryptically told his family when he returned. Of the only two dozen men who knew of the existence of the recently launched MK-UL-TRA, nine were at Deep Creek Lake that weekend.[15] Olson was one of them. After nearly a week, Olson was still disoriented, not his usual self. He needed a doctor, one who knew about MK-ULTRA. There was only one, Dr. Harold Abramson, who had also been conducting his own LSD

---

12   Ibid., 54

13   H.P. Albarelli, *A Terrible Mistake* (Walterville, OR: TrineDay, 2009), digital version, 396.

14   See Jeanne McDermott, *The Killing Winds: The Menace of Biological Warfare* (Berkeley: Arbor House, 1987), 140.

15   Kinzer, 115.

experiments. Olson had met Abramson once before, at a Manhattan hotel meeting attended by a Federal Bureau of Narcotics (FBN) agent, George Hunter White, and CIA contract agent Jean Pierre Lafitte. White, an aggressive supporter of interrogation, came out of Camp X, the Canadian "school of murder and mayhem," as White dubbed it, North America's first paramilitary training camp. Among its courses were the art of guerilla warfare and introduction to assassination. Among White's trainees were future members of the CIA's upper echelon: Angleton, Helms, Wisner.

A body fell from room 1018A of the Statler Hilton Hotel shortly before 2:30AM on the morning of Saturday, November 28, 1953. It was Frank Olson, nine days after his unwitting consumption of LSD mixed in a drink of Conteur. Did he jump on his own accord or was he pushed? He had been in the company of CIA men to see Dr. Abramson, missing Thanksgiving dinner with his family. Allegedly involved in the defenestration of Olson was Jean Pierre Lafitte, the contract agent Olson met months earlier.

Why, then, is it so far-fetched to consider the use of hypnosis and other forms of mind control by our lowly wandering bishops if the apparatus of "national security," "for the good of the country," and "fighting godless communism" was entirely unethical, let alone illegal? With the utmost secrecy around Bluebird, Artichoke, MK-ULTRA, and its successors like Operation Midnight Climax – wherein prostitutes seduced men for information with their bedroom antics being watched and recorded – and the astonishing amoral lengths those projects were carried out, it is no surprise covert intelligence, under the auspices of those same phrases like "national security," has dominated the messaging from the executive branch since Lyndon Johnson assumed presidential duties on November 22, 1963. JFK, LBJ, and Dick Nixon all were forced out of office in some fashion: JFK by assassin bullets; LBJ, pressured by the unpopular Vietnam War, stepped down after only one full term; Nixon, by resignation, leaving Warren Commission veteran Gerald Ford, the only unelected president in the country's history, to finish Nixon's term. Scandal, subterfuge, obfuscation – all for the good of the country. It took almost thirty years and six presidents before one could complete a second term (Ronald Reagan).

* * *

And so we now meet Dr. William J. Bryan, a California hypnotist who operated a hypnotherapy practice until he lost his license in 1969 for sexual misconduct with four female patients who were under hypnosis at the time. At his funeral in Hollywood in 1977, one of the pallbearers was Bryan's attorney, the famed Melvin Belli, who represented Jack Ruby at his Dallas murder trial in 1964.

In 1955, Bryan founded the American Institute of Hypnosis, Bryan's avenue to propagate his work, which included a scholarly journal. He published *Religious Aspects of Hypnosis* in 1962, the same year John Frankenheimer's film version of Richard Condon's novel *The Manchurian Candidate* was released. Bryan claimed to be a consultant on the film, though his involvement is unverified. In her article, "Manchurian Candidates: Forensic Hypnosis in the Cold War," Dr. Alison Winter of the University of Chicago posited Bryan, after his work as a military psychiatrist during World War II, joined the OSS to research memory and confession, before becoming involved in MK-ULTRA, honing what Bryan called "hypno-conditioning."[16] Bryan was certain Communist countries achieved advanced psychological warfare tactics, "far more dangerous than the atom bomb," he said.[17] Bryan specialized in legal hypnosis; he was hired by F. Lee Bailey as a consultant on the successful prosecution of Albert DiSalvo, the Boston Strangler.[18] In his book *Project Artichoke*, David M. Silvey expounds on a relationship between FBN agent George Hunter White and Bryan regarding the infamous Zodiac killings that gripped California through the 1960s and 70s. What is even more intriguing for our purposes is Bryan's purported identification with the Old Catholic Church and association with Dave Ferrie, according to researchers Duffy and Parker as cited in H.P. Albarelli's book, *A Secret Order*.[19] Whether such a connection is true, Bryan's book, *Religious Aspects of Hypnosis*, draws fascinating parallels between the act of praying to God (Great Spirit) and hypnotic trance under medical supervision. One can imagine someone like a David Ferrie gravitating to hypnosis given his vocation to the priesthood as a young man. His habitual recourse to praying the rosary throughout his life is indicative of this.[20]

Peter Evans, author of *Nemesis*, suggested William Joseph Bryan hypnotized 24-year-old Palestinian Sirhan Sirhan prior to the shooting of Robert F. Kennedy in the Ambassador Hotel kitchen on June 5, 1968.[21] Sirhan, who made mention of Franz Mesmer while in prison before his murder trial, continually insisted he could not remember the incident,

---

16   A. Killen and S. Andriopoulos, "On Brainwashing: Mind Control, Media, and Warfare," *Grey Room*, No. 45, (Fall 2011), 111.

17   Ibid., 112.

18   Ibid., 113.

19   *A Secret Order*, digital version, 691.

20   Cf. Joan Mellen, *A Farewell to Justice* (New York, Skyhorse, 2013), 112.

21   John Hiscock, "New Life in Sirhan Defense," *Los Angeles Times*, 31 January 2005.

claiming that he was hypnotized. The key defense witness at Sirhan's trial, Berkeley law and psychiatry professor Dr. Bernard L. Diamond, testified on behalf of the defense. Diamond approached the topic of hypnosis with Sirhan this way:

> "Sirhan, you know what hypnosis is?"
>
> "Isn't it domination of the weaker will by the stronger?"
>
> "No,' said Diamond, 'it isn't that at all. It's simply a way of demonstrating one's own ability to concentrate, and the hypnotist is not dominating over the will of the other. No one can be hypnotized against his own will, and the hypnotist really just gives suggestions and encouragement to a person so that he can use his own willpower to strengthen his own abilities. There's a lot of phoney baloney about hypnosis."[22]

In a somewhat inconvenient conclusion for the defense, Diamond believed Sirhan hypnotized *himself* prior to the shooting of RFK. Diamond said, "I see Sirhan as small and helpless, pitifully ill, with a demented psychotic range, out of control of his own consciousness and his own actions, subject to bizarre, disassociated trances in some of which he programmed himself to be the instrument of assassination, and then, in an almost accidentally inducted twilight state, he actually executed the crime, knowing next to nothing about what was happening."[23] With echoes of Elmer James, Sirhan Sirhan worked as a stable boy at Santa Anita Race Track with ambitions to become a jockey. In 1966, a morning horseback riding accident at Graja Vista Del Rio in Corona, California ended those dreams.

But that wasn't Sirhan's only connection with the equine industry. An overlooked figure in the Sirhan case is Reverend Jerry Owen (nee Oliver Brindley Owen), nicknamed "The Walking Bible" for his savant-like ability to quote any verse of the Bible. Like most "evangelists" documented here, Owen had his own checkered past to say the least, including a "Sex and Salvation" tour with a 16-year-old girl and morals charge from 1945 that got him kicked out of "We the People Crystal Lake Gospel Park Church" in Milwaukie, Oregon. By 1968, according to authors Turner and Christian, he was "giving free pony rides to children who promised to memorize a Bible verse and attend church on Sunday."[24] Owen was running Wild Bill's Stables in Santa Ana. He told police he randomly picked

---

22   R.B. Kaiser, *"RFK Must Die!"* (New York: E.P. Dutton, 1970), 429.
23   Ibid., 661.
24   William W. Turner and Jonn Christian, *The Assassination of Robert F. Kennedy* (New York: Random House, 1978), 8.

up a hitchhiking Sirhan Sirhan in Los Angeles the day before the California primary – and that was the extent of his interaction. During Sirhan's trial, however, witnesses testified that Owen *did* know Sirhan well before – one testified seeing Owen and Sirhan riding horses on the Santa Ana River levees weeks earlier. Later, Owen claimed to be friends with the sister of Arthur Bremer, who attempted to assassinate Democratic presidential candidate George Wallace in 1972.

In 1966, Sirhan became a member of the Rosicrucian Order, namely the Ninth Degree of the Grand Lodge, the secret society Earl Anglin James's successor of the Old Catholic Orthodox Church, Guy F. Claude Hamel, joined a year earlier in Toronto. Diamond suggested Sirhan's ability to put himself into a self-induced trance was motivated by his association with the Rosicrucians.

Recall the sign Delphine Roberts carried protesting desegregation: "It is our sacred duty to preserve *the white race of Jesus.*" For a Catholic like Roberts who's taught Jesus was a Jew born of the House of David, we have seen how it rather reflects Christian Identity and Rosicrucian thought. "Jesus was born of *Gentile* parents through whose veins flowed Aryan blood, and in whose hearts and minds had been implanted the teachings of the Essene Brotherhood, as well as the more secret teachings of the Great White Brotherhood," H. Spencer Lewis writes in the Rosicrucian book, *The Mystical Life of Jesus.*[25] It's possible Roberts was inspired by Banister, who claimed to be a past master of Graham Surghnor Lodge #383, and a member of both the Scottish Rite and Jerusalem Temple in New Orleans.[26] However, when asked by this author, the recorder for the Jerusalem Shriners did not find any record of Banister as a member.[27] In any case, the Rosicrucian Order is the chief "channel for the dissemination of the secret doctrines and teachings" of the Masters of the "Great White Brotherhood."[28] Blavatsky was able to communicate with these perfected entities, The Masters, as described in her book, *Isis Unveiled.*

Sirhan asked for two books in prison: *The Secret Doctrine* by Blavatsky, and *Talks On: At the Feet of the Master* by Charles Webster (C.W.) Leadbeater (1854-1934), a Blavatsky disciple whom Blavatsky personally converted to Theosophy. These two archaic works immersed in the occult seem like odd requests coming from a 24-year-old devoted Palestinian

25   H. Spencer Lewis, *The Mystical Life of Jesus* (San Jose: The Rosicrucian Press, 1929), 53 (emphasis in original).

26   Agency: HSCA; Record Number: 190-100906-1011; Agency File Number: 0077271 [5 of 6].

27   E-mail to author, 25 February 2023.

28   H. Spencer Lewis, *Rosicrucian Questions and Answers* (San Jose: The Rosicrucian Press, 1929), 63.

nationalist as Sirhan. But they certainly reveal Sirhan's interests in the topic, augmented by his membership in the Rosicrucians. Leadbeater, a co-Freemason (from a lodge that admits both men and women), claimed to be a clairvoyant, able to contact The Masters on the astral plane, and fancied himself Senior Knight of the Round Table. He was the author of an additional number of books: *The Hidden Life in Freemasonry, Spiritualism and Theosophy*, and *The Science of the Sacraments: An Occult and Clairvoyant Study of the Christian Eucharist*, in which he championed an esoteric view of the sacrament of Holy Communion, the Catholic dogma of the bread and wine becoming the body, blood, soul, and divinity of Jesus Christ. Leadbeater penned this book when he was "Regionary Bishop of The Liberal Catholic Church for Australasia." In other words, this highly influential figure in Theosophy, Rosicrucianism, and the occult in general was yet another bishop in the Old Roman Catholic Church.

Leadbeater, Earl Anglin James and Charles Brearley share the same line of apostolic succession, from that of Arnold Harris Mathew, archbishop primate of the Old Catholic Church of Great Britain and Ireland. Leadbeater was consecrated in 1916 by one James Ingall Wedgwood, founding bishop of the Liberal Catholic Church, who according to Peter Anson, "managed to combine [the] traditional doctrines [of the Old Catholic Church] with Co-Masonry, Rosicrucianism, and Theosophy."[29]

In a letter to the leading theosophist of the day, Annie Besant, Leadbeater wrote, "[Wedgwood] desires most earnestly to offer the [Old Catholic] movement to the World Teacher as one of the vehicles for His force, and a channel for the preparation of His Coming. I took him therefore to the LORD MAITREYA at the Festival (Asala, the occult festival), and He was graciously pleased to accept the offer, and to say that He thought the movement would fill a niche in the scheme, and would be useful to Him. From what He said I inferred that He Himself had so guided events as to produce this curious result, that a branch of the Catholic Church, having the Apostolic Succession in a form which cannot be questioned, should be entirely in the hands of the Theosophists, who are eager and willing to do exactly as He wishes.... With His permission [the Lord Matriyea] Wedgwood has consecrated me as a Bishop, on the understanding that I am at perfect liberty to wear my ordinary dress, and am in no way bound to perform any ecclesiastical ceremonies or to take any outward part in the work unless I see it useful to do so, but to act as an intermediary between the LORD and this branch of His Church."[30]

---

29   Anson, 346.
30   Anson, 348, quoting *Extracts from Letters of C.W. Leadbeater to Annie Besant, 1916-1923*.

Along with Besant and Marie Russak, Wedgwood founded the Order of the Temple of the Rosy Cross. Once the order broke up, Russak became involved in the Ancient Mystical Order Rosae Crucis (AMORC), the Rosicrucian organization of which Sirhan Sirhan joined in 1966.

Being essentially borderless in its theology and doctrines, drawing on numerous faith traditions, the Liberal Catholicism of Leadbeater and Wedgwood emphasized an "all are welcome" strategy to attract congregants: "This Church aims at combining the traditional sacramental form of Catholic worship – with its ritual, its deep mysticism, and its abiding witness to the reality of sacramental grace – with the widest measure of intellectual liberty and respect for the individual conscience."[31] Leadbeater lived in Australia, at the head of a commune of more than fifty people, most aged 9-25. His private residence was floor-to-ceiling copper, and he said Mass either in the basement chapel or in Sydney at St. Alban's Liberal Catholic Church. Legend has it that St. Alban founded the first Masonic lodge in Britain, in 287 A.D.[32]

* * *

Hypnosis also factors in the killing of Martin Luther King, Jr., whose death along with the Brothers Kennedy completes a morbid triangle of a trinity of American assassinations in less than five years. Strangely, Earl Anglin James surfaces yet again – entirely voluntarily and without logic – when he announces to anyone who would listen that he was the father of King's accused assassin, James Earl Ray (in reality, Ray's father was George Ellis Ray).[33] "I think the guy [Earl Anglin James] is pretending to be nuts, possibly as a cover," Queen's University Classics professor, Richard Bernabei, wrote to assassination researcher Harold Weisberg. Still, ten years after the death of King and months of Ray on the run – including an extended stopover in Toronto – the HSCA asked federal agencies for their records on Earl Anglin James.

Bernabei's letter to Weisberg about James, dated October 23, 1968, is worth quoting further:

> [Richard] Sprague came up with an interesting lead as to who might have supplied false Canadian passports to "Ray." He suggests Earl Anglin James. Sprague sent me a copy of a Toronto Star article by reporter Earl McRae. EAJames runs a diploma mill in Toronto; appears to be crazy, but I think he may be faking.

31   Ibid., 352.
32   Ibid., 357, n.3.
33   FBI Report, SA Edward J. Carney, 10/7/68, p. 25.

The funny thing is that one of my students is a fried (sic) of McRae, the *Star* reporter. Months ago my student told me that McRae described Earl James as a forger, though McRae does not mention forgery in his articles. I suspect that he knows something about Earl James that he dares not print for fear of a lawsuit – I recently made a try at getting in touch with McRae, and I will pick his brains if I can.

What interests me is that my student made no mention of Earl James as a weirdo cleric and operator of a diploma mill – he only mentioned that James was a forger. I suppose that he got that info directly from McRae, for McRae does not print it.

By the way, Ferrie called Earl James seven times in 1962-63. Probably you know that.

When James Earl Ray was named as King's assassin, Earl James came forth and proclaimed that he was Ray's father. I think the guy is pretending to be nuts, possibly as a cover.

I may also be able to get information on Earl James through a couple of inmates at a penitentiary here. I know a couple of people there who might be willing to help. If it works out I might get some real inside dope. We'll see.[34]

But how did hypnosis play a factor? Three months before King's death at the Lorraine Motel on Mulberry St. in Memphis, James Earl Ray was on Crenshaw Blvd. in Gardena, south of Los Angeles. Ray was using the alias 'Eric S. Galt' when he met with Rev. Xavier von Koss, head of the International Society of Hypnosis, who attempted to put Ray under hypnosis. For $20, von Koss advertised in the *Los Angeles Times* for a time in 1968 (and which disappeared shortly after King's murder) he could unlock the "Innermost Hidden Secrets of HYPNOTIC MIND-POWER."[35] But von Koss could not crack Ray's subconscious. "[Ray] had stated he had wanted to use hypnosis to solve problems,"[36] the self-proclaimed "internationally recognized authority on hypnosis and self-hypnosis" stated.[37] von Koss handed off three popular self-help books to Ray/Galt: *How to Cash in on Your Hidden Memory Powers*; *Self-Hypnotism: The Technique and Its Use in Daily Living*; and the enduring classic, *Psycho-Cybernetics*.

---

34   Dick Bernabei, 1968 letter 39, The Weisberg Archive, Beneficial-Hodson Library, Hood College.

35   Matt Pearce, "When James Earl Ray came to LA, he found a place where he could blend in," *Los Angeles Times*, 4 April 2018.

36   Phillip F. Nelson, *Who REALLY Killed Martin Luther King Jr.?* (New York: Skyhorse, 2018), 408.

37   William Bradford Huie, *He Slew the Dreamer* (Jackson: University of Mississippi Press, 2018), 155.

In addition to Rev. von Koss, Ray met with a clinical psychologist, Mark O. Freeman, and is alleged in William Huie's biography, *He Slew the Dreamer*, to have interacted with the Church of Scientology, the John Birch Society, and the Liberty Lobby/John Birch Society-backed Orange County chapter of American Friends of Rhodesia.[38] According to Jeffrey Caufield, "The far right saw Rhodesia as a model for the separation of the races." Caufield notes further, "According to Jack Martin, a former [Guy] Banister employee, Kent Courtney was also a supporter of Rhodesia. Martin stated that 'Courtney and his followers do business with the known Neo-Nazi-right-wing-conservatives of Rhodesia, and the Union of South Africa, the Neo-Nazis-Afrikaners.'"[39]

Xavier von Koss, 1930

As for Xavier von Koss, he was born in Sweden in 1910. In 1930, he made passing headlines in the Southwest when he rode a pony from Fort Worth to Los Angeles. He claimed to be a descendant of the Habsburg.[40] He disappeared from the public record entirely after the James Earl Ray/ Eric S. Galt drama and Ray's conviction. The International Society of Hypnosis is a society of one, Xavier von Koss. Moreover, it is a title nearly identical with the diploma mill of Sir Sidney Lawrence, the International Hypnotists, of which Earl Anglin James was dean.

---

38   Matt Pearce, "When James Earl Ray came to LA, he found a place where he could blend in," *Los Angeles Times*, 4 April 2018.
39   Caufield, 687.
40   "Descendant of Habsburg on Horseback Trip," *Albuquerque Journal*, 25 June 1930.

CHAPTER FIFTEEN

THE END?

The wicked plots against the righteous
And gnashes at him with his teeth.

– Psalm 37:12

In the early 1970s, Joe Coffey, a New York detective working under the city's longtime DA Frank S. Hogan, uncovered a plot involving a Genovese crime family soldier colluding with others home and abroad to sell black-market stolen or counterfeit securities worth $14.5 million and $3.7 million in counterfeit bonds. The case was chronicled in Richard Hammer's 1982 bestseller, *The Vatican Connection* (and was the basis for Puzo and Coppola's first draft of what became *The Godfather, Part III*).[1]

One of the swindlers cultivated powerful relationships within the Vatican. Austrian Leopold Ledl allegedly gained the confidence of octogenarian French cardinal Eugene Tisserant, whose "influence cannot possibly be underestimated," a 1953 CIA profile on Tisserant stated.[2] According to the account Ledl later told Coffey and the FBI, Tisserant lamented during an after dinner conversation at the Vatican's Hotel Columbus about the shrinking size of the Vatican's coffers, preventing church funds from reaching far-flung missions, and supporting Italy's Christian Democratic government, which backed the Vatican's tax-free status, something the rival Communist party sought to reverse.[3] Tisserant wondered aloud if his Austrian dinner guest – Ledl – might happen to come upon first-class securities of American companies? Possibly even counterfeit, in the ballpark of, say, about $950 million? Such a number would alleviate the financial woes with interest, Tisserant explained. The fake securities would be used as collateral for dollar-for-dollar financing. So when the Vatican would loan or invest, it could make billions based on that collateral of phony stocks. Those involved would pay out $625 million to the crooks,

---

1   Mario Puzo and Francis Ford Coppola, *The Godfather, Part III* (First Draft), 10 May 1989.
2   CIA, RIF 640446, Box 129, Folder 1, p. 6.
3   See Richard Hammer, *The Vatican Connection* (New York: Henry Holt & Co., 1982), 283-284ff.

with a kickback of $150 million. The Vatican Bank and the Bank of Italy would be the two financial channels. At least, that was how Ledl laid it out.

Tisserant is an interesting character to suggest such a scheme. For more than two decades he was Secretary of the Congregation for the Oriental Churches, which made him the chief Vatican authority, next to the pope, of Eastern Catholic churches, and the Catholic Church in regions such as Egypt, Cyprus, Turkey, Greece, the Middle East, the Ukraine, Hungary, and Bulgaria. This was during a time of great political and upheaval in nearly all of the geographical areas, many captive nations to the USSR, that fell under the dicastery. In short, Tisserant was in an unsung position of power. He was deeply immersed in the political intrigue over the German invasion of Russia in 1941, so much so he conceived of the Tisserant Plan: Catholic missionaries, some disguised as merchants, would follow on the heels of the Nazi invasion and "convert" Soviet Russia.[4] Of course, the invasion was a catastrophic failure for the Axis and sent the Reich spiraling towards defeat. Tisserant, however, was less concerned about National Socialism. A greater enemy, "godless communism," loomed on the horizon like an apocalyptic nightmare. It was a matter of huge import for the Church, exemplified in Pius XI's 1937 encyclical condemning atheistic communism, *Divini Redemptoris*. As the post-World War II landscape emerged in the wake of Nazi horrors, Tisserant "was so anti-communist that he felt communists did not deserve Christian burial."[5] The Nazis may have been the enemy, but at least they were not the Communists.[6]

It also must be noted that Tisserant represented Pope John XXIII in an August 1962 meeting with Metropolitan Nikodim in Metz, France. "The gist of Nikodim's message was that the Russian Orthodox Church would consider sending observers to the [Second Vatican Ecumenical] Council provided an assurance was given in advance it would be a strictly apolitical event (that is, that it would not condemn atheistic Communism). Since the principle of 'no condemnations' had already been established as one of the ground-rules of the Council, this assurance could be given."[7]

Although Tisserant died in 1972, the securities fraud plan he supposedly hatched with Ledl continued. In Turin, a meeting purportedly

---

4 Eric Fratti, trans. Dick Cluster, *The Entity* (New York: St. Martin's Press, 2008), 264.
5 Ibid., 272.
6 It should be noted Tisserant was concerned the Church was slow to condemn German atrocities, writing to the cardinal archbishop of Paris: "I fear that history will reproach the Holy See with having practiced a policy of selfish convenience and not much else."
7 Peter Hebblethwaite, *John XXIII: Pope of the Century* (London: Continuum, 1984, 1994), 215.

took place to test the quality of the counterfeit securities. Ledl claimed the newly appointed president of the Vatican Bank, American archbishop Paul Marcinkus, arrived in a BMW. Tisserant's former assistant, whose name has never been unmasked, was there. So was an alleged monsignor, Alberto Barbieri. The $14.5 million dollars in fake securities were delivered as a deposit. To prove the Vatican's complicity, Ledl produced for the American investigators two letters, one from the Sacra Congregazione dei Religiosi dated June 29, 1971, detailing the purchase plan of the securities over five installments. The signature at the bottom is illegible, with no name typed under it. The document appears legitimate and on the face of it certainly confirms Ledl's tale, but is also just vague enough to question its veracity.

Still, it was enough for the FBI to make moves, including seeking out their fellow American who had lived in the Vatican for nearly two decades, Archbishop Marcinkus. They offered immunity deals to some of the conspirators, hopscotching Europe to corner others, with Leopold Ledl in Vienna their ultimate target. When they arrived in Austria, the American federal investigators found Ledl was actually in a Vienna prison on a different – but not entirely unrelated – matter. There, he told his side of the story and alerted the feds to the confirmation letter from the Vatican.

The investigators then worked channels to arrange a meeting with Marcinkus. It was an unprecedented and delicate matter to approach, needing help from New York's Cardinal Cooke to arrange introductions. The FBI had no jurisdiction in the Vatican. Since the Lateran Treaty of 1929, a concordat hammered out by Mussolini and Pope Pius XI that defined Vatican City State – the 110 acres surrounded by Rome – inhabitants within Vatican City were subject to the sovereign state's own laws, like any other country. The only way to get a meet-

First Lady Jacqueline Kennedy with Pope John XXIII in Rome in 1962. Behind the pope – Monsignor Paul Marcinkus, later archbishop president of the Vatican Bank

ing with Marcinkus would be if the Vatican allowed them in as a courtesy. Eventually, on April 28, 1973, William Aronwold and other American investigators from the FBI and New York Organized Crime Strike Force met with the Holy See's Deputy Secretary of State, Archbishop Giovanni Benelli, and reticent members of his staff. The American investigators were stonewalled. It was essentially the same with Marcinkus three days later. "Look, I don't have to tell you anything! But I will," he relaxed, smiling. "Because I want to cooperate with the FBI."

He dismissed the allegations. He denied meeting Ledl. Marcinkus said an associate of Ledl, Mario Foligni, alias the "Count of San Francisco," sought to solicit the Vatican Bank in exorbitant deals. The feds left. While they did not have evidence to indict Marcinkus, a federal grand jury in New York indicted sixteen Americans and Europeans for stock fraud, including one Vincent Rizzo; Ricky Jacobs, a notorious dealer in counterfeit securities; "Count" Foligni in Italy; and Leopold Ledl. Hammer notes Foligni held an honorary doctorate in theology: "His titles and degrees were about as legitimate as any of Ledl's and he had come by them in much the same way."[8] It is likely Foligni collected these titles from Earl Anglin James.

How did Ledl bluff his way into a facade of international success? Years earlier and rather by accident – so Ledl says – Ledl was in Switzerland seeking investors for a brush he patented when he met King Mwami Mwambutsa IV of Burundi, exiled there when Hutu officers led a military coup d'etat and overthrew the East Central African constitutional monarchy in October 1965. A former Belgian colony, Burundi is situated south of Rwanda, a region historically plagued by ethnic violence between Hutu and Tutsi tribes. Mwambutsa IV was hoping to wrest power from the rebels and put his son, Ntare V, on the throne. Mwambutsa offered to make Ledl an honorary consul at a discounted price, along with the rank of diplomat, and personal financial counselor to the exiled royal house. Ledl accepted – "it would increase his stature immeasurably in an easily impressed world"[9] – and he helped incite a coup to fulfill Mwambutsa's goal.

Here was a three-fingered butcher whose sole success in life to that point was a patent on a brush. Now, in this fraudulent diplomatic role, Leopold Ledl propelled into new social strata. He grew to like the racket of buying and selling phony titles and diplomas. Richard Hammer explains:

8   Hammer, 205.
9   Ibid., 203.

If anything was certain it was that within a very few years, the Honorary Consul Dr. Ledl had become very rich, indeed, and very well connected. He had moved his family from Vienna into a luxurious wooded estate, valued at over $1 million, in Maria Anzbach, Austria, and had hired private tutors for his growing daughters. He was serving his guests the best food and wines, and the bar was always stocked with the best liquor, though he drank only milk. He was driving the best cars, traveling first-class all the way. And he even claimed a few more titles – counsel of the patriarchate of Alexandria, and counselor of the archbishopric for Central Africa.[10]

And where did Ledl get the forged paperwork that ultimately got him arrested? Like a good salesman, Ledl packaged the consular title with an honorary doctorate from the National University of Canada. Ledl had met Earl Anglin James by way of an unnamed Hungarian acquaintance of the Knights of Malta, according to Ledl. But as we have seen, one can easily be misled by phony chivalric orders. Although he was born in Belgrade, Yugoslavia, not Hungary, Ledl's most probable contact was Count Archbishop Lorenzo Michel de Valitch of the Sovereign Order of Cyprus, which fancied itself a legitimate affiliation with the Sovereign Military Order of Malta. Later, de Valitch would come under suspicion by Italian intelligence for his role in the ethnic conflicts in the Balkans.[11]

As for Leopold Ledl, he was convicted in 1973 for fraud and extortion: the sales of fake honorary Burundian consul titles – one for $35,000, and another that came armed with an honorary doctorate, price: $100,000.[12] A search for Ledl's whereabouts yielded little information; it is believed he lived in Vienna under an assumed name.[13] Moreover, we have seen another connection to bogus Burundi consulships: Count Dr. Pericles Voultsos-Vourtzis of the Sovereign Order of St. Dennis of Zante and lay representative in the U.S. of the Old Holy Catholic Church.

There are other connections to note. Also indicted in the securities scheme was Santa Monica card club owner Manuel Richard "Ricky" Jacobs, perhaps the premiere dealer in counterfeit and stolen securities in the United States in his day. He was charged with five others, including mobster Johnny Roselli, in the Beverly Hills Friars Club swindle of the 1960s, in which Roselli and Jacobs rigged games using an elaborate system of electronic devices and coded signals. In one year, the club's exclu-

---

10   Hammer, 277.
11   Email correspondence with Peter Levenda, April 20, 2023.
12   Hammer, 322.
13   Email correspondence with librarian K. Winkler, Bibliothekarischer Auskunftsdienst, Vienna, Austria, 27 March 2023.

sive clientele lost about $400,000 cumulatively – about $3.3 million in today's money.

The Italian parliament's commission on Propaganda Due (P2) identified Jacobs as friends and accomplices of Tampa boss Santo Trafficante.[14] In addition, at an economic conference at the Bayerischer Hof in Munich in 1971, Jacobs introduced Ledl and accomplice Maurice Ajzen to a well-dressed American in his mid-50s as his financial adviser. He did not state the man's name, nor did the man offer it. Later, Coffey showed Ajzen photographs of top U.S. government officials. Finally, Ajzen made a match: Treasury secretary John B. Connally, Jr. Prior to joining the Nixon Administration, Connally was governor of Texas and fellow motorcade passenger with the President and Mrs. Kennedy on November 22, 1963. That he was purportedly Jacobs's financial adviser is not out of the realm of possibility: Connally handled other personal portfolios, such as the estate of oil tycoon Sid W. Richardson. He was also out of reach for the New York District Attorney's office or the FBI to pursue further. Coffey was told: "You are to forget you ever heard the name John Connally in connection with this case. You are not to pursue this line of investigation. You have nothing. You will get nothing. You are not to look for anything. And that's an order."[15]

After his time at Treasury John Connally became one of Nixon's closest advisers, even briefly considered to replace the disgraced VP Spiro Agnew in 1974. Under presidents Nixon and Ford, Connally was a member of the President's Foreign Intelligence Advisory Board, and co-chaired the Committee for the Defense of the Mediterranean, which sponsored seminars featuring speeches by Clare Boothe Luce and CIA director William Colby. A supporter of Connally's initiatives and ambitions was Michele "the Shark" Sindona. Sindona introduced Connally to Milanese banker Roberto Calvi, the beleaguered general manager of the Banco Ambrosiano whose schemes with the Vatican Bank would result in his 1982 murder. Calvi and his wife were even visitors at Connally's Texas ranch.[16]

Dominick Mantell was another one of the sixteen indicted in the Vatican Connection. Originally part of the Maggadino family in Buffalo, Mantell was transferred to Tampa under the protection of Santo Trafficante.

Archbishop Marcinkus, son of a Lithuanian window-washer, came from Capone's turf, Cicero, Illinois, rising to become the highest-rank-

---

14   "Commissione Parlamentare D'Inchiesta Sulla Loggia Massonica P2," Doc. XXIII, n.2, 1984, 54.

15   Hammer, 284.

16   Larry Gurwin, *The Calvi Affair: Death of a Banker* (London: Macmillan, 1983), 192.

ing American to work in the Vatican. In *Double Cross*, co-authored by the godson of Chicago gangland boss Sam Giancana with Giancana's brother, Chuck, we read about Sam's apparent closeness with longtime Chicago cardinal archbishop Samuel Stritch, leading proponent of Catholic Action who also oversaw the first U.S. post of Opus Dei, the extremely conservative theological and social movement founded by St. Josemaria Escriva. It was Stritch, according to the book, who recommended Marcinkus to work in the Vatican. Giancana employed a priest, appropriately named "Father Cash," as both a local courier and to launder his money through the Vatican Bank where Marcinkus was eventually – and conveniently – placed to wash the funds. After his murder in 1975, police found a framed photo of Giancana with Pius XII. Giancana's tomb, in an enormous family mausoleum, occupies a piece of Mount Carmel Catholic Cemetery.

In the little known book *Citizen Spy*, author Robert W. Morgan claims one Fred Kerr, associate of Meyer Lansky and Arizona crime boss Joe Bonanno, confessed how the money laundering process through the Vatican Bank operated out of Chicago during the tenure of Archbishop John Cardinal Cody (1965-1982). Kerr insists both Marcinkus and banker Roberto Calvi at the Banco Ambrosiano, of which the Vatican was the largest shareholder, were deeply involved in and fully aware of the Mafia's laundering practices.

Leopold Ledl tells us Earl Anglin James's personal motto was, "As long as you live, you have to live."[17] "Sir James was not at all stingy," Ledl explains in his 1990 autobiography, *Per Conto del Vaticano*. He then drops a remarkable admission: "For every doctoral title sold by the National University of Canada, in fact, [James] paid the sum of two thousand dollars into the bank account 'for the coup d'etat of King Ntare."[18]

This is a crucial admission – one never before uncovered in previous research – that reveals much about the mad bishop's methods and objectives. Of course, the planned coup failed. Shortly afterwards, Ntare V was assassinated in 1972. He was 24 years old. The resulting chaos led to a wave of ethnic cleansing that claimed 300,000 lives. But by then, Leopold Ledl was already invested in the Vatican securities scheme. Today, Burundi is one of the least developed countries in the world. Based on its GNI (gross national income) as of this writing, Burundi is the poorest country in the world. But that meant little to Earl Anglin James. He lived the way he lived, ensconced in the musty apartment of his mother, continuing to

---

17   Leopold Ledl, *Per Conto del Vaticano* (Naples: Tullio Pironti, 1990), 52-53ff.
18   Ibid.

earn his existence by deceiving naive and uneducated individuals primarily from developing nations.[19]

And it begs the question: What other plots and coups did the mad bishop financially support?

---

19   "Cheque book diplomacy," *The Guardian*, 2 July 1974. James specifically targeted people in Africa and India, where he oversaw another diploma mill out of the Toronto apartment, the World Jnana Sadhak Society.

EPILOGUE

I will ransom them from the power of the grave;
I will redeem them from death:
O death, I will be thy plagues;
O grave, I will be thy destruction:
repentance shall be hid from mine eyes.

– Hosea 13:14

Earl Anglin James died in 1977. National University of Canada died with him. He left behind a son he never saw, an ex-wife (or more) whom he never loved. Of the church he oversaw as primate archbishop, there was no congregation to mourn his passing, no cathedral church to hold his funeral, no bishop's undercroft to bury him. Of the 2,100 degrees he amassed over fifty years, there was not one college or university who counted him as an alumnus. Of the hundreds, if not thousands who sought him out, he could count none as friend.

He was a scion of the ignoble, whose network hovered over three American assassinations that forever changed the country. James was one of the conduits the plotters used to cover their crimes: via fake orders, titles, degrees, and religious affiliations – things that impressed a certain social stature in the mid-20th century that allowed them to get away with it. They were chameleons hiding in plain sight. Besides, it was the age of the Red Menace, and certainly something as vile as assassination could only have been actualized by a Judeo-Communist Conspiracy.

The plotters usurped these institutions to preserve a certain view of America that the liberal Irish Catholic yankee John F. Kennedy was about to shatter with his Civil Rights Act. The racists and anti-Semites in the Deep South who longed for another Civil War, if not World War III, found a willing cabal of anti-communist fascists in Guy Banister's associates in New Orleans. Through James, this network connected with other like-minded bigots hiding behind pseudo-chivalric orders and honors to incite a hardcore underground dedicated to ousting the Kennedy vision. The ensuing government coverup, in this author's estimation, was less about hiding its own guilt than it was diverting away from the real reason for the assassination: civil rights. The great scar on the United States is its legacy of slavery, and if the general public was privy in 1963-1964 that the assassination was carried out by segregationists in the well-connected racist right, calling themselves "patriots," fortified by an extremist view of evangelical Christianity, backed by a group of hawkish retired generals, financed by like-minded conservative Dallasites of great influence, and spurred by the zealotry that vengeance begets, the social fallout would have been greater than any riot this country endured. In this context, the later killings of Martin Luther King, Jr. and Robert F. Kennedy were motivated by the same ideology. The same ideology that spawned one radical right domestic attack after another in the ensuing decades, including the storming and defilement of the United States Capitol Building on January 6, 2021.

As the Zapruder film showed, the shooters only concentrated on JFK, who until the last second before impact believed he was in control of his own destiny. It was all an illusion. When he died, so it was thought, so too would have been the ugly idea of integration. After all, a Texan was now in the White House. Surely he would bury that idea of civil rights – he was "our man in the White House!" I asked my mentor from John Carroll University, Dr. Thomas Nevin, who remembered well November 22, his impression that the shot that blew open JFK's head was intended to be the shot heard around the world that would trigger a new War for Southern Independence:

> That could well be. Ironic, that LBJ knew he had to pass the Civil Rights bill in 1964, said it would cost the Dems the South for a generation (it's been longer than that) and that bill furthered the multi-culturalism that has posed a major issue for America: what happens when a culture changes so much that it can no longer recognize itself? Is this the very definition of decadence, of Rome by the 3rd century of the Christian era? This is what Nietzsche meant in claiming Christianity was the vampire of the Empire, the agent of a cultural breakdown. Interesting, too, that Johnson oversaw the greatest defeat in America's military-colonial history.[1]

Furthermore, we see the influence of the occult in how each of these assassinations were conducted and covered up: traces of theosophy, spiritualism, mesmerism, and hypnotism. These elements would have appealed to the mind of an Earl Anglin James or David Ferrie and their retinue. On the surface, the calls Ferrie placed to James were likely related to his con-

1   Email correspondence with author, 7 May 2023.

secration by Stanley, and the ensuing drama over various excommunications. However, as this work has shown, there were deeper machinations behind becoming bishops and claiming diplomas: this underworld had darker, sinister motivations.

Moreover, one cannot underestimate David Ferrie, who bridged the occultish worldview of the wandering bishops with the anger of the southern extremists and anti-communists. As a young man, Ferrie had the privilege of a stellar education. He graduated a year early from a premier Jesuit high school. That rigorous academic workload coupled with no-nonsense discipline would have informed his outlook for the rest of his life. His drug use, sexual offenses, pedophilia, and homosexuality collided with this strict religious upbringing. He was no fool. His passions, talents and own human failings may have swept him up in what became an unstoppable tsunami of plotting and hatred that came to fruition on November 22. A client of G. Wray Gill, Clara "Bootsie" Gay, said she saw drawings of Dealey Plaza when Ferrie's desk was emptied the Tuesday after the assassination. Thomas Beckham said upon orders from Ferrie he delivered a package to Lawrence Howard in Dallas that contained diagrams, photographs, and cash. Ferrie himself made a strange trip the night of the assassination to the two port cities of Houston and Galveston. When news leaked he was the subject of the New Orleans DA's investigation of the assassination, he told them, "I'm a dead man! From here on, believe me, I'm a dead man!" Sure enough, just before Garrison was prepared to indict Ferrie for conspiracy to kill the president, Ferrie was found dead in his bed. He was 48. The autopsy report concluded death resulted from a brain hemorrhage – a natural cause. Two suicide notes were found in Ferrie's house. But was he "suicided"? "No matter what happens," David Ferrie told Raymond Broshears, "I will never commit suicide." Broshears emphasized Ferrie was adamant about that.

* * *

The 1960s saw the destruction of the Kennedy kingdom by three mortal blows: the crippling stroke of patriarch Joseph P. Kennedy, Sr. in 1961; the fatal shot to JFK's head in 1963; and the bullet that smashed through the mastoid bone of RFK in 1968. On a large cabinet near where Robert F. Kennedy fell in the Ambassador Hotel, someone scrawled the Arthurian phrase "The Once and Future King!" in crayon. Like his brother, RFK was mortally wounded from a shot to the head. Head wounds abound in medieval literature, and it is no different in Arthurian lore: in

Morte Arthure, an alliterative poem from around 1400 AD, three heroes endure head wounds: Lancelot, Gawain, and Arthur. Lancelot survives; Gawain and Arthur do not. Larissa Tracy notes how these blows to the heads of Lancelot, Gawain and Arthur set into motion the eventual fall of Camelot. "By striking at the head – the king and his most trusted knights – the poet criticizes the kingship of Richard II (1377-1399) weakened by the rebellion of barons, warning against tyranny in a poignant reflection of late fourteenth-century political turmoil that ultimately ended in usurpation."[2]

An appendage to the Kennedy mystique is the Chappaquiddick accident and death of Mary Jo Kopechne that destroyed any hope of an Edward Kennedy presidency. It could not be made clearer that whatever the vision the Kennedys had would not survive. In this scenario, it is not the Kennedy brothers who will initiate a new frontier for America but a brotherhood long couched in what America was and should be – a once and future America – established long before the FitzGeralds and Kennedys sailed from Ireland's principality of Thomond onto American shores: "In a world of pain, suffering, and ignorance, Freemasons must become the band of wise brothers fuelling the Light that directs man to the 'great spirit' within."[3]

Freemasonry was a heresy, condemned in a papal bull by Clement XII in 1738. Canon 2335 in the Code of Canon Law read: "Persons joining associations of the Masonic sect or any others of the same kind which plot against the Church *and legitimate civil authorities* contract ipso facto excommunication simply reserved to the Apostolic See."[4] Freemasons were conspirators, then, plotting against not only Holy Mother Church, but against legitimate civil authorities – in our case, the lawfully elected and legitimate President of the United States of America. On their side, Freemasonry viewed the Catholic Church as charlatans, black magicians, and certainly not *legitimate claimants of apostolic succession* as the Church of Rome believes itself to be. If John Kennedy was Wanted For Treason by the Hunts and other sons of the great state of Texas, was he a traitor to the United States, or to those who ultimately were plotting against him?

James Shelby Downard has meticulously documented the occultic, ritualistic nature of President Kennedy's murder in his writings. In his

2   Larissa Tracy, "'Into the Hede, throw the helme and creste': Head Wounds and a Question of Kingship in Stanzaic Morte Arthur, in *Wounds and Wound Repair in Medieval Culture*, ed. Larissa Tracy and Kelly DeVries (Leiden: Brill, 2015), 497.

3   "The Journey of a Freemason," District Grand Lodge of Lebanon, https://dgll.org/the-journey-of-a-freemason/.

4   Robert Bradley, SJ, "Catholicism vs. Freemasonry – Irreconcilable Forever," https://www.ewtn.com/catholicism/library/catholicism-vs-freemasonry-irreconcilable-forever-946 (Emphasis mine).

seminal work on the assassination, "Sorcery Sex, Assassination and the Science of Symbolism," Downard writes, "The ultimate purpose of that assassination was not political or economic, but sorcerous; for the control of the dreaming mind is the underlying motive in this entire scenario of lies, cruelty and degradation."[5] This is echoed in the landmark 1968 work *Farewell America* by the pseudonymous James Hepburn: "President Kennedy's assassination was the work of magicians. It was a stage trick, complete with accessories and false mirrors, and when the curtain fell the actors, and even the scenery, disappeared."

Downard goes on to describe the trident-shaped layout of Dealey Plaza, across from the Trinity River, as a "Sun Temple,"[6] the site of the original Mason building in Dallas – a city near the 33rd latitude and on the 33rd north parallel – designed as a pyramid with its capstone missing, where Jim Marrs and other researchers are convinced multiple assassins were planted to take out the president in a "triangulation crossfire" arrangement before his motorcade vanished under the "triple underpass." When Walter Cronkite told the nation on CBS, "three shots were fired at President Kennedy's motorcade in downtown Dallas," was he aware of the symbolic connotations with the Masonic tale of Hiram Abiff? In the story, Abiff was chief architect (master mason) for King Solomon, who is ambushed by other masons wanting to know his secrets as master mason. Hiram Abiff refuses to say anything, and three times Abiff is struck by a different mason's tool. He is killed by the last blow.

These three ruffians – Jubela, Jubelo and Jubelum – are the "'unworthy craftsman' of Temple burlesque, 'that will be blamed for nothing.'" When the infamous "three tramps" are paraded across Dealey Plaza by Dallas Police minutes after the assassination, appropriately photographed from multiple angles, the symbolism is striking: the ceremonial procession of Jubela, Jubelo and Jubelum in the flesh. The identities of these men were never revealed, and were released from custody without explanation. Blamed for nothing.[7]

Dealey Plaza, named after the father of *Dallas Morning News* publisher, Ted Dealey, who bore no love for JFK, became the proscenium for the ritualistic slaughter of the "scapegoat Sun King. He was the sacrifice in the

---

5   See James Shelby Downard, "Sorcery, Sex, Assassination and the Science of Symbolism," p. 27. and "King Kill/33°". David Icke also discusses this at length: *The Biggest Secret*, ch. 19 "The Goddess and the King" (Ryde: Bridge of Love Publications, 1999) and *...The Truth Shall Set You Free* (Ryde: Bridge of Love Publications, 1995).

6   Icke, 408.

7   Cf. Kris Millegan, ed., *Fleshing Out Skull & Bones: Investigations Into America's Most Secret Society* (Walterville, OR: TrineDay Press, 2004), p. 197.

ancient ritual of the Killing of the Sun King: the 'Ceannaideach' which is Gaelic for Wounded Head. Kennedy, of course, was shot in the head."[8] Lee Oswald may have proclaimed himself to be "just a patsy," a scapegoat for defecting to the Soviet Union, as he said, but as with so much in the assassination, there was a flip side to that coin, another scapegoat: the President of the United States. Thomas Szasz wrote about the use of a scapegoat in ancient history in a passage that is worth quoting in full:

> Thousands of years ago ... religion and medicine were a united and undifferentiated enterprise; and both were closely aligned with government and politics – all being concerned with maintaining the integrity of the community and of the individuals who were its members. How did ancient societies and their priest-physicians protect people from plagues and famines, from the perils of impending military encounters, and from all the other calamities that threaten persons and peoples? They did so, in general, by performing certain religious ceremonies.
>
> In ancient Greece (as elsewhere), one of these ceremonies consisted of human sacrifice. The selection, naming, special treatment, and finally the ritualized destruction of the scapegoat was the most important and most potent "therapeutic" intervention known to "primitive" man.
>
> When the ancients saw a scapegoat, they could at least recognize him for what he was: a *pharmakos*, a human sacrifice. When modern man sees one, he does not, or refuses to, recognize him for what he is; instead, he looks for 'scientific' explanations – to explain away the obvious.[9]

Plato, in *The Republic*, believed that the Just Man "will be scourged, racked, bound, will have his eyes put out, and will at last be crucified." Of course, one cannot help but think of Christ, the ultimate *pharmakos* in Kennedy's Catholic religion. But still more – the crucifixion of Christ, the slain president's faith taught him, went beyond the actual physical crucifixion in Jerusalem. It was of great spiritual meaning, the Son of God giving his life as a ransom for the many. In this way, Christ was a spiritual victim – in Latin, *hostia*. In the execution of John Kennedy, the flawed mortal man passed into tragic myth, a transformation that only aided his executioners; it is nearly impossible now to view the assassination as it ac-

---

8   Icke, 410.
9   Thomas Szaz, *Ceremonial Chemistry* (Garden City, NY: Anchor Press/Doubleday, 1974), 19, 20.

tually unfolded at 12:30PM. Instead, we can only look back through myths that have obscured the truth.

The Masonic Brotherhood views itself as the legitimate successors of the medieval Knights Templar, founded in 1118 by a contingent of Frankish knights to ostensibly defend the Christian kingdom of Jerusalem, with a Cistercian monk, the esteemed Bernard of Clairvaux, as its spiritual guide. The order became immensely powerful beyond its apparently humble origins, and its infamous disbanding by the pope, subsequent torture of the knights, and eventual burning at the stake of its last Grand Master, Jacques DeMolay, spawned great legends about the Templars over the centuries. Our own wandering bishops from Earl Anglin James down considered themselves keepers of the Templar flame, the legitimate successors to the defenders of Christendom, its treasures, and its secrets. Legend has it that when the flames surrounded de Molay, the Grand Master uttered an ominous curse:

> *S'en vendra en brief temps meschie*
> *Sus celz qui nous dampnent a tort;*
> *Diex en vengera nostre mort.*
>
> *Let evil swiftly befall*
> *Those who have wrongly condemned us;*
> *God will avenge our death.*

Indeed, thirty-three days later Clement V was dead, followed eight months later by the other Templar hunter, King Philip IV of France. The surviving Templars were granted the divine retribution de Molay promised; this truly was a sacred order, one given divine favor to usher that secret knowledge, that gnosis, through the centuries until the end of time. No one is greater than this collective brotherhood who are at once priests, prophets, and kings. And heaven help he who thinks otherwise.

Secret societies thus have long memories. It is perhaps no coincidence, then, from this esoteric perspective, that Pope Clement V issued *Pastoralis praeeminentiae*, his papal bull disbanding the Order, on November 22, 1307.

Slide down the banister, go get your coat
Ferry 'cross the Mersey and go for the throat.
                              - Bob Dylan, "Murder Most Foul"

Index

Brasol, Boris 36
Brearley, Charles 1, 48, 60, 134, 136
Bremer, Arthur 172
Brien, Dan 61-64
Bringuier, Carlos 112, 142
Broken Wings: A Collection of Poems 136
Broshears, Raymond 1, 70, 81, 82, 84, 115, 187
Brothers, William H.F. (Father Francis of Woodstock) 3, 32, 110, 111, 157, 174
Browder, Eddie 151
Brownlee, Morris 97
Brown, Richard 34
Brundage, Percival 97, 98, 103
Bryan, William J. 169, 170
Budd, Ralph W. 42
Bunde, Louis 3, 156, 160, 161
Bundy, McGeorge 123
Burns, Robert Alfred 31, 32, 139
Butler, Ed 112, 113, 142, 145
Byrd, David Harold 3, 40, 96, 157-160
Byrd, Richard 40

C

Cabell, Charles P. 55, 106
Cabell, Earle 157
Cable News Network (CNN) 7
Caliguire, Ralph 25
Calles, Plutarco Elias 32
Calvin Coolidge College 2, 60, 103
Calvi, Roberto 182, 183
Camacho, Manuel Alvaro 155
Capell, Frank 85
Capone, Albert Francis 23, 56, 161, 182
Carfora, Henry Carmel 31, 32, 33, 132
Carpenter, Arthur E. 143
Carroll News, The 8
Casey, Diana Ruth 23
Casey, William 36
Casparis, Hans 98
Castro, Fidel 7, 8, 37, 52-57, 87, 105, 106, 108, 113, 142, 151
Castro, Raul 56
Caufield, Jeffrey 65, 75-82, 85-87, 89,

90, 91, 96, 100, 108, 110, 111, 113, 115, 142, 146, 176
Central Intelligence Agency (CIA) 7, 36-40, 52, 54, 55, 57, 97, 98, 106, 117, 121, 123, 129, 142, 149, 156, 167-169, 177, 182
Certain Arrogance: The Sacrifice of Lee Harvey Oswald and the Cold War Manipulation of Religious Groups, A 39, 98
Chaudhuri, Bhabes Chandra 104
Christian, Jonn 145, 171
Citizen Spy 183
Citizens' Report. 112
Civil Air Patrol (CAP) 96, 105
Claudius I (fake Pope) 139
Clement V (Pope) 191
Clement XII (Pope) 188
Clement XV (fake Pope) 137, 138, 139
Cody, John Cardinal 183
Coffey, Joe 177, 182
Coffield, H.H. (Pete) 3, 157, 158
Colby, William 182
Coleman, Walter 90
Collin, Michael 138
Collins, Frederick W. 21
Condon, Richard 170
Conein, Lucien 123
Congress of Racial Equality (CORE) 100
Connally, John B. Jr. 90, 182
Cooke, Terence 35, 179
Cooney, John 120, 128
Coppola, Francis 177
Corrigan, Leo F. 156
Corso, Phillip 3, 85, 86
Coughlin, Charles 35, 36
Courtney, Kent 82, 176
Craig, Roger 75
Crichton, John Alston 3, 158, 159
Crisman, Fred L 74, 75
Cronkite, Walter 150, 189
Crowley, Aleister 67, 68
Crow, William Bernard 66, 67
Crozier, Brian 120
Cuban Revolutionary Council (CRC) 105-108